Paul
Forrestal

CUISINE IMAGINAIRE

Menus for Delicious Vegetarian Entertaining

ROSELYNE MASSELIN

BBC BOOKS

PUBLISHED BY BBC BOOKS
a division of BBC Enterprises Limited,
Woodlands, 80 Wood Lane,
London W12 0TT

First published 1993
© Roselyne Masselin 1993

ISBN 0 563 36413 0

Designed by Peter Bridgewater
Photographs by Graham Kirk
Home Economist Allyson Birch

Set in Baskerville and Gill Sans by
Ace Filmsetting Ltd, Frome, Somerset
Printed and bound in Great Britain by
Clays Ltd, St Ives Plc
Colour separation by
Dot Gradations Ltd, Chelmsford
Jacket printed by
Belmont Press Ltd, Northampton

Acknowledgements

I would like first to thank my dear friend Clive for his support and ever-lasting enthusiasm in all the projects that I have undertaken over the many, many years that I have known him. He will never realise how much he has helped me. I would also like to thank all members of my family for their support and concern.

On the work front, I would like to thank all my colleagues, assistants and helpers, many of whom became good friends and with whom I have worked over many years in the past at the Vegetarian Society and now with my own catering business and cookery school.

I would like to thank Sarah Brown, Jo Wright, Leila, Pam, Susan Urqhart, Tony Morrin, Janice, Paul, Rosie Billings, Julian, Christine and Greg and Colleen Hobson, all of whom have helped me tremendously over the years.

I would like to thank Jo Middleditch for her skilled assistance in all aspects of my work both with *Catering Imaginaire®* and at *La Cuisine Imaginaire* cookery school. I would like to thank Louisa for her recent assiduous and enthusiastic work. I would also like to thank all the helpers who have worked with my catering company.

I would like to thank Mitzie Wilson at *BBC Good Food*, Heather Holden-Brown at BBC Books and Valerie Buckingham for her expert editing.

I would like to thank my agents Shan Morley Jones and later Laura Fleminger for getting me through the difficult times in the writing of this book.

I would, of course, like to thank Peter for his care and love.

CONTENTS

$\mathscr{I}$ NTRODUCTION

● WHAT IS CUISINE IMAGINAIRE ABOUT?

I launched CUISINE IMAGINAIRE *three years ago, to determine my own style of creative vegetarian cookery;* CUISINE IMAGINAIRE *is a light and creative style of vegetarian cooking and describes vegetarianism for the 1990s with the emphasis placed on style and presentation.* CUISINE IMAGINAIRE *borrows ideas from* nouvelle cuisine*: it brings colours and textures to the fore; the food is presented in an* à la carte *style to match, in quality, other gourmet meat-based cuisines.*

CUISINE IMAGINAIRE *moves away from heavy wholefood combinations and allows taste and style to take prime importance.* CUISINE IMAGINAIRE *is a book for special occasions and treats. I concentrate on the best results so I use white bread, cream, etc. where I judge necessary, instead of their wholefood counterparts. I do not recommend you eat like this every day – this is a special occasions cookbook. There are, however, menus to suit everyone – the health-conscious and the not-so-health-conscious.*

Each menu has been created to offer a balance of flavours, colours and textures, so if you wish to substitute recipes, bear this in mind. The dishes that are completely egg-free and dairy-free are marked with the symbols ◆ and ★ respectively, in the boxed menus.

The menus are varied, well presented and will appeal to vegetarians and non-vegetarians alike. The recipes are not too technical, so that everyone can enjoy cooking the dishes: I hope that you will find them inspiring.

ROSELYNE MASSELIN
January 1993

How to use this book

● **THIS BOOK IS VERY CLEAR AND SIMPLE TO USE**

There is a section on ingredients at the beginning of this book which will help you with the recipes. There are, for example, explanations for miso, bouquet garni, tamari, seitan, etc.

This section is followed by one on equipment. Don't think that you have to update all your kitchen equipment; there are only a few items which make life easier, such as a blender and a food processor which you definitely need.

Food presentation and garnishes are covered in the last introductory section. There are tips on cutting techniques and garnishings to make the very most of the dishes you prepare.

The book is then divided into four sections of seasonal menus: Spring Menus, Summer Menus, Autumn Menus and Winter Menus, which are then followed by menus for special occasions such as: Exotic Finger Buffet, Summer Buffet, Winter Buffet, Easy Entertaining (light and easy pre-theatre supper), Christmas Menu, and Family Celebration Menu.

● **SOME OF THE MORE UNUSUAL INGREDIENTS USED**

OILS

Certain oils are more suitable for particular uses and foods. In the following recipes I have used a variety of oils including grapeseed, walnut, toasted sesame, hazelnut, groundnut, sunflower, corn and olive oil which have been specifically chosen for their individual qualities and tastes.

When olive oil is listed, use a rich green virgin or extra virgin olive oil for the finest results.

With walnut and hazelnut oils it is well worth investing in the finest quality, cold-pressed oils which are obtained from the early pressings of the nuts, as they are rich in flavour. To preserve their flavour, these extractions should be kept in the refrigerator.

VINEGARS

It is worth spending money on good quality vinegars as they provide a superior flavour.

Vinegar is an indispensable ingredient in the kitchen as it is a flavouring agent for salad dressings and sauces as well as an important component in marinades and some hot dishes.

There is a wide range of herb, fruit and wine vinegars available giving a wonderful variety of flavours and colours. I have used a selection from the common wine vinegars through to the more unusual raspberry and champagne vinegars.

FLAVOURINGS

The flavourings that are stipulated in my recipes have been chosen to give the dishes their character. I therefore suggest that you do not substitute them with an alternative.

STOCK CUBES

When choosing stock cubes look at the ingredients panel and avoid those containing monosodium glutamate.

BOUILLON POWDER

Bouillon powder has a lighter flavour than stock cubes and is the closest to home-made vegetable stock. Just dissolve it directly in the dish or in hot water, as suggested in the recipe.

BOUQUET GARNI

You may use the ready-prepared bouquet garni sachets or you may prefer to make your own bouquet garni. Either tie a bundle of herbs together or chop and enclose in a small muslin or cheesecloth purse, a mixture of bay leaves, parsley, thyme and any other suitable herbs.

FRESH HERBS

If you are not so lucky to have a garden full of fresh herbs you can buy them in small packets from most supermarkets. They are expensive but here is a way to store them for at least a week so that you can use them in more than one recipe. Place the herbs in a mixing bowl, immerse them in chilled water for 2–3 hours, drain well to remove every trace of water, return to a glass bowl or plastic container, cover with food wrap and store in the refrigerator.

CONTINENTAL PARSLEY

Also known as flat leaf parsley, continental parsley has a slightly different flavour from the curly varieties, giving the dishes a continental hint. If you are unable to obtain it use the curly variety instead but do try your local Italian delicatessen first!

GINGER JUICE

To obtain ginger juice, finely grate some crisp, unpeeled root ginger on the medium grate of the grater and then squeeze out the resulting juice with your hands. I can guarantee you will be amazed at the quantity released.

● SOYA BEAN PRODUCTS

TAMARI AND SHOYU

Tamari and shoyu are naturally fermented soya sauces unlike many of the 'soy sauces' on the market which contain caramel to flavour and colour them. It is worth buying the naturally fermented varieties both for their much superior flavour and nutritional content – being rich in protein and minerals. Shoyu is made from soya beans, wheat and salt and is less concentrated than tamari which has a stronger flavour and is made simply from soya beans, salt and water and is therefore gluten-free. Both are delicious used as bases for marinades, sauces and salad dressings, and added to savoury dishes.

MISO

Miso is made by the fermenting of soya beans and rice, barley or wheat for 1–2 years with the addition of sea salt to form a thick paste. It is a complete protein (since it benefits from the amino acids from the soya bean as well as those from the grain it is fermented with) so is extremely nutritious as well as rich in minerals and some B vitamins.

In some of my recipes I have used barley miso, in others rice miso; barley miso has a strong flavour whereas rice miso is more subtle. Both are used to flavour stock, casseroles and sauces.

TOFU

Tofu is the set curds of the soya bean. There are three types of tofu: silken, regular and smoked.

Silken tofu has the appearance and texture of set yoghurt and can only be used in creamed mixtures such as cheesecakes, ice-creams and whips.

Regular tofu has a denser texture and can be cut into the desired shape and size. It should be marinated for the best flavour and then used threaded on kebabs, etc.

Smoked tofu is naturally smoked and has a 'smoky' flavour!

All three types are very low in fat and high in protein. Tofu is increasingly available from major supermarkets as well as wholefood shops.

TEMPEH

Tempeh is made from soya beans and, in a similar process to cheese, has been fermented to produce a close textured yet grainy high protein product, which absorbs the flavour from sauces well.

● WHEAT PRODUCTS

SEITAN

Seitan is spun wheat gluten and is made to have a 'meaty' and therefore 'chewy' texture. It is high in protein and is often sold already naturally flavoured with shoyu and a touch of fresh ginger, which gives it a pleasant flavour.

● PASTRY

FILO PASTRY

Frozen filo pastry is readily available from major supermarkets and ethnic shops. I find it is best to defrost the pastry for 3–4 hours at room temperature before using so it is freshly thawed. When working with filo pastry remember to keep remaining pastry sheets covered to prevent them from drying out and cracking.

● GRAINS

COUSCOUS

Couscous is made by processing semolina into tiny pellets by steaming, drying and cracking the grains. It has a light texture and taste when cooked and is ideal for stuffings and fillings. It is available from major supermarkets and wholefood shops.

BULGUR WHEAT

Bulgur wheat is a wheat grain which is steamed and dried before being milled. It has a heavier texture than couscous with a stronger and slightly nutty flavour. It is available from major supermarkets and wholefood shops.

POLENTA

Polenta is a staple food in Italy where it is often used to make a thick savoury porridge. Polenta has a fine granular texture similar to semolina. To obtain the finest quality, bright yellow variety purchase it from an Italian delicatessen.

● DAIRY PRODUCTS

EGGS

Unless otherwise stated all eggs used in my recipes are size 3 and are free-range.

CHEESE

I have used a wonderful selection of soft, semi-hard and hard cheeses in my recipes. Some cheeses contain rennet (an enzyme found in calves' stomachs which is added to curdle and set the milk) and therefore not vegetarian. Look out for the increasing range of vegetarian cheeses which indicate they contain a non-animal rennet.

CRÈME FRAÎCHE

Crème fraîche is an important ingredient in French cooking. It is a cream which is treated with a culture to give a light acidity without sourness, and is used in sauces, terrines and sweet dishes.

● FRESH VEGETABLES/FRUITS

WILD RASPBERRIES AND STRAWBERRIES

Ask your greengrocer to order wild raspberries and strawberries for you.

WILD MUSHROOMS

Order them from your greengrocer if they are not available in the supermarkets which now offer a variety of delicious mushrooms. To prepare, wipe over gently with a damp cloth.

● SEAWEEDS

There are many varieties of seaweeds with differing tastes and uses; some have a strong sea flavour while others are mild and sweet. They are high in protein, contain essential amino acids and are rich in minerals and trace elements. Wholefood shops sell them ready cleaned and dried. Unopened they store indefinitely. Once opened store in an airtight container.

HIZIKI

Hiziki (also spelt hijiki) is a useful, sweet-flavoured seaweed extremely rich in iron and calcium. It comes in the form of fine shreds.

NORI

Nori, which comes in sheets, is the most popular seaweed available and is very high in protein and minerals. It should be toasted prior to use although some nori sheets are sold already toasted.

Nori is also sold in the form of nori powder which is toasted and ground to a fine texture. In this form, it can be sprinkled over casseroles or soups, and added to dishes for greater flavour and nutritional value.

ARAME
Arame is mildly-flavoured, thin-shredded strips of seaweed.

AGAR-AGAR
Agar-agar is obtained from a variety of seaweeds and is a natural unflavoured vegetable gelatine available in powder or flake form. Both can be used but the flakes take a lot longer to dissolve than the powder, so follow methods in recipes. Gelatine is not a vegetarian ingredient.

● EQUIPMENT REQUIRED

LARGE PASTRY BRUSH
A large pastry brush makes jobs such as buttering filo pastry or egg washing so much easier and quicker. It looks similar to a 2.5 cm (1 inch) wide paintbrush and can be found in good kitchen shops or catering equipment shops.

WHISKS
The whisk is my favourite tool: I have three types ranging in size and weight. A small whisk is useful for sauces and amalgamating ingredients. The larger whisks may be used for batters and cake mixes.

BLENDER VERSUS FOOD PROCESSOR
Both the blender and food processor are an absolute must in a vegetarian kitchen!

Both blend liquids such as sauces and soups but a blender gives a much smoother texture and is therefore useful for smooth soups and coulis-type sauces. (Look out for blenders with a coffee grinder attachment – see below.)

When a recipe suggests you use a food processor to blend liquids it is because a coarser texture is required. As well as blending liquids, a food processor does a number of other useful jobs such as grinding nuts, making breadcrumbs and grating cheese.

COFFEE GRINDERS
Coffee grinders, which are sometimes sold as an attachment to a blender, are ideal for grinding small quantities of nuts, seeds and spices which would take a lot of effort with a pestle and mortar.

MOULDS
I have used a variety of moulds, namely darioles, college pudding moulds (small and medium), individual brioche tins, charlotte tins, heart-shaped moulds and crumpet rings as well as pastry cutters, giving a variation in shapes and adding extra interest to the dishes. You will be able to purchase the above from good kitchen equipment shops or catering equipment shops. Remember that your supplier will usually be able to order most size moulds.

MEASURING SPOONS

All spoon measurements given are level measuring spoons.

● FOOD PRESENTATION AND GARNISHES

CHOPPING VEGETABLES

VEGETABLE STRIPS

Julienne: Julienne are very fine thin strips 3 mm/⅛ inch wide and up to 8 cm/3¼ inches long.

Matchsticks: Matchsticks are strips approximately 4 mm/⅙ inch wide and 5 cm/2 inches long.

Batons: Batons are shorter and wider than matchsticks and are about 5 mm/¼ inch wide and 4.5 cm/1¾ inches long. Bâtonnets are slightly smaller than batons.

TURNED CARROTS OR OTHER VEGETABLES (E.G., POTATOES, COURGETTES, TURNIPS)

Cut the vegetables in half lengthways, into 3–5 cm (1¼–2 inch) lengths. Hold each piece steady with your fingertips and, with a small knife, trim all the sharp edges. Work from the top to bottom in a quick curving movement, turning the vegetables slightly between each cut. The finished vegetables should be of a uniform, elongated walnut size and 'barrel' shaped. For courgettes, some of the skin may be left on for decorative effect. Use the parings for soups.

SHREDDED ONION

To shred an onion first trim, peel and halve it. Place each onion half flat side down and cut very thin slices across following the natural formation lines of the onion.

CANELLÉ COURGETTES

Choose young courgettes if possible. Cut grooves all around the courgettes with a canellé knife, leaving 5–7.5 mm (½–¾ inch) intervals in between the grooves.

CARROT FLOWERS

Peel the carrots and cut 5 deep grooves with a canellé knife at equal intervals around the carrots. Cut the carrots in thin slices across.

HALF-MOONS (FOR VEGETABLES SUCH AS MOOLI (WHITE RADISH/DAIKON) AND TURNIPS)

Peel the vegetable and cut in half north to south. Place the cut side on the chopping board and cut in thin slices across.

PEELING AND SEGMENTING AN ORANGE

PEELING

Using a serrated knife cut a slice from the top and bottom of the fruit through to the flesh. Stand the orange on a chopping board and cut away the rind, pith and skin working in lengths from top to bottom. Follow the curve of the fruit carefully to avoid cutting away any of the flesh.

SEGMENTING

Hold the peeled orange over a bowl to capture any juices and slide the knife down one side of a segment, cutting it away from the skin. Cut down the other side of the segment and pull out the section. Repeat with the remaining segments to leave the flaps of skin like the pages of a book.

ORANGE AND LEMON CURLS

Wash the fruit thoroughly then, using a zester, scrape around the skin to give curls.

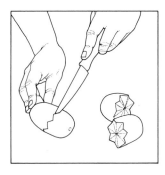

VANDYKED KIWI

To vandyke a kiwi or other fruits, use a pointed knife and cut around the middle of the fruit in a zig-zag fashion then carefully separate the halves.

CHILLI FLOWER

A chilli flower is made the same way as a spring onion tassle. Cut down from the pointed tip through to the centre of the chilli to make 8–12 petals, leaving the seeds intact. Place in icy cold water and leave, allowing the petals to curl.

PEPPER OR TOMATO TRIANGLE

Using a 3 cm (1 ¼ in) square piece of pepper or tomato flesh with skin on, make 2 equal incisions from either side to make a capital 'N', leaving the tops intact so as not to cut into slices. Twist the first bar under and place its end over the end of the last bar to form a triangle.

TOMATO ROSE

Cut the skin off in one piece in a spiral as if peeling an apple, removing as little flesh as possible. Roll up the resulting skin tightly, shiny side outwards to form a rose. If you like, place two watercress leaves either side of the tomato rose to make a lily.

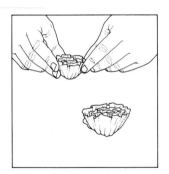

FILO PASTRY ROSE

Scrunch up a small piece of filo pastry to form an irregular pattern. Butter the top of the pie, place the extra pastry on top, brush with butter and bake. Once cooked, the pastry will look decorative and similar to a flower. It also works well with a large piece of pastry.

GHERKIN OR STRAWBERRY FANS

To fan gherkins, strawberries and other fruits, thinly slice them lengthways leaving the top/stalk attached. Flatten the slices gently to form a fan shape.

BUNDLES AND TIES

SPRING ONION OR CHIVE BUNDLES

The green tops of spring onions or chives can be used to bundle together vegetables, pancakes, filo pastry purses, etc. The tops of these vegetables should be steamed first for 1 minute.

LEMON AND ORANGE TIES

To make orange or lemon ties cut a long piece of skin from the fruit using a canellé knife; blanch by dipping in boiling water and simmering for 2 minutes, and use as ties for pancakes, etc.

REFRESHING HERBS

Garnishing a plate with limp herbs is worse than no garnish at all! To use herbs as a garnish to their best effect they ideally need to be freshly picked, which is not always possible. So to refresh limp herbs, immerse them totally in chilled water for 2–3 hours, drain well to remove every final drop of water, return the herbs to the bowl, cover with food wrap and place in the refrigerator where they will revive within 1–2 hours.

FEATHERING AND DAZZLING CREAM

To feather/dazzle cream on a coulis sauce draw a knife through the cream to streak and give a feathered effect.

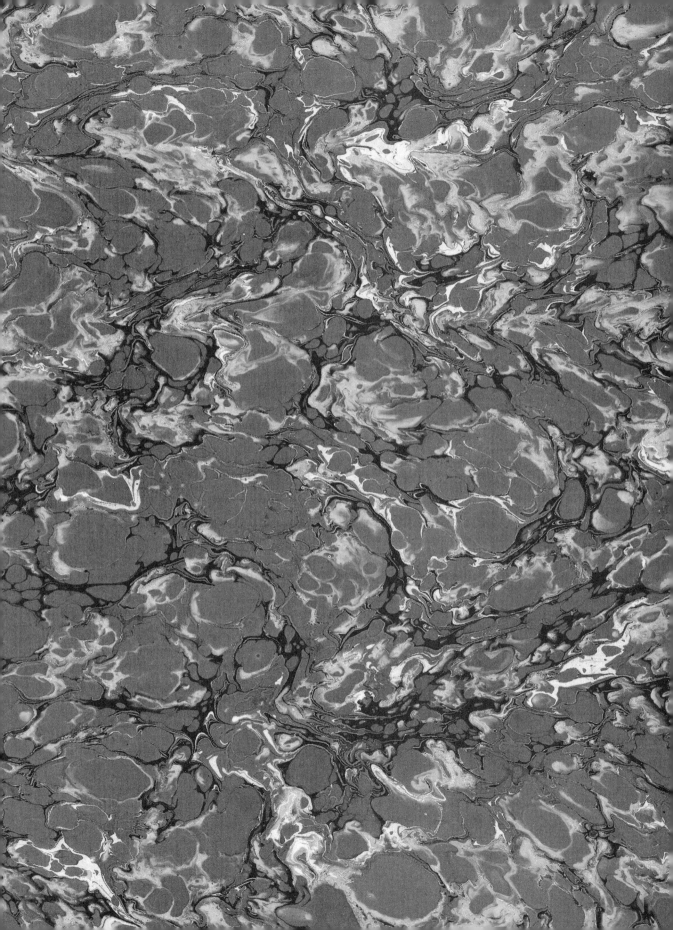

1

SPRING
MENUS

❶ Spring Menu

Art Deco Polenta Triangles
served with Fresh Herb, White Wine
and Tomato Sauce

~

Fresh Thyme, Courgette and
Artichoke Gratinée ◆

~

Tutti-frutti Ice-cream served with
Lemon and Apricot Sauce ◆

~

This is an enticing menu which starts with Italian polenta served with a very flavoursome and fruity tomato sauce. This is followed by a Fresh Thyme, Courgette and Artichoke Gratinée which, although simple, is made with such a combination of fresh ingredients that it is full of flavours. The menu finishes with Tutti-frutti Ice-cream which offers a richness totally different from that of other ice-creams as it has a base of creamed cashew nuts, curd cheese and tofu.

ART DECO POLENTA TRIANGLES SERVED WITH FRESH HERB, WHITE WINE AND TOMATO SAUCE

SERVES 6

Polenta is the name of a traditional Italian dish and is also the name of cornmeal flour. Here it is cooked with water as one would porridge, flavoured with butter and left to set; it is then cut into decorative triangular shapes which are dipped into egg and cornmeal, then fried until golden. The soft texture and flavour of the cornmeal is counteracted by that of the Fresh Herb, White Wine and Tomato Sauce; the combination makes a very special starter with an excellent colour and texture contrast.

It is best to buy polenta from an Italian delicatessen as it is only there that you will find the very coarse and bright yellow variety which is necessary for this dish.

- *600 ml (1 pint) water*
- *25 g (1 oz) butter, salted or unsalted*
- *1 × 2.5 ml spoon (½ teaspoon) salt*
- *100 g (4 oz) polenta*

FOR THE COATING

- *2 eggs, beaten*
- *75 g (3 oz) polenta*

FOR FRYING

- *2 × 15 ml spoons (2 tablespoons) olive oil*
- *25 g (1 oz) butter*

FOR THE FRESH HERB, WHITE WINE
AND TOMATO SAUCE

- *1 × 15 ml spoon (1 tablespoon) olive oil*

- *1 onion, peeled and finely chopped*
- *2 cloves garlic, crushed or finely chopped*
- *1 bayleaf*
- *1 sachet bouquet garni*
- *1 × 400 g (14 oz) tin tomatoes*
- *85 ml (3 fl oz) Italian white wine*
- *2 × 15 ml spoons (2 tablespoons) tomato purée*
- *1 vegetable stock cube, crumbled*
- *1 × 15 ml spoon (1 tablespoon) fresh chopped basil*
- *1 × 5 ml spoon (1 teaspoon) fresh chopped oregano*
- *salt and freshly ground pepper, to taste*

TO GARNISH

- *fresh basil*

Bring the water and butter to the boil in a medium-sized saucepan. Once boiling, add the salt and the polenta, sprinkling it gradually into the boiling water. Turn the heat down to medium then boil fast for 3 minutes, uncovered; turn it down again, place a lid on and cook until all the liquid has been absorbed, about 5 minutes. Place the pan in a double boiler (or in another pan of simmering water, which is covered with foil, so the heat is not lost) and cook for 20 minutes.

Transfer the cooked polenta into a lightly greased 18 × 18 cm (7 × 7 inch) square dish or tin and spread to 2 cm (¾ inch) thickness; cool slightly then cool thoroughly in the refrigerator.

- **MAKE THE SAUCE**

Heat the oil and fry the onion until translucent. Add the garlic, bayleaf, bouquet garni, tin of tomatoes, white wine, tomato purée and stock cube and simmer for 20 minutes.

Remove the bayleaf, break up the tomatoes with a wooden spoon, add the fresh basil and oregano, and season to taste; simmer for another 5 minutes. Keep the sauce warm.

Once the polenta is cold and set, turn it out on to a chopping board and cut into 9 neat squares; cut each square into 2 triangles. Dip each triangle first in beaten egg and then in the dry polenta. Fry half the pieces at a time in half the olive oil and half the butter for 1–2 minutes on each side or until the coating is crisp and golden. Drain on kitchen paper and repeat the process with the other half of the triangles, olive oil and butter.

- **TO SERVE**

Serve the polenta triangles arranged on warm plates, topped with the hot tomato sauce and garnished with a sprig of basil.

FRESH THYME, COURGETTE AND ARTICHOKE GRATINÉE

SERVES 6

*T*his light dish relies on the use of fresh seasonal vegetables to give it a very pleasant flavour and texture. Jerusalem artichokes have a particularly good texture and a nutty flavour; you should be able to buy them from your greengrocer but if not available use fresh small new potatoes instead. As soon as Jerusalem artichokes are peeled or scraped, place them in cold water to stop them from discolouring. If fresh broad beans are not available, use tinned flageolet beans instead.

* *750 g (1½ lb) fresh broad beans*
* *450 g (1 lb) Jerusalem artichokes, peeled*
* *3 × 15 ml (3 tablespoons) sunflower oil*
* *750 g (1½ lb) courgettes, chunkily chopped*
* *750 g (1½ lb) leeks, chopped (including almost all of the green tops)*
* *350 g (12 oz) french green beans, trimmed and cut in half*
* *6 medium tomatoes, peeled and chopped*
* *3 × 15 ml spoons (3 tablespoons) fresh chopped parsley*

* *3 × 5 ml spoons (3 teaspoons) fresh chopped thyme*
* *salt and freshly ground black pepper, to taste*
* *150 g (5 oz) mature Cheddar cheese, grated*

TO GARNISH

* *2 × 5 ml spoons (2 teaspoons) fresh chopped thyme*

Preheat the oven to gas mark 6, 400°F (200°C).

Take the broad beans out of their pods and boil in water until tender; this will take between 10 and 20 minutes depending on how fresh the beans are. In another pan, steam the artichokes for 10–12 minutes or until just tender; drain and slice into 5 mm–1 cm (¼–½ inch) slices.

Heat the oil in a very large frying-pan or pan and stir-fry the courgettes on a high heat until golden; lower the heat to medium high, add the leeks and french beans and cook for another 3 minutes. Add the tomatoes and cook, semi-covered, until the tomatoes have broken down to a pulp; this should take approximately another 2–3 minutes. Add the broad beans and Jerusalem artichokes with half the fresh herbs. Cook together for another 5 minutes. Season well.

Divide the mixture between six fairly shallow round ovenproof dishes, 200 ml (⅓ pint) in capacity. Scatter the rest of the fresh herbs over the vegetables and top with the grated cheese.

Bake in the preheated oven for 15–20 minutes or until golden on the top; then flash under a hot grill for 30 seconds to give a gratinée effect. Serve hot, each garnished with a little fresh thyme sprinkled on the top, with a mixed leaf salad as accompaniment.

TUTTI-FRUTTI ICE-CREAM

SERVES 6

Makes 550 g (1¼ lb) ice-cream

his ice-cream is not meant to bear a great resemblance to the traditional tutti-frutti ice-cream that one has become used to, but it does have similarities as it is made with a selection of plenty of fruits and contains pistachios.

- 25 g (1 oz) pistachios
- 25 g (1 oz) hazelnuts
- 150 ml (¼ pint) water
- 1 × 2.5 ml spoon (½ teaspoon) gelozone
- 175 g (6 oz) firm/regular tofu, chopped
- 50 g (2 oz) cashew nuts, ground to a fine paste in a coffee grinder
- 175 g (6 oz) curd cheese
- 50 g (2 oz) dried apricots, finely chopped
- 25 g (1 oz) sultanas, finely chopped
- 3 drops vanilla essence
- 2 drops almond essence
- 2 × 15 ml spoons (2 tablespoons) honey

FOR THE LEMON AND APRICOT SAUCE

- 50 g (2 oz) dried apricots
- 600 ml (1 pint) water
- piece of lemon rind, approximately 2.5 cm (1 inch) square

TO DECORATE

- 40 g (1½ oz) pistachios, skinned (for method see below) and finely chopped
- 15 g (½ oz) icing sugar

Place the pistachios and hazelnuts on a baking sheet and place in a preheated oven at gas mark 6, 400°F (200°C) for about 8 minutes or until you can see that their skins are beginning to crack. Transfer them into a clean tea-towel and rub the nuts against one another so they shed their skins. Discard the skins and chop the nuts until fairly fine.

Place the water and gelozone in a small saucepan; bring almost to boiling point, stirring all the time, but do not allow to boil. Transfer the mixture into a blender and add the tofu and cashew nut paste. Blend until completely smooth. Transfer the mixture into a mixing bowl, add the curd cheese and mix until completely smooth. Add the apricots, sultanas, vanilla and almond essences, pistachios, hazelnuts and honey and mix thoroughly until evenly distributed.

Place in an ice-cream maker or a freezer-proof container and freeze for 4 hours or until firm.

Make the lemon and apricot sauce. Place the apricots, water and lemon rind in a medium saucepan and bring to the boil; cook for 40 minutes. You should be left with 450 ml (¾ pint) cooking liquid; if not add cold water to make up the amount. Cool the mixture and blend in a blender until completely smooth. Chill in the refrigerator.

Remove the ice-cream from the freezer and let it stand for 30 minutes at room temperature or 1 hour in the refrigerator before serving; then scoop out two small scoops per person and serve on a bed of Lemon and Apricot Sauce. Scatter the chopped pistachios over the top and sprinkle the icing sugar through a sieve around the ice-cream. Serve immediately.

② *Spring Menu*

HIZIKI AND CUCUMBER BÂTONNETS
IN FRESH GINGER AND SESAME MARINADE ♦★

~

TRIO OF WILD MUSHROOMS
IN BUTTERFLY CASES

~

LAYERED FRUIT TERRINE
ON RUM AND ORANGE SAUCE ♦★

~

*T*he starter is very unusual as it uses one of the many
different types of sea vegetable available as its base.
The marinade is made with some strong flavourings, namely
toasted sesame oil and fresh ginger juice, which give this
starter its far eastern exotic appeal. Overall, the starter is very
light, fragrant and delicious and makes an excellent 'a priori'
to the rich main course of Trio of Wild Mushrooms in
Butterfly Cases made from puff pastry. The dessert is also
light, unusual and highly flavoured, making this menu well
balanced and very successful.

HIZIKI AND CUCUMBER BÂTONNETS IN FRESH GINGER AND SESAME MARINADE

SERVES 6

*E*very time I demonstrate this recipe, there is always someone smiling in the audience, and sitting there thinking, 'I will never like this dish, in a million years . . .' and that person is always the most surprised of all when he or she becomes enchanted by the result. And if you are also thinking you won't like it, well don't be too hesitant about making it, because you'll love it . . .

Hiziki seaweed can be purchased from good wholefood shops. In order to get the most flavour out of fresh root ginger choose roots which look clean, crisp, plump and fresh (when snapped in the middle the ginger shouldn't be stringy and should smell sweet and lemony).

- 15 g (½ oz) hiziki seaweed
- 150 ml (¼ pint) water
- 2 × 5 ml spoons (2 teaspoons) tamari

FOR THE MARINADE

- 2 × 15 ml spoons (2 tablespoons) sunflower oil
- 1 × 5 ml spoon (1 teaspoon) toasted sesame oil
- 1 × 15 ml spoon (1 tablespoon) fresh lemon juice
- ½ × 15 ml spoon (½ tablespoon) cider vinegar

- 1 × 15 ml spoon (1 tablespoon) tamari
- 2 spring onions, peeled and finely chopped (including most of the green tops)
- freshly ground black pepper
- 2½ × 15 ml spoons (2½ tablespoons) finely grated fresh root ginger
- ½ cucumber, cut into matchsticks

TO GARNISH

- 2 spring onions, peeled and finely chopped (including most of the green tops)
- a few fresh mint or coriander leaves

Soak the hiziki in the water and tamari in a small saucepan for 10 minutes, then bring to the boil, cover and simmer for 15 minutes; by then the water should have been absorbed by the seaweed or have evaporated. If not, remove the lid and boil until it has done so.

Meanwhile make the marinade. Mix the sunflower oil, toasted sesame oil, lemon juice, cider vinegar, tamari, spring onions and black pepper together in a mixing bowl. Pick up the grated root ginger in your hand and squeeze and collect as much of the juice as possible. Add the juice to the marinade ingredients and mix well; discard the fibres.

Cut the warm hiziki into 2.5 cm (1 inch) long pieces and add to the marinade. Leave to cool.

Fifteen minutes before serving add the cucumber matchsticks, mix delicately and leave to stand for 10 minutes; stir once more and leave to stand for another 5 minutes.

● **TO SERVE**

Divide the mixture between six large starter plates, placing it in the centre of the plate in the shape of a raised bonfire. Pour a sixth of the marinade over each seaweed mixture, and leave to disperse all over the plate. Serve with the spring onion garnish scattered over and around the 'bonfire'. Garnish with the fresh mint or coriander leaves placed at equal intervals, looking outwards towards the edge of the plates. Serve with crisp toast cut into triangular shapes.

T R I O   O F   W I L D   M U S H R O O M S   I N   B U T T E R F L Y   C A S E S

SERVES 6

*T*hese puff pastry cases are filled with rich wild mushrooms in a cream and whisky sauce. Since mushrooms are filling, the combination of three wild mushrooms makes this dish more than satisfying, so serve with light side vegetables such as steamed baby new potatoes, carrot batons and green beans.

Each wild mushroom has its own delicate flavour and should be prepared carefully as follows: oyster mushrooms – discard part of the stalk and shred both the cap and stalks; shiitake – discard the hard part of the stalk and shred both the cap and the rest of the stalk; field – wipe with a damp cloth to remove dirt and shred the caps and the stalks; chanterelles – remove the hard part of the stalks, and if any, scrape the rest of the stalks and shred the caps or leave whole (if the mushroom is small). Do not immerse any of the above mushrooms in water to clean, just wipe them with a damp cloth before chopping.

Do not substitute the cream with fromage frais or yoghurt as those low-fat alternatives will curdle in this instance.

- *750 g (1½ lb) puff pastry*
- *beaten egg, to glaze*

FOR THE FILLING

- *50 g (2 oz) butter*
- *175 g (6 oz) shallots, chopped finely*
- *1 kg (2¼ lb) mixture of three different prepared wild mushrooms, e.g. oyster, shiitake, field or chanterelle*
- *1½ × 5 ml spoon (1½ teaspoons) fresh chopped dill weed*

- *600 ml (1 pint) double cream*
- *2 × 15 ml spoons (2 tablespoons) whisky*
- *salt and freshly ground black pepper, to taste*

TO GARNISH

- *1 × 15 ml spoon (1 tablespoon) fresh chopped chives*
- *tomatoes, water-lily style (see page 16), optional*

Preheat the oven to gas mark 9, 475°F (240°C).

Roll out the pastry to a 20 × 40 cm (8 × 16 inches) rectangle; cut this into six 10 × 10 cm (4 × 4 inches) squares and the rest of the leftover pastry into another six rectangles. Fold each of the squares in half diagonally and make a cut through both layers of the triangle, 1 cm (½ inch) away from the edge, towards the point of the triangle. Leave an area of 5 mm (¼ inch) at the point where the cuts almost meet, uncut. Unfold each of the triangles, so each opens up as a square and brush the cut edges with a little of the beaten egg. Lift both loose corners (which will form the sides of the case) and fold one so it goes underneath the other and neatly meets the edge of the base of the case; fold the other so it meets the other edge of the base of the case, on the other side. Stick the edges with a fork, making a decorative pattern and brush with beaten egg.

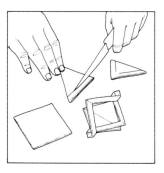

Repeat the process with all six cases. Cut six 'lids' from the leftover pastry, mark these with a fork and brush lightly with beaten egg.

Transfer both the cases and lids on a lightly greased baking sheet and bake in the preheated oven for 5 minutes; turn the oven down to gas mark 5, 190°F (375°C) and bake for a further 15 minutes or until the pastry is crisp overall. Note: you will need to take the lids out after 10–15 minutes. Keep all the cases and lids hot.

● MAKE THE FILLING

Melt the butter and fry the shallots until tender and golden brown. Add the mushrooms, fry quickly for 5–10 minutes then cook in a semi-covered pan for 10 minutes.

Add the dill weed, cream, whisky and seasoning; bring to the boil and cook for another 6 minutes.

● TO SERVE

Place each pastry case on a separate plate and fill with the mixture to excess, allowing some of the mixture to overflow on one side of the cases on to the plates. Semi-cover the top by placing the pastry lids at an angle and garnish by sprinkling some of the chives over. If you wish, place a tomato rose and watercress, lily-style (see page 16), on each plate.

LAYERED FRUIT TERRINE ON RUM AND ORANGE SAUCE

SERVES 6

This makes an exquisite light pudding which looks stunning. It consists of fruits set in a fresh fruit 'jelly', all in the shape of a 450 g (1 lb) loaf; the terrine is then turned out and cut into neat slices, displaying layers of various colourful fruits.

Agar-agar, which is used to set this terrine, is found in good wholefood shops and makes a very pleasant vegetarian alternative to gelatine as its set texture is soft, clear and not sticky. The setting shouldn't, however, be too soft or you will have difficulty in making slices out of the terrine! My advice is that when measuring agar-agar you use measuring spoons and fill them just above the rim; this way the recipe will be a great success. (Don't be tempted to use too much agar-agar on the other hand or the terrine will have a slightly rubbery texture.)

If the agar-agar mixture starts setting in the pan as you are layering this terrine, reheat it slowly to re-melt (do not reheat too much or the quantity of liquid will be reduced).

- *2 × 5 ml spoons (2 teaspoons) agar-agar powder or 6 × 5 ml spoons (6 teaspoons) agar-agar flakes*
- *600 ml (1 pint) white grape juice*
- *1½ × 15 ml spoons (1½ tablespoons) caster sugar*
- *1 × 15 ml spoon (1 tablespoon) crème de cassis*
- *2 oranges, peeled and segmented, see page 15*
- *175 g (6 oz) dark grapes, halved and pipped*
- *2 kiwi fruits, peeled and sliced*

- *2 large bananas*

FOR THE RUM AND ORANGE SAUCE

- *1 × 5 ml spoon (1 teaspoon) arrowroot*
- *300 ml (½ pint) orange juice*
- *1 × 15 ml spoon (1 tablespoon) honey*
- *1 × 15 ml spoon (1 tablespoon) dark rum*

TO DECORATE

- *18 strawberries, cut into fans (keep the green tops), see page 16*

Place the agar-agar in a saucepan and gradually add the white grape juice, mixing well. Bring to the boil and simmer for 3 minutes; if you are using agar-agar powder you should simmer the mixture for 12 minutes. Add the sugar and simmer for a further 10 seconds to make sure that it is totally dissolved. Take the pan off the heat and add the *crème de cassis*. Leave to cool a little.

Line a 450 g (1 lb) loaf tin with food wrap and place a layer of orange segments across the base of the tin. Using a small ladle, carefully pour just enough of the grape juice mixture to cover the orange segments. Leave to set; this first layer will take the longest to set (approximately 30 minutes). As agar-agar does not need to be chilled in a refrigerator to set, it is best not to move the tin so that the orange segments remain still. When set, make the second layer: cover the surface of the jelly with the halves of grapes, placed face down. Cover with more of the grape juice mixture and this time leave to set in the refrigerator. For the third layer, place the kiwi fruit slices over the jelly and cover with more grape juice mixture and leave to set in the refrigerator. Peel and slice the bananas and layer them on top of the set jelly. Cover with the grape juice mixture and leave to set in the refrigerator. Repeat all the layers once and finally leave to set in the refrigerator for 3–4 hours.

- **MAKE THE SAUCE**

Place the arrowroot in a small saucepan and gradually add the orange juice, stir until there are no visible lumps. Bring to the boil, stirring all the time and simmer for 1–2 minutes until the arrowroot clears. Remove from the heat and stir in the honey and rum; leave to cool.

- **TO SERVE**

Pour some of the sauce over six plates. Turn out the terrine on to a chopping board and carefully cut into six slices. Place each slice, cut side down, on to the sauce and decorate each plate with three strawberries, placed at equal intervals around the terrine, looking outwards.

③

𝒮 P R I N G 𝓜 E N U

LEMON AND CORIANDER
MARINATED AUBERGINES ◆★

~

LAYERED PANCAKE GALETTE WITH
BABY LEEK AND FENNEL SAUCE

~

SPIKED KIWIS IN TEARS OF GREEK YOGHURT ◆

~

I like this menu because it is light, colourful and, of course, tasty. The starter consists of slices of aubergines in a fresh, delicious coriander marinade. The pancake galette is multi-coloured as it has layers of red tomatoes and fennel alternating with green leek and watercress purée. The light and enjoyable dessert is very simple to make, and looks very pretty on the plate.

LEMON AND CORIANDER MARINATED AUBERGINES

SERVES 6

Here is a low-fat way of preparing aubergines. When marinated, the aubergines take on the flavour of the dressing quite intensely to produce a dish that is delicious and unusual. After being in contact with the lemon juice, the aubergines turn to a pretty purple colour and this looks great on the plate with the green marinade.

- 750 g (1½ lb) aubergines
- 1.2 litres (2 pints) water
- 6 × 15 ml spoons (6 tablespoons) white wine vinegar
- 4 × 15 ml spoons (4 tablespoons) fresh lemon juice
- 2½ × 15 ml spoons (2½ tablespoons) virgin olive oil

- 2 large cloves garlic, crushed
- 6 × 15 ml spoons (6 tablespoons) fresh chopped coriander
- salt and freshly ground black pepper

TO GARNISH

- 6 lemon wedges
- 12 sprigs fresh coriander

Cut the aubergines lengthwise into slices 7.5 mm (⅓ inch) thick. Bring the water to the boil and cook the aubergines for 14–17 minutes, making sure the slices are immersed. The colour of the flesh will change from white to green. Do not touch the slices as they are boiling but test them for tenderness after 14 minutes – the texture should be soft. Drain well in a colander and carefully place on a clean tea-towel to dry them.

Make the marinade by mixing all the other ingredients together. Transfer the aubergine slices into a large jam jar or '*bocal*' and pour the marinade over. Leave to marinate at room temperature for a few hours then place in the refrigerator for the last few hours. In total, the aubergine slices should marinate for approximately 12 hours.

● **T O   S E R V E**

Carefully lift one aubergine slice at a time out of the jar and place on a serving plate. Place another aubergine slice or two on to each plate and pour some coriander dressing over and around it. Garnish each plate with a wedge of lemon and two sprigs of fresh coriander. Serve with garlic toasts or crisp French bread.

L A Y E R E D   P A N C A K E   G A L E T T E
W I T H   B A B Y   L E E K   A N D   F E N N E L   S A U C E

SERVES 6

*T*his pancake galette has very colourful red and green layers of fennel and tomato alternating with leek and watercress. The pancakes should be large enough, measuring 19 cm (7½ inches) minimum, to allow for cutting easily into 6 portions. Serve this light savoury with new parsley potatoes and a side salad.

FOR THE PANCAKE BATTER

- 450 ml (¾ pint) semi-skimmed milk
- 3 eggs
- 2 × 5 ml spoons (2 teaspoons) sunflower oil
- ¼ × 5 ml spoon (¼ teaspoon) salt
- 175 g (6 oz) wholemeal flour

FOR THE FILLING NO. I

- 450 g (1 lb) fennel
- 25 g (1 oz) butter
- 1 clove garlic, crushed
- 1 kg (2 lb) medium tomatoes, peeled and chopped
- 1 × 5 ml spoon (1 teaspoon) sugar
- salt and freshly ground black pepper
- 225 g (8 oz) Cheddar cheese, grated

FOR THE FILLING NO. 2

- *15 g (½ oz) butter*
- *750 g (1½ lb) young leeks, chopped*
- *200 ml (⅓ pint) water mixed with 2 × 5 ml spoons (2 teaspoons) bouillon powder*
- *1 bunch watercress*

salt and freshly ground black pepper

FOR THE LEEK AND FENNEL SAUCE

- *25 g (1 oz) butter*
- *350 g (12 oz) young leeks, chopped*
- *1 head florence fennel, chopped*
- *600 ml (1 pint) water*
- *4 × 5 ml spoons (4 teaspoons) bouillon powder*
- *salt and freshly ground black pepper*

TO GARNISH AND SERVE

- *50 g (2 oz) Cheddar cheese, grated*
- *2 tomatoes, each cut into 6 wedges*
- *few leaves continental parsley or watercress sprigs*

● **MAKE THE PANCAKE BATTER**

Place the milk, eggs, oil and salt in a blender and blend until smooth. Add the flour and blend again until completely smooth. Leave to stand.

● **MAKE THE FILLINGS**

For the filling No. 1. Cut the fennel in half lengthwise and trim the top; remove the core and dice the fennel bulb. Melt the butter in a fairly large frying-pan and stir-fry the fennel until tender but do not brown. Add the garlic, tomatoes and sugar and cook, uncovered, for 10–15 minutes, stirring from time to time until the mixture has reduced by a third and is thick enough to be spread in between layers of pancakes. Season well.

For the filling No. 2. Melt the butter and gently fry the leeks until tender in a covered pan, this should take no more than 6–8 minutes. Add the water and bouillon powder, bring to the boil and simmer for another 5 minutes. Remove the large stalks from the watercress and roughly chop the rest. Add to the pan, cook for 1 minute and season well. Take the pan off the heat, cool a little and process in a food processor until the mixture is a little smoother.

● **MAKE THE SAUCE**

Melt the butter and gently fry the leeks and fennel until tender. Add the water and bouillon powder, bring to the boil and simmer for 10 minutes. Cool the sauce a little and blend in a blender until completely smooth. Transfer back into a clean pan, season well and reheat.

● **MAKE THE GALETTE**

Preheat the oven to gas mark 3, 325°F (160°C). Make 9 pancakes, each measuring 18–20 cm (7½–8 inches) in diameter, in a fairly large frying-pan. Place one pancake on a greased round baking sheet (18–20 cm (7½–8 inches) in diameter); cover with a quarter of the tomato sauce, level it and sprinkle a quarter of the grated cheese over it. Cover with another pancake, then a quarter of the leek and watercress mixture and another pancake. Repeat the layers three more times and finish with a plain pancake placed over the final layer of leek and watercress purée. Finish by sprinkling 50 g (2 oz) grated Cheddar cheese over the top pancake and place in the preheated oven for 20–25 minutes or until the pancake layer is heated through and the cheese is golden on top. Leave to stand for 5–8 minutes.

● TO SERVE

Cut into six portions and garnish each with 2 wedges of fresh tomatoes and a sprig of continental parsley or watercress. Serve with a little of the leek and fennel sauce poured by the side.

SPIKED KIWIS IN TEARS OF GREEK YOGHURT

SERVES 6

*T*his light dessert combines kiwi fruits, raspberries and Greek yoghurt to make a refreshing platter. The Greek yoghurt should be piped into tear shapes using a very small nozzle.

- 225–350 g (8–12 oz) Greek yoghurt
- 25 g (1 oz) soft brown sugar
- 9 kiwi fruits
- 225 g (8 oz) fresh raspberries
- 40 g (1½ oz) icing sugar

FOR THE RASPBERRY COULIS

- 450 g (1 lb) fresh or frozen raspberries
- 100 g (4 oz) soft brown sugar

Hang the Greek yogurt in a sieve lined with a cheesecloth or muslin to remove some of the moisture; leave to stand for 2½ hours, then mix with the soft brown sugar.

Make the raspberry coulis. Place the raspberries in a medium saucepan, add the sugar and 3 × 15 ml spoons (3 tablespoons) water; cook on a low to medium heat for 6 minutes or until soft. Cool a little, then sieve to remove all pips. Cool completely.

Remove the base and the top end of the kiwi fruits; peel and vandyke each one across, half-way down the middle, so you end up with two vandyked 'egg-cup' shapes (see page 15).

● TO SERVE

Place a few tablespoons of the coulis on each of the plates and place 3 halves of kiwis in the centre of each plate. Place 3 raspberries on the outside of each kiwi fruit. Pipe tears of Greek yoghurt all around the plate and sieve a little icing sugar over the plate just before serving.

❹

𝒮PRING 𝓜ENU

TRUFFLED AND BRANDIED FIELD MUSHROOMS ♦

~

CONTINENTAL FLAGEOLET
AND POTATO TIMBALE ♦

~

SOFT MERINGUE SOUFFLÉD PETIT PINEAPPLE ★

~

This menu probably sounds the most French of all in the book. The field mushrooms are cooked in a very slow and tasty way in their own juice. The timbale which follows has many layers and a mellow flavour and should be served with light vegetables or a side salad. The delicious pudding looks great with its white and spiky soft meringue topping and is served straight from the oven when the meringue is golden and the fruit salad underneath just warm and syrupy.

TRUFFLED AND BRANDIED FIELD MUSHROOMS

SERVES 6

This recipe relies on the slow cooking of field mushrooms which take their flavour from the brandy and tamari sauce. When served, these mushrooms have a crunchy topping and a soft base which should be cooked somewhere between *al dente* and soft. If no truffles are available, use 1 × 5 ml spoon (1 teaspoon) nori seaweed powder instead.

- 40 g (1½ oz) butter
- 6 large field mushrooms (approximately 13 cm (5 inches) wide)
- 1½ × 15 ml spoons (1½ tablespoons) tamari
- 5 × 15 ml spoons (5 tablespoons) water
- 1 × 5 ml spoons (1 teaspoon) brandy
- 1 clove garlic, crushed
- salt and freshly ground black pepper
- 2 spring onions, finely chopped

FOR THE FILLING

- *225 g (8 oz) button mushrooms*
- *15 g (½ oz) butter*
- *3 cloves garlic, finely chopped*
- *2 × 15 ml spoons (2 tablespoons) chopped fresh continental parsley*
- *40 g (1½ oz) breadcrumbs*

- *1½ × 15 ml spoons (1½ tablespoons) tamari*
- *salt and freshly ground black pepper*
- *15 g (½ oz) black truffles*

TO GARNISH

- *6 leaves fresh continental parsley*

Melt the butter and fry the field mushrooms in a partly covered pan for 10 minutes, on a low to medium heat. Turn the mushrooms over, cover the pan and cook for a further 10 minutes on a very low heat. Mix the tamari with the water and add the liquid to the pan together with the brandy, garlic and seasoning. Cook on a low to medium heat for 20 minutes, making sure that the pan is well covered so it does not lose any moisture. Baste the mushrooms with the cooking liquid from time to time.

● MAKE THE FILLING

Place the button mushrooms in a food processor and process until fine. Melt the butter and cook the mushrooms on a low heat for 10 minutes in an open pan, stirring occasionally. Add the garlic and continental parsley and cook for another 3 minutes. Add the breadcrumbs, tamari and seasoning and stir over the heat until the mixture has dried out a little. Chop the truffles into fine slivers then chop across to give small dice; add and mix well.

Take the whole field mushrooms out of their pan and place on a baking sheet (reserve the cooking liquid). Top each mushroom with a sixth of the breadcrumb mixture and flash under a medium hot grill until the breadcrumbs are crisp on top.

Slowly reheat the reserved cooking liquid, add the spring onions to the sauce and cook for 3 minutes, covered, adding 1–2 × 15 ml spoons (1–2 tablespoons) more water if necessary.

● TO SERVE

Place the mushrooms on plates and pour the juice around them. Garnish with continental parsley.

CONTINENTAL FLAGEOLET AND POTATO TIMBALE

SERVES 6

*T*his dish started as an adaptation to a Gratin Dauphinois but is now far from being anything that resembles it; it has become a very colourful and healthy alternative. When making this dish, make sure that every layer is well flavoured as it is too late to season once it is turned out.

- 150 g (5 oz) flageolet beans, soaked overnight
- 350 g (12 oz) green beans, topped and tailed
- 275 g (10 oz) mature vegetarian Cheddar cheese, grated
- 2 × 5 ml spoons (2 teaspoons) bouillon powder
- salt and freshly ground black pepper
- 4 × 15 ml spoons (4 tablespoons) fresh chopped continental parsley
- 1.5 kg (3 lb) King Edward potatoes, unpeeled
- 1 kg (2 lb) medium to large fresh tomatoes, sliced

FOR THE SAUCE

- 1 × 15 ml spoon (1 tablespoon) virgin olive oil
- 1 onion, peeled and finely chopped
- 1 × 400 g (1 × 14 oz) tin tomatoes
- 2 × 15 ml spoons (2 tablespoons) tomato purée
- 300 ml (½ pint) water
- 1 vegetable stock cube
- few drops Tabasco
- 1 × 15 ml spoon (1 tablespoon) fresh chopped thyme and basil

TO SERVE

- 6 sprigs fresh basil

Preheat the oven to gas mark 5, 375°F (190°C).

Place the flageolet beans in a medium saucepan, cover with 2.5 cm (1 inch) water and bring to the boil. Simmer for 30–35 minutes or until tender. Drain. Meanwhile, steam the green beans for 8 minutes. Place the flageolets and the green beans in a food processor, add 50 g (2 oz) of the cheese, bouillon powder and seasoning and process until smooth. Take the mixture out of the food processor, add the parsley and mix well.

Lightly oil the base and sides of a 2.5 litre (4½ pint) straight-sided ovenproof soufflé dish. Boil the potatoes until tender. Drain and slice into 5 mm (¼ inch) slices.

Place a third of the tomato slices, slightly overlapping, on the base of the dish and sprinkle a third of the remaining 225 g (8 oz) cheese over them. Cover with a layer of cooked potatoes, arranged in a circular, overlapping fashion. Spoon half the green bean and flageolet mixture over the potatoes and level with the back of a spoon. Arrange another layer of potatoes on top. Repeat the layers and finish with an extra layer of tomatoes and cheese. Bake for 40 minutes.

● MAKE THE SAUCE

Heat the oil and fry the onion until soft. Add the tin of tomatoes, tomato purée, water, stock cube and Tabasco and bring the contents of the pan to the boil. Simmer for 25 minutes and cool a little. Blend in a blender until smooth. Return the sauce to the pan, add the fresh herbs and reheat; simmer for another 3 minutes.

● TO SERVE

Remove the timbale from the oven and allow it to stand for 10 minutes, then loosen the edges and turn it out on to a serving platter. Cut into six portions and serve on a bed of tomato sauce. Garnish each plate with a sprig of fresh basil.

SOFT MERINGUE SOUFFLÉD PETIT PINEAPPLE

SERVES 6

*T*his delicious dessert combines sweetness, lightness and exotic flavours. When preparing these souffléd baby pineapples for a dinner party, make sure you have assembled and weighed the ingredients for the meringues before the meal, then all you need to do is whip the egg whites, add the sugar, spoon the meringue over the fruit salad – already in the pineapples – and flash the shells in the oven. The fruit salad filling will come out just warm and deliciously syrupy. The dwarf pineapples are just the right fruits to use as a shell as they are very sweet and hold exactly the right amount of mixture to make a perfectly sized pudding.

- *3 dwarf pineapples*
- *6 passion fruits*
- *3 kiwi fruits*
- *6 banana apples (if not available use small bananas)*
- *1 large mango*

FOR THE MERINGUE

- *3 egg whites*
- *175 g (6 oz) white sugar*
- *extra sugar for sprinkling on top of the meringue*

Preheat the oven to gas mark 7, 425°F (210°C).

Cut each dwarf pineapple in half lengthwise to create two boat-shaped shells; leave the green tops on. Scoop the flesh out of the pineapple with the help of a grapefruit knife; remove and discard the core then dice the flesh into small pieces.

Prepare the other fruits: remove all seeds and flesh from the passion fruits; peel and dice the kiwi fruits, banana apples and mango into small pieces. Fill the pineapple shells with the fruit salad mixture.

Prepare the meringue. Whisk the egg whites until stiff; add the sugar, a dessertspoon at a time, and carry on whisking between each addition until all the sugar is incorporated.

Five minutes before serving, place two large tablespoons of the meringue over each pineapple and spike it with a fork or skewer so it looks like the spikes of the pineapple. Place on a baking sheet. Sprinkle a little of the extra sugar over the meringues and place the baking tray in the preheated oven for 3–4 minutes or until golden and set; do not worry if the meringue peaks get a little brown, as all they do is caramelise and taste fine.

Serve each pineapple half on a plate straightaway.

❺

ℐPRING ℳENU

CROWN OF CREAMED ASPARAGUS ♦

~

SORREL AND COTTAGE CHEESE CHARLOTTE

~

LEMON TARTLETS

~

This is a menu which uses ingredients such as asparagus, sorrel and lemon to give a sense of lightness to the meal. It is, however, a well-balanced meal which starts with a little creamy timbale surrounded by lightly cooked asparagus. The main course is a charlotte with a fresh spinach and cottage cheese filling and the menu finishes with tartlets based on lemon pâte sablée and a lemon and yoghurt filling.

CROWN OF CREAMED ASPARAGUS

SERVES 6

These asparagus timbales have a very delicate flavour and a pretty pale green colour. The plates are simply but effectively garnished with asparagus tips, criss-crossed with slices of tomato.

Follow precisely the quantities given below to ensure a delicate and creamy setting. Also make sure that you buy fine asparagus and that you have a minimum of 36 asparagus tips in your bunch.

- 750 g (1½ lb) green asparagus
- 3 × 15 ml spoons (3 tablespoons) champagne vinegar
- 2 × 15 ml spoons (2 tablespoons) sunflower oil

FOR THE TIMBALES

- 300 ml (½ pint) water
- 2¼ × 5 ml spoons (2¼ teaspoons) agar-agar powder or 6¾ × 5 ml spoons

- (6¾ teaspoons) agar-agar flakes
- 2½ × 5 ml spoons (2½ teaspoons) bouillon powder
- salt and freshly ground black pepper
- 150 ml (5 fl oz) double cream

TO GARNISH

- 18 thin wedges of tomato, de-seeded and centre part taken out
- 6 sprigs fresh chervil

Trim 2.5 cm (1 inch) off the asparagus spears and steam for 15 minutes. Divide the asparagus into two equal quantities.

Take the first quantity and cut the tips and any tender parts (discard any woody parts) into 4.5 cm (1½ inch) pieces. Make sure you have at least 18 tips in this quantity. Mix the champagne vinegar, sunflower oil and a good pinch of salt together in a small mixing bowl; add the tips (only) of asparagus to the vinaigrette and leave aside. Reserve the tender parts separately.

● MAKE THE TIMBALES

Take the second quantity and roughly chop all parts of the asparagus. Place in a blender with the water and blend until completely smooth; pass through a sieve and retain only the pulp. Place the agar-agar and bouillon powder in a small saucepan and stir in the aparagus purée gradually. Bring to the boil, cover the pan, turn the heat down and simmer for 12 minutes. Stir from time to time and push whatever sticks to the side of the saucepan down back into the mixture; this is probably agar-agar which is not mixing and this will affect the setting. Season to taste and check the quantity of liquid left; you should have 450 ml (¾ pint) of liquid but if not, add a little water to make up the quantity. Transfer the mixture into a mixing bowl and add the cream. Season again, if necessary. Leave to cool a little.

Pour the asparagus mixture into 6 small ramekin dishes 100 ml (3½ fl oz) in capacity. Carefully place the reserved asparagus pieces (the tender parts, not the tips, from the first quantity) around each ramekin, so they form a crown. Leave to cool and set.

● TO SERVE

Loosen the sides of the ramekin dishes with the point of a knife; turn out on to plates and garnish each plate with 3 of the reserved asparagus tips in vinaigrette, criss-crossed with a wedge of tomato. Pour some of the vinaigrette around the timbales and over the tips and place a sprig of chervil on top of each timbale. Serve with crisp bread and butter, melba toast or triangles of toast.

SORREL AND COTTAGE CHEESE CHARLOTTE

SERVES 6–8

*T*his is a savoury version of a charlotte and here the mould is lined with bread. The sorrel gives this dish unusual and delicious pungency but if not available use the same weight of spinach instead. The filling is based on cottage cheese and so is quite a low-fat mixture. The charlotte is served on a bed of tasty tomato sauce which makes a stunning colour contrast.

15 g (½ oz) butter

225 g (8 oz) fennel, finely diced

50 g (2 oz) sorrel leaves, finely chopped

225 g (8 oz) spinach leaves, finely chopped

225 g (8 oz) cottage cheese

3 eggs, beaten

450 ml (¾ pint) milk

1 × 5 ml (1 teaspoon) English mustard

pinch cayenne pepper

salt and freshly ground black pepper

450 g (1 lb) medium sliced white bread, buttered

100 g (4 oz) pine kernels

FOR THE TOMATO COULIS

1 × 15 ml spoon (1 tablespoon) butter

1 onion, peeled and finely chopped

2 cloves garlic, crushed

1 × 400 g (1 × 14 oz) tin tomatoes

2 × 15 ml spoons (2 tablespoons) tomato purée

300 ml (½ pint) water

2 × 5 ml spoons (2 teaspoons) bouillon powder

1 bayleaf

salt and freshly ground black pepper

TO GARNISH

6 sprigs fresh chervil

Preheat the oven to gas mark 5, 375°F (190°C).

Melt the butter and gently fry the fennel until tender. Add the sorrel and spinach and cook for a further 5 minutes until tender, stirring all the time. Take the pan off the heat. Drain the whey off the cottage cheese. Transfer the cottage cheese into a bowl and add the sorrel mixture. Mix well and season to taste.

Place the eggs in another mixing bowl, add the milk, mustard, cayenne pepper and seasoning and beat well using a whisk.

Cut the crusts off the bread and cut the slices in half diagonally so you end up with two triangles out of each slice.

Line the base and grease a 1.75 litre (3 pint) charlotte mould and line it with the bread, buttered side against the mould. Start by placing two triangles over the base first then line the sides by overlapping the triangles so that there are no gaps until the tin is thoroughly lined. Reserve about 4 slices of bread.

Fill the charlotte with the sorrel mixture, sprinkling the pine kernels between the bread slices and the sorrel mixture. Pour the savoury egg custard over the sorrel and spinach mixture and leave to stand for 20 minutes to allow it to soak into the bread. Then force the egg custard to disperse evenly through the sorrel mixture by dipping the prongs of a fork through the savoury sorrel and egg mixture. Cover with 2 to 4 slices of reserved triangles of bread. Leave to stand for another 10 minutes. Bake in the preheated oven for 55 minutes or until completely set. Let the mould stand for 15 minutes then loosen the edges carefully with a knife before turning out.

● **MAKE THE TOMATO COULIS**

Melt the butter and fry the onion until soft; add the garlic and cook for another 2 minutes. Add the tin of tomatoes, tomato purée, water, bouillon powder and bayleaf and bring the contents of the pan to the boil. Turn the heat down and simmer for 25 minutes. Remove the bayleaf, cool a little and blend the coulis until smooth. Reheat in a clean saucepan and season to taste. Keep warm.

● **TO SERVE**

Cut the charlotte into thick slices and serve on a bed of hot tomato coulis with a sprig of fresh chervil.

LEMON TARTLETS

SERVES 6

*T*his is a low-fat version of *tarte au citron*, and is delicious and tangy as it uses yoghurt instead of cream. The pastry is a *pâte sablée* – therefore short and crumbly – flavoured with a little lemon essence. To give a good lemon flavour in the tartlets, lemon zest is used; I prefer to use organic lemons as I find that their flavour is better and also because the zest has not been chemically treated. Do not refrigerate these tartlets once cooked or the pastry will soften.

FOR THE PASTRY

● *15 g (½ oz) ground almonds*
● *150 g (5 oz) plain white flour*
● *40 g (1½ oz) soft brown sugar*
● *pinch of salt*
● *75 g (3 oz) butter, softened*
● *2 egg yolks, beaten*
● *few drops of lemon essence*
● *a little egg white, to brush the pastry*

FOR THE FILLING

● *3 eggs*
● *75 g (3 oz) soft brown sugar*
● *zest of 2 lemons*
● *450 ml (¾ pint) plain natural yoghurt*

TO DECORATE

● *15 g (½ oz) icing sugar*
● *6 large strawberries in fans, see page 16*

Preheat the oven to gas mark 6, 400°F (200°C).

● **MAKE   THE   PASTRY**

Mix the ground almonds, flour, sugar and salt in a large mixing bowl. Mix well then add the butter, working it into the flour with your fingertips. Add the egg yolks and lemon essence and gather into a smooth dough. Do not overwork the dough otherwise the pastry will be tough.

    Divide the pastry into six parts and shape each into a smooth ball; flatten slightly and roll out to a circle measuring 13 cm (5 inches) in diameter. Dust your work surface lightly first with a little flour to stop the pastry from sticking but do not flour twice as this will affect the balance of ingredients in the pastry. It is preferable to flour your rolling pin to make sure there is no pastry sticking to it. Line 6 tartlet tins, measuring 9 cm (3½ inches) in diameter and 2 cm (¾ inch) deep, and flute the edges with your fingers. Place on the middle shelf of the preheated oven and bake for 15 minutes. Remove, allow to cool slightly then lightly brush the pastry with beaten egg white. Return the tartlets to the oven for 3 minutes to dry out the egg white as this will stop the pastry from going soft on contact with the filling. Cool in their tins.

● **MAKE   THE   FILLING**

Turn the oven down to gas mark 2, 300°F (150°C). Place the eggs and sugar in a mixing bowl and whisk together for 2 minutes until creamy. Add the lemon zest and yoghurt and beat again. Pour the mixture into the prepared flan cases and bake for 1 hour. Cool thoroughly.

● **TO   SERVE**

Place the tartlets on to serving plates and just before serving dust with a little icing sugar, letting some fall around the edge of the tartlets to decorate the plate. Place a fanned-out strawberry on the edge of each tartlet.

SPRING MENU ⑥
right Chestnut Mushroom and Armagnac Terrine served with Cream and Brandy Sauce
centre Legumes de Printemps in Filo Baskets *left* Syrupy Lemon and Apricot Many-Layer Pudding

6

$\mathscr{S}$ PRING $\mathscr{M}$ ENU

CHESTNUT MUSHROOM AND ARMAGNAC
TERRINE SERVED WITH CREAM
AND BRANDY SAUCE

~

LEGUMES DE PRINTEMPS IN FILO BASKETS ♦

~

SYRUPY LEMON AND
APRICOT MANY-LAYER PUDDING ♦

~

*This is a light menu which starts with a tasty terrine
made with a combination of two different mushrooms.
The main course is a combination of crisp vegetables cooked in
a flavoursome miso and tamari sauce set in filo pastry baskets.
The meal ends with a layered light apricot pudding which
turns out well.*

CHESTNUT MUSHROOM AND ARMAGNAC TERRINE

SERVES 6

These delicious soft terrines are made with nutty chestnut mushrooms and ordinary creamed mushrooms; whole brandied mushrooms are also added to give them further texture. In order to make this terrine successfully don't wash the mushrooms (just wipe with a damp cloth), otherwise the terrine will be watery.

FOR THE MUSHROOM TERRINES

- *225 g (8 oz) chestnut mushrooms*
- *225 g (8 oz) button mushrooms*
- *25 g (1 oz) butter*
- *3 eggs*
- *1 × 15 ml spoon (1 tablespoon) tamari*
- *3 × 15 ml spoons (3 tablespoons) soured cream*
- *5 × 15 ml spoons (5 tablespoons) double cream*
- *salt and freshly ground black pepper*

FOR THE FILLING	FOR THE CREAM AND BRANDY SAUCE
● *10 g (¼ oz) butter*	● *3 × 15 ml spoons (3 tablespoons)*
● *24 button mushrooms*	*Armagnac*
● *½ × 15 ml spoon (½ tablespoon)*	● *1 × 15 ml spoon (1 tablespoon)*
brandy	*double cream*
● *½ × 15 ml spoon (½ tablespoon) tamari*	● *2 × 5 ml spoons (2 teaspoons) tamari*
● *2 × 15 ml spoons (2 tablespoons) fresh*	● *3 × 15 ml spoons (3 tablespoons) water*
chopped continental parsley	
● *salt and freshly ground black pepper*	TO GARNISH
	● *12 leaves continental parsley*

Preheat the oven to gas mark 6, 400°F (200°C). Line and lightly grease 6 ramekins 150 ml (¼ pint) in capacity.

Process the mushrooms for the terrine in the food processor until fine. Melt the butter in a large frying-pan and cook the mushrooms on a medium heat for 15 minutes, stirring from time to time. This is to dry out the mushroom mixture so do not cover the pan. Allow the mushrooms to cool a little.

Beat the eggs until smooth; add the tamari, soured cream, double cream and seasoning and mix well. Stir in the mushrooms. Leave to stand.

● **MAKE THE FILLING**

Melt the butter in a small saucepan, add the whole button mushrooms and cook on a medium heat for 2 minutes. Turn the heat down and add the brandy, tamari, continental parsley and seasoning and cook for another 3 minutes.

● **MAKE THE SAUCE**

Mix all the ingredients together and slowly bring to the boil, stirring all the time. Simmer, covered, for 6 minutes then cool.

Place a bain-marie on the middle shelf of the oven and heat until the water is steamy.

Divide the egg and mushroom mixture between the prepared ramekins. Place three of the whole button mushrooms in the centre of each of the ramekins and press them down until they are immersed. Place the filled ramekins in the bain-marie and bake for 20–25 minutes or until set. Take the ramekins out of the water and leave to cool completely.

● **TO SERVE**

Turn out a ramekin on to each plate and pour a little sauce over and around the terrine. Do not pour too much of the sauce on the plate and do not attempt to cover its base. Garnish each terrine with one of the leftover whole button mushrooms, cut in half, and two leaves of fresh continental parsley.

Legumes de Printemps in Filo Baskets

SERVES 6

*T*hese filo baskets look very impressive and are filled with delicious baby vegetables cooked in a tasty savoury miso and tamari sauce. The filo baskets may be prepared in advance and kept in an airtight tin for two days. Some packets of filo pastry contain 24 sheets, others contain only a few, so check the contents of your packet before starting this recipe.

- *30 sheets filo pastry*
- *100–125 g (4–5 oz) melted butter*

FOR THE FILLING

- *1.25 kg (2½ lb) mixture of prepared baby vegetables: dwarf corn, baby courgettes, button mushrooms, broccoli florets, baby carrots, baby turnips, peas, etc.*
- *40 g (1½ oz) butter*
- *4½ × 5 ml spoons (4½ teaspoons) arrowroot*
- *1½ × 15 ml spoons (1½ tablespoons) barley miso*
- *1½ × 15 ml spoons (1½ tablespoons) tamari*

- *1½ × 15 ml spoons (1½ tablespoons) tomato purée*
- *450 ml (¾ pint) water*
- *salt and freshly ground black pepper*

FOR THE SAUCE

- *1 × 15 ml spoon (1 tablespoon) barley miso*
- *1½ × 5 ml spoons (1½ teaspoons) arrowroot*
- *300 ml (½ pint) water*

TO GARNISH

- *6 sprigs of chervil*

Preheat the oven to gas mark 7, 425°F (220°C).

Defrost the filo pastry in the refrigerator or at room temperature. Place 6 upturned college pudding moulds 200 ml (⅓ pint) in capacity, greased on the outside, on a baking sheet.

Brush each sheet of filo pastry with the melted butter and cut in half. Place one half over a mould letting the filo pastry drop on to the baking sheet if necessary, as this will make a rim. Place the second half of pastry sheet on to the first one at a slightly different angle to the first, overlapping it. Repeat with another three sheets of filo pastry, then repeat the process with the other 5 cups. Note: if your baking sheet is not big enough to take 6 cups, bake 3 cups at a time. Bake in the preheated oven for 10–15 minutes until golden brown, turning the oven down to gas mark 5, 375°F (190°C), if the pastry appears to become too brown. Take the cups out of the oven and leave to stand for 5 minutes. Carefully turn the cups out and remove the moulds from the pastry. Do not worry if one layer of pastry comes off as you do so.

● **MAKE THE FILLING**

Cut the dwarf corn and baby courgettes into 2 cm (³/₄ inch) long pieces; cut the broccoli into small florets and thinly slice part of their base; slice the baby carrots into 5 mm (¹/₄ inch) thick slanted slices: cut the baby turnips into 1–2 cm (¹/₂–³/₄ inch) thick pieces; leave the peas whole.

Melt the butter and sauté the vegetables together for 5 minutes on a medium heat; cover and cook for a further 5 minutes or until tender.

Whisk the arrowroot, miso, tamari, tomato purée and water together in a mixing bowl. Add this mixture to the vegetables and bring to the boil, stirring all the time. Simmer for 3–4 minutes and season to taste.

● **MAKE THE SAUCE**

Place the miso, arrowroot and water in a mixing bowl and whisk until smooth. Transfer it into a small saucepan, bring to the boil, stirring all the time, then turn the heat down and simmer for 2 minutes. Keep it hot.

Reheat the baskets, if necessary, in a preheated oven to gas mark 5, 375°F (190°C) for 4–5 minutes; do not leave the baskets in the oven for too long otherwise they will dry out and may crack.

● **TO SERVE**

Pour a little of the sauce over 6 warmed plates, just enough to glaze the plate. Place the baskets over the sauce and divide the filling between them. Garnish with a sprig of chervil over one edge of the baskets. Serve with a mixture of rice and wild rice cooked together.

SYRUPY LEMON AND APRICOT MANY-LAYER PUDDING

SERVES 6

*T*his colourful dessert is delicious and consists of alternating layers of apricot and light breadcrumbs. Serve with Greek yoghurt.

- *175 g (6 oz) dried apricots, soaked overnight in 450 ml (¾ pint) water*
- *120 ml (4 fl oz) honey*
- *120 g (4½ oz) white breadcrumbs*
- *grated rind and juice of 1 lemon*
- *215 g (7½ oz) wholewheat flour*
- *3 × 5 ml spoons (3 teaspoons) baking powder*

- *120 g (4½ oz) solid white vegetable fat, chilled*
- *4 × 15 ml spoons (4 tablespoons) milk*

TO DECORATE

- *6 leaves fresh mint*

Lightly grease a 1.25 litre (2¼ pint) pudding basin and line its base. Cut the apricots into fine slivers and cook in their soaking juice for 10 minutes, uncovered, so the liquid reduces.

Drain the apricots (reserve the liquid for serving with the pudding), and mix them with the honey, 40 g (1½ oz) of the breadcrumbs and the lemon rind. Leave aside.

Place the flour in a separate mixing bowl and add the baking powder; mix well to distribute the powder evenly. Grate the fat into the flour, making sure that it falls freely into the flour and does not re-form as lumps. Add the lemon juice, milk and the rest of the breadcrumbs and, using a palette knife, form the mixture into a soft dough. Roll out the dough into 3 circles, one fitting the base of the pudding bowl and the two others graduating in size to fit the middle and the top of the dish.

Start layering by spooning a good layer of the apricot mixture into the base of the pudding bowl. Cover it with the smallest layer of pastry and repeat the process twice, finishing with pastry. Cover with a layer of greaseproof paper, greased on the inside, and a layer of foil. Tie with string and steam for 2½ hours. Leave to stand for 15 minutes and turn out on to a serving dish.

● **TO SERVE**

Cut into slices and serve on individual plates on a bed of sieved juice left over from the cooking of the apricots. Pour a little Greek yoghurt on to each plate, decorate with a leaf of fresh mint and serve.

7

SPRING MENU

THREE-LAYER CARROT AND ASPARAGUS MOUSSE RAINBOW

~

BUTTER BEAN 'BLANQUETTE STYLE' IN FILO PRESENTATION BOX

~

CAKE OF PEAR AND ALMOND WITH COINTREAU AND APRICOT SAUCE

~

This menu starts with a rainbow mousse which is simple to make and is accompanied by a tasty dill vinaigrette. The success of the main course is due partly to the contrast between the soft texture of the casserole and the crunchiness of the pastry. The light pear and almond cake is served warm with a Cointreau and apricot sauce.

THREE-LAYER CARROT AND ASPARAGUS MOUSSE RAINBOW

SERVES 6

Makes a deep 450 g (1 lb) loaf terrine

This is a soft terrine made of two layers interlacing one another, giving the impression of many more layers. A layer of bread is placed between the carrot layer and the asparagus layer to prevent the layers melting into each other and this gives this terrine its rainbow effect. The terrine is served on a bed of tasty dill vinaigrette.

LAYER NO. 1

- 225 g (8 oz) fresh asparagus
- 150 ml (¼ pint) water
- 1 egg
- salt and freshly ground black pepper

LAYER NO. 2

- 225 g (8 oz) carrots, peeled and diced
- a touch of orange rind
- 150 ml (¼ pint) double cream
- 2 eggs
- salt and freshly ground black pepper

- 4 slices of medium sliced white bread, buttered

FOR THE VINAIGRETTE

- 3 × 15 ml spoons (3 tablespoons) dill vinegar
- 6 × 15 ml spoons (6 tablespoons) sunflower oil
- salt and freshly ground black pepper

TO GARNISH

- 18 steamed spears asparagus
- 18 thin strips orange rind 4 cm (1½ inches) long

Preheat the oven to gas mark 6, 400°F (200°C) and line a deep 450 g (1 lb) loaf tin with greased baking parchment. Place a bain-marie in the oven.

● MAKE THE FILLINGS

For the Layer No. 1. Steam the asparagus for 12–15 minutes or until tender. Trim and discard the woody parts of the asparagus, if any. Blend the asparagus together with the water until completely smooth. Add the egg and plenty of seasoning and blend again until smooth.

For the Layer No. 2. Steam the carrots for 15–18 minutes or until tender and just beginning to soften. Transfer into a food processor and process until very fine but not completely puréed, so there is some texture left. Transfer into a mixing bowl and add the touch of orange rind, double cream, eggs and seasoning. Mix well with a whisk.

Pour a little less than half the quantity of the carrot mixture on the base of the loaf tin; cover with two pieces of bread without crusts, cut out to fit exactly the shape of the loaf tin. This bread layer will stop the asparagus mixture from slipping through to the carrot mixture. Carefully pour the asparagus mixture over the bread and cover with another layer of buttered bread, again cut out to fit the tin exactly. Pour the rest of the carrot mixture over the bread and place the loaf tin in the bain-marie; the water should be steaming and come two-thirds of the way up the tin. Bake for 40 minutes and leave to cool thoroughly in the bain-marie.

Make the vinaigrette. Mix the dressing ingredients together in a small mixing bowl.

● TO SERVE

Turn the terrine out on to a platter. Cut into 2 cm (¾ inch) slices and pour a little of the dressing around each slice. Garnish each plate with 3 asparagus tips (cut out from the spears) and criss-cross with the orange strips. Serve cool.

BUTTER BEAN 'BLANQUETTE STYLE' IN FILO PRESENTATION BOX

SERVES 6

*T*he blanquette is presented in a box of filo pastry and apart from making the dish look extremely pretty and keeping the casserole hot, this also provides a very good texture contrast to the otherwise soft casserole. It is also fun to make these boxes because they are very quick to make.

The blanquette should be well seasoned. As well as a liaison of cream and egg, I add a little flour to stop the buttery court bouillon from curdling. If sugar snap peas are not available, use mangetout or runner beans (both threaded) instead.

FOR THE FILO PRESENTATION BOXES

- *15–18 sheets of filo pastry*
- *100 g (4 oz) butter, melted*

FOR THE BLANQUETTE FILLING

- *25 g (1 oz) butter*
- *175 g (6 oz) leeks, chopped into 2 cm (¾ inch) pieces*
- *175 g (6 oz) baby carrots (no longer than 7.5 cm (3 inches), cut in half lengthways*
- *100 g (4 oz) heart of a white celery, chopped into 2 cm (¾ inch) pieces*
- *2 medium turnips, cut into thin half-moons*
- *100 g (4 oz) baby sweetcorn, cut in half lengthways*
- *175 g (6 oz) sugar snap peas, topped and tailed*

- *75 g (3 oz) French green beans, topped and tailed and cut in half*
- *350 g (12 oz) courgettes, part peeled with a canellé knife and chunkily chopped*
- *bouquet garni of two good bunches of parsley and 2 bayleaves*
- *600 ml (1 pint) water*
- *2 vegetable stock cubes, crumbled*
- *1 × 400 g (14 oz) tin of butter beans, drained*
- *5 medium tomatoes, peeled and chopped*
- *1 × 15 ml spoon (1 tablespoon) white flour*
- *150 ml (¼ pint) double cream*
- *3 egg yolks*
- *salt and freshly ground black pepper*

TO GARNISH

- *fresh sprigs chervil*

Preheat the oven to gas mark 6, 400°F, (200°C).

Brush a sheet of filo pastry with the melted butter, place another buttered sheet on it and fold into thirds; you now have 6 layers. Cut into a strip measuring 4.5 × 33 cm (1¾ × 13 inches). Butter the outer side and place it against the inside walls of a crumpet ring mould 10 cm (4 inches) in diameter. Repeat six times. Fold some more buttered filo pastry over and over three times so you have three layers. Cut six 9 cm (3½ inch) rounds out of this pastry to make lids and use some leftover single layered pastry to make six filo pastry roses (see page 16). Place a filo pastry

rose in the centre of each lid and place two or three boxes and the lids at a time in the preheated oven for 5 minutes. Remove the lids, if cooked, then check to see that the sides of the boxes are not falling in. Cook for a further 10 minutes then remove the rings away from the pastry; leave to cook for a further 2 minutes to dry the pastry out. Remove and keep warm.

● **MAKE THE BLANQUETTE FILLING**

Melt the butter in a large pan and fry the leeks until tender. Add the carrots, celery and turnips and fry for 4 minutes, stirring from time to time. Add the sweetcorn and sugar snap peas and cook for a further 4 minutes. Add the French green beans, courgettes and bouquet garni and cook, uncovered, for 5 minutes. Add the water, stock cubes, butter beans and tomatoes and cook for another 5 minutes.

Mix the flour, cream and eggs together in a separate mixing bowl. Take the pan off the heat and add the egg and cream mixture. Put the pan back on the heat and reheat slowly, bringing the contents of the pan gradually up to boiling point, stirring slowly all the time. Season well and take the pan off the heat.

● **TO SERVE**

Place the filo pastry presentation box on a warm serving plate and ladle in the blanquette mixture. Overfill the box so the filling spills over the sides. Cover with the lid placed slightly at a slant on one side so it shows the contents of the box. Bring some of the better baby carrots to the top and garnish with fresh chervil.

CAKE OF PEAR AND ALMOND WITH COINTREAU AND
APRICOT SAUCE

SERVES 6

*T*hese are lovely cakes served with a well-flavoured Cointreau and apricot sauce. Don't let the sugar syrup cook for longer than the time suggested otherwise you will end up with a caramelised cake topping!

FOR THE PEAR
AND ALMOND TOPPING

- 750 g (1½ lb) pears, peeled and thinly sliced across
- 50 g (2 oz) caster or soft brown sugar
- 75 g (3 oz) sultanas
- 85 ml (3 fl oz) water
- 25 g (1 oz) flaked almonds
- 1 × 15 ml spoon (1 tablespoon) Cointreau

FOR THE CAKE

- 75 g (3 oz) caster sugar
- 175 g (6 oz) unsalted butter, softened
- 2 eggs, beaten
- 215 g (7½ oz) plain white flour
- 1½ × 5 ml spoons (1½ teaspoons) baking powder

FOR THE COINTREAU AND
APRICOT SAUCE

- 9 × 15 ml (9 tablespoons) apricot jam
- 450 ml (¾ pint) water
- 1½ × 15 ml spoons (1½ tablespoons) Cointreau

TO DECORATE

- 30 whole almonds
- 6 sprigs fresh mint

● MAKE THE TOPPING

Cook the pears in a small dry frying-pan or shallow pan on a low to medium heat, do not worry if the pears begin to brown. After a while the pears will lose some of their moisture and at that point they will be nearly cooked. Add the sultanas and stir well, uncovered, to reduce the moisture content. Place the sugar and the water in a small saucepan, bring to the boil and simmer for 3½ minutes. The liquid will become a sugar syrup. Pour over the pears and sultanas, add the Cointreau, turn the heat off and stir.

● MAKE THE CAKE

Preheat the oven to gas mark 5, 375°F (190°C).

Mix the caster sugar and the butter with a whisk until light in colour and fluffy in texture. Add the eggs and whisk well again; sieve the flour and baking powder over the mixture and whisk in gradually. Do not overbeat once the flour is added. Place 6 × 10 cm (4 inch) crumpet rings on a baking sheet and grease the base and the sides of the rounds. Spoon the cake mixture into the rounds and level. Spoon the pear, sultana and Cointreau mixture over the cake and sprinkle the almonds over the top. Bake in the oven for 25 minutes or until just cooked in the middle.

● MAKE THE COINTREAU AND APRICOT SAUCE

Place the apricot jam in a small saucepan and add the water. Bring to the boil and simmer for 6 minutes. Sieve the mixture so you have a smooth sauce and add the Cointreau, mixing well. Keep the sauce warm.

● TO SERVE

Leave the cakes to cool down for 3 minutes then loosen around the edges with a small knife and transfer on to individual plates. Pour 3 × 15 ml spoons (3 tablespoons) of the sauce over each cake. Serve warm, decorated with some whole almonds evenly spaced around and a sprig of mint.

SPRING MENU ⑦
top Three-Layer Carrot and Asparagus Mousse Rainbow *below left* Butter Bean 'Blanquette
Style' in Filo Presentation Box *right* Cake of Pear and Almond with Cointreau and
Apricot Sauce

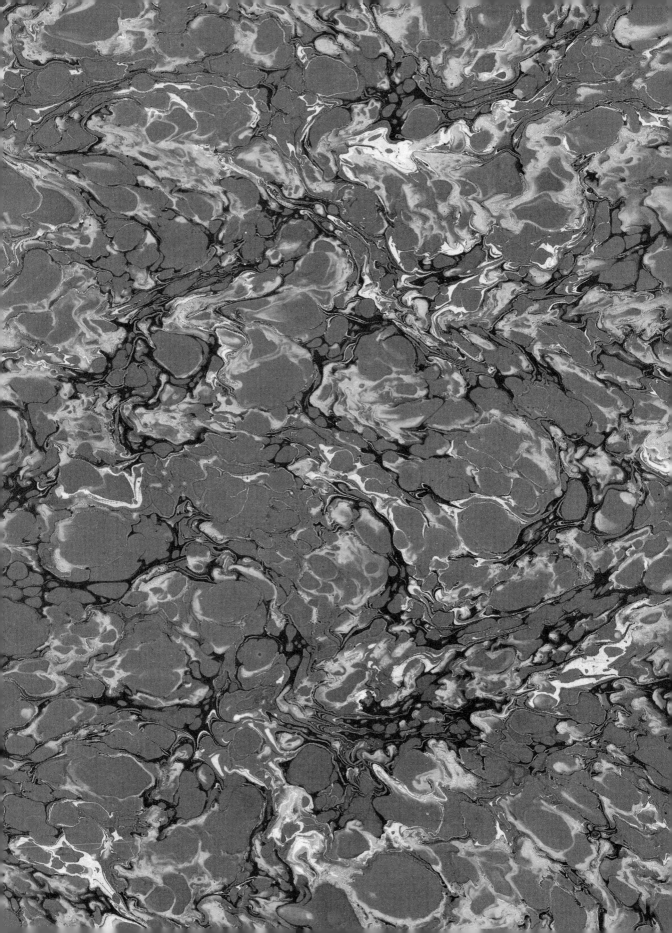

2

SUMMER

MENUS

❶ SUMMER MENU

MARINATED DILL COURGETTES WITH CURLY
RED ONION AND PICKLED CUCUMBER ♦★

~

INDIVIDUAL LENTIL AND AUBERGINE
CHARLOTTES SERVED WITH HOT
TOMATO COULIS

~

BROKEN HEARTS IN PASSION CREAM ♦

~

Here is an inviting menu; I like the cool refreshing starter of baby courgettes in a sharp and reviving marinade, the delightful layered savoury charlottes and a finish of curd cheese hearts presented on a paw-paw and passion fruit coulis. This menu may in fact be cooked at any time of the year provided you respect the need for very fresh and crisp vegetable ingredients. The tomato coulis may be prepared the day before; the starter, the main course preparation and assembling, and the pudding may all be prepared a few hours prior to the meal.

MARINATED DILL COURGETTES
WITH CURLY RED ONION AND PICKLED CUCUMBER

SERVES 6

This starter looks colourful on the plate as the mildly flavoured red onion brightens up the plate wonderfully.

To look interesting the vegetables need to be cut as follows: shred the red onion to look curly; dice the pickled cucumber finely or its flavour will be too overpowering; and thinly slice the baby courgettes lengthwise then chop across. Baby or small courgettes should be used as the skin of large courgettes may be bitter.

If you are unable to find wholegrain garlic and chive mustard, use a plain wholegrain mustard instead and add a touch of crushed garlic to the dressing.

- 550 g (1¼ lb) baby or small courgettes

FOR THE MARINADE

- 1 large pickled dill cucumber, finely diced
- 3 × 15 ml spoons (3 tablespoons) sunflower oil
- 3 × 15 ml spoons (3 tablespoons) dill vinegar
- 2 × 5 ml spoons (2 teaspoons)

- wholegrain garlic and chive mustard
- salt and freshly ground black pepper
- ¼ red onion, shredded thinly

TO GARNISH

- 1 large pickled dill cucumber, finely diced
- ¼ red onion, shredded thinly
- 18 leaves continental parsley

Prepare the courgettes: cut the courgettes in thin slices lengthwise, discarding the first slice to remove most of the green skin. Cut each slice into pieces 4 cm (1½ inches) wide across. Steam the courgette slices for 6 minutes; they should have just changed colour and be soft in texture.

MAKE THE MARINADE

Mix the pickled dill cucumber, sunflower oil, dill vinegar, wholegrain garlic and chive mustard, and salt and black pepper together with a fork in a mixing bowl.

Add the courgettes, stirring once or twice with a spoon to ensure that the slices are all coated with the dressing, and leave to cool for 30 minutes at room temperature. Stir again and chill in the refrigerator for another 30 minutes. Add the red onion and chill for another 30 minutes.

TO SERVE

Divide the mixture on to six white dinner plates, placing the courgettes in a heap in the centre of each plate. Pour the dressing around, making sure that some of the pickled dill cucumber and red onion are scattered around the mound of courgettes. Garnish with more pickled dill cucumber and red onion scattered over to add crunchiness. Finish garnishing by evenly placing three to five leaves of flat leaf continental parsley over the dressing. Serve with some warm French bread and butter.

INDIVIDUAL LENTIL AND AUBERGINE CHARLOTTES

SERVES 6

These charlottes are not unlike individual turned-out moussakas but the result is lighter and more colourful. You can make one large charlotte if you prefer but as you cannot cut it into neat slices it is better to make them individually. To bake the charlottes, large Le Creuset, ramekin dishes or deep straight-sided dishes 200–300 ml (7–10 fl oz) in capacity may be used. If you use the smaller size lay the ingredients above the rim; they will settle in the cooking process and turn out as easily.

Although I use a fair amount of olive oil in this recipe, the charlottes are not too high in fat as most of the oil will be drained on kitchen paper. Also, apart from the aubergine slices, none of the other ingredients has any fat content.

The charlottes should be served on a bed of tomato coulis with a selection of hot vegetables or a mixed salad. They can also be successfully served cold for a more casual summer dinner party. The tomato coulis can be made ahead of the savoury charlottes. Use ripe and red tomatoes to give the best colour.

- 175 g (6 oz) green lentils
- 3 large aubergines, each cut into 12 slices across
- 10 × 15 ml spoons (10 tablespoons) Greek olive oil
- 1 large onion, peeled and finely chopped
- 3 cloves garlic, peeled and crushed
- 175 g (6 oz) mushrooms, chopped
- 1 × 5 ml spoon (1 teaspoon) fresh chopped oregano
- 2 × 5 ml spoons (2 teaspoons) Marmite
- salt and freshly ground black pepper
- 450 ml (15 fl oz) natural yoghurt
- 3 eggs, beaten
- 3 large beef tomatoes

FOR THE TOMATO COULIS

- 1 × 15 ml spoon (1 tablespoon) olive oil
- 1 small onion, peeled and finely chopped
- 750 g (1½ lb) fresh ripe tomatoes, de-seeded and chopped
- 2 × 15 ml spoons (2 tablespoons) tomato and garlic purée
- 200 ml (7 fl oz) water
- 2 × 5 ml spoons (2 teaspoons) bouillon powder
- salt and freshly ground black pepper

TO GARNISH

- 12 sprigs parsley (ordinary or flat leaved)
- 6 tomato roses, see page 16

Preheat the oven to gas mark 5, 375°F (190°C)

Place the lentils in a medium saucepan, cover with 2.5 cm (1 inch) of water, bring to the boil, turn the heat down, cover and simmer for 30 to 40 minutes or until tender. Note: some lentils will take longer to cook than others; the fresher they are, the less time they will take to cook. Drain well.

Remove the top and bottom ends of the aubergines and cut each aubergine into 12 slices across. Fry six of the aubergine slices in 1½ × 15 ml spoons (1½ tablespoons) of olive oil on a high heat; the colour should be brown throughout. Turn the slices over, turn the heat down, and continue frying until the other side is brown too. (By turning the heat down, you will not need to add more oil.) Drain on kitchen paper and repeat the process with the rest of the oil and the aubergine slices. Note: If you don't want to fry the aubergine slices, place them on a baking sheet, brush them with olive oil and grill until golden brown. Repeat the same process with the rest of the aubergine slices.

Heat the remaining 1 × 15 ml spoon (1 tablespoon) olive oil and fry the onion and garlic together until golden brown. Add the mushrooms and cook until tender. Add the lentils, oregano and Marmite and cook together in a semi-covered pan on a low heat for 10 minutes, stirring from time to time. Season well.

Beat the yoghurt and eggs together in a mixing bowl and season. Remove the top and bottom ends of the tomatoes and slice each into four thick slices across.

Lightly grease six large ramekin dishes, line the bases with greaseproof paper and start layering: use two aubergine slices to cover the base of each dish, making sure that the slices go right to the edges of the dish; cover the slices with half of the lentil mixture divided between the ramekins. Cover with half the yoghurt and egg mixture then place a slice of tomato on each dish. Repeat the layers, finishing with a slice of tomato. Bake in the preheated oven for 20–25 minutes or until set.

● **MAKE THE TOMATO COULIS**

Heat the oil and fry the onion in a medium saucepan until tender. Add the tomatoes, tomato and garlic purée, water and bouillon powder, bring to the boil, turn the heat down and simmer for 25 minutes until the tomatoes have completely broken down.

Cool the mixture a little then blend in a blender until completely smooth. Sieve the mixture to remove any pips, season to taste and reheat up to boiling point before serving.

Remove the charlottes from the oven, leave to stand for 5 minutes then delicately ease them out by sliding a knife between the terrine and the dish.

● **TO SERVE**

Turn the charlottes out on to individual plates and pour the tomato sauce over half the surface of the plate. I find that having tomato sauce all around is a little heavy-handed and doesn't look as pretty. Serve any extra coulis in a sauce boat. Garnish with two sprigs of ordinary or flat leaf parsley on either side of the charlottes and a tomato rose sitting on top. Serve with hot vegetables or a mixed side salad.

BROKEN HEARTS IN PASSION CREAM

SERVES 6.

*H*ere is a sumptuous dish for the romantics of today! It consists of a curd cheese heart on a coulis of passion fruit and paw-paw. Use heart-shaped moulds approximately 9 cm (3½ inches) wide and 2.5 cm (1 inch) deep.

- *175 g (6 oz) curd cheese*
- *750 g (1½ lb) Greek yoghurt*
- *1½ × 5 ml spoons (1½ teaspoons) finely grated lemon rind*
- *4 × 15 ml spoons (4 tablespoons) clear Mexican honey*

FOR THE COULIS

- *4 passion fruits*
- *1½ ripe paw-paws, peeled and de-seeded*
- *175 ml (6 fl oz) orange juice*

FOR THE FRUIT KEBABS

- *Half a paw-paw, peeled, de-seeded and chopped into 12 chunky pieces*
- *12 dark grapes, pipped and kept whole*
- *1 kiwi fruit, peeled and chopped into 12 chunky pieces*
- *12 medium strawberries (keep the green tops on)*

Mix the curd cheese, Greek yoghurt and lemon rind until smooth. Place a double layer of muslin or a single layer of cheesecloth over a large sieve or colander and place the mixture in it. Leave in a cool place for 4 hours. Discard the juice and transfer the mixture back into the mixing bowl, add the honey and mix well. Divide between six heart-shaped moulds, each lined with a double layer of muslin or a single layer of cheesecloth. Place in the refrigerator for 1½ hours.

● MAKE THE COULIS

Cut the passion fruits in half and scoop out the seeds and flesh; place them into a sieve and sieve all the juice away from the seeds. Discard the seeds and flesh. Place the passion fruit juice in a blender, add the chopped paw-paw and orange juice and process until completely smooth.

● MAKE THE FRUIT KEBABS

Thread the fruits on to six kebab skewers, placing the strawberries at each end.

● TO SERVE

Turn the hearts out on to large plates and pour the coulis delicately around each one. Sit the fruit kebabs in the middle of the hearts so they break each one in two. Serve straightaway.

❷ SUMMER MENU

CREAMED LETTUCE SOUP WITH FLAGEOLET

~

TURNED PASTA RIBBONS WITH TRICOLOUR
PEPPER AND FRESH BASIL SAUCE

~

'AIRY FAIRY' YOGHURT BOMBE SERVED WITH
GALIA MELON AND WILD RASPBERRIES

~

This creamy lettuce soup makes an excellent starter to a summer dinner party because it has a light texture, a slight sharpness and a very inviting pale green colour. In this menu, it is followed by fresh tagliatelle accompanied by a very tasty sauce and presented in an unusual and colourful manner. The Yoghurt Bombe is flavoured with lemon rind and honey and is not frozen but left to set; its white colour contrasts well with the chilled green melon and the red raspberries to make a delicious finish to this meal.

CREAMED LETTUCE SOUP WITH FLAGEOLET

SERVES 6

The best lettuce to use is a soft, round lettuce although a French butterhead lettuce makes a good alternative. *Crème fraîche* is an ideal accompaniment to this blend of creamed lettuce and flageolet because it has both a great richness and a hint of sourness.

- 175 g (6 oz) flageolet beans, soaked overnight
- 25 g (1 oz) butter
- 2 soft, round lettuces, cleaned and shredded
- 1½ vegetable stock cubes, crumbled
- 5 × 15 ml spoons (5 tablespoons) crème fraîche
- good pinch salt and freshly ground black pepper

TO GARNISH

- *3 × 15 ml spoons (3 tablespoons)* crème fraîche *mixed with 3 × 15 ml spoons (3 tablespoons) milk*

- *2 × 15 ml spoons (2 tablespoons) fresh chopped chives*

Drain the beans thoroughly and place them in a pan, cover them with 750 ml (1½ pints) water and bring to the boil. Boil fast for 10 minutes then reduce the heat to a simmer, cover and cook for 30–35 minutes or until soft. The fresher the beans, the less time they will take to cook.

Drain, reserving the cooking water; if you have less than 600 ml (1 pint) of liquid left, make up the quantity with a little water.

Melt the butter and fry the lettuce until soft. Add the cooked beans, 450 ml (¾ pint) of the reserved cooking liquid and the stock cubes and bring to the boil. Simmer for 15 minutes.

Cool a little then blend in a blender until completely smooth. It will take a little while to get the beans completely creamy. Add some of the remaining 150 ml (¼ pint) of the cooking liquid if necessary, to achieve a good consistency.

Place the *crème fraîche* in a mixing bowl; add a few tablespoons of the blended soup to it, stir well to loosen the mixture, then add the rest of the mixture. Transfer it into a clean saucepan, season to taste and reheat on a low to medium heat, stirring all the time. When the soup is coming up to the boil, reduce the heat to very low and wait for the first boil then remove from the heat.

● **TO SERVE**

Serve in warmed soup bowls with a swirl of the *crème fraîche* garnish mixture with a light sprinkling of chives on the top.

TURNED PASTA RIBBONS
WITH TRICOLOUR PEPPER AND FRESH BASIL SAUCE

SERVES 6

*T*his dish presents three nests of fresh tagliatelle with a very tasty tricolour pepper and basil sauce in between each nest. It is accompanied with a pesto sauce and is garnished with fresh basil leaves. Although I find that fresh tagliatelle is best for this dish, you may use fresh spaghetti or fresh spaghettini instead.

When making the sauce for this dish, make sure that you remove all the white pith from the peppers to avoid any bitterness. Also, choose ripe red tomatoes otherwise the sauce will lack colour. If you find celery salt is not available, make your own by grinding 2 × 5 ml spoons (2 teaspoons) celery seeds with 15 g (½ oz) sea salt in a coffee grinder until fine.

FOR THE TRICOLOUR PEPPER AND
FRESH BASIL SAUCE

- *3 × 15 ml spoons (3 tablespoons)
  olive oil*
- *2 small onions, peeled and finely chopped*
- *3 cloves garlic, peeled and crushed*
- *2 small green peppers, de-seeded
  and finely diced*
- *2 small yellow peppers, de-seeded and
  finely diced*
- *2 small red peppers, de-seeded and diced*
- *750 g (1¾ lb) fresh ripe tomatoes,
  peeled and chopped*
- *2 × 15 ml spoons (2 tablespoons)
  tomato purée*
- *3 × 15 ml spoons (3 tablespoons) fresh
  chopped continental parsley*

- *2 × 5 ml spoons (2 teaspoons) fresh
  chopped marjoram*
- *1 × 15 ml spoon (1 tablespoon)
  bouillon powder*
- *½ × 5 ml spoon (½ teaspoon) celery salt*
- *1½ × 15 ml spoons (1½ tablespoons)
  fresh chopped basil*
- *salt and freshly ground black pepper*

FOR THE PASTA

- *750 g (1¼ lb) fresh tagliatelle*
- *15 g (½ oz) butter*
- *75 g (3 oz) Cheddar cheese, grated*

TO SERVE AND GARNISH

- *2 × 15 ml spoons (2 tablespoons)
  ready-made pesto sauce*
- *18 fresh basil leaves*

● MAKE THE PEPPER AND BASIL SAUCE

Heat the olive oil and fry the onion and garlic until soft and the onion is translucent. Add the peppers and tomatoes and cook, covered, until the tomatoes have broken down and are reduced to a pulp; this will take 10–15 minutes. Add the tomato purée, parsley, marjoram, bouillon powder and celery salt, and simmer, covered, for another 10 minutes.

● COOK THE PASTA

Meanwhile, boil the pasta for as many minutes as are suggested on the packet and drain. Transfer into a mixing bowl, add the butter and cheese and stir until dissolved. Cover and keep hot over a pan of simmering water while you finish making the sauce but do not leave over the water for too long or the cheese will start cooking and then will become hard on cooling.

Complete the sauce by adding the basil and seasoning to taste. Cook for another minute.

● TO SERVE

Divide the pasta between 6 plates then divide each quantity into three; swirl each third of pasta around a fork and place the heaps of pasta on the outside of the plate, at equal intervals, so that you are left with three gaps in between each mound of pasta. Place 1–1½ ml spoons (1–1½ tablespoons) of the pepper and basil sauce in between the mounds and spoon out 2 × 5 ml spoons (2 teaspoons) of pesto sauce in the centre 'hole' on the plate. Garnish each plate with basil leaves by each mound of pasta and serve with a side salad on side plates.

'AIRY FAIRY' YOGHURT BOMBE
SERVED WITH GALIA MELON AND WILD RASPBERRIES

SERVES 6

*T*his dessert is made with yoghurt, cheeses, lemon rind and whipped egg whites; the mixture is left to set in a large sieve and then turned out. It looks like a bombe but is not frozen. Although easy, it should be started approximately 3½ hours before the start of the meal to allow it to set properly. This will also give you plenty of time to prepare the rest of the meal.

- *450 ml (¾ pint) strained Greek yoghurt*
- *100 g (4 oz) curd cheese*
- *100 g (4 oz) cottage cheese, sieved*
- *rind of 1 lemon*
- *rind of ½ orange*
- *2 × 15 ml spoons (2 tablespoons) honey (not Mexican, it is too strong)*
- *2 egg whites*

TO DECORATE AND SERVE

- *1 ripe Galia melon, peeled, de-seeded and cut into slices*
- *225–350 g (8–12 oz) wild raspberries*
- *sprig mint, lemon-scented geranium leaves or sweet cicely, optional*

Mix the Greek yoghurt, curd cheese, cottage cheese, lemon and orange rind together in a large mixing bowl and whisk until the mixture is completely smooth. Add honey to taste. Whisk the egg whites until firm and fold them gently into the yoghurt and cheese mixture.

Line a large sieve with a piece of cheesecloth and pour the mixture into it. Leave to stand over a bowl (to collect the liquid that results) in a cool place or the refrigerator for 2½ hours. Discard the resulting juice.

● **TO SERVE**

Turn the bombe out on to a platter. Decorate all around with wedges or slices of melon and place some wild raspberries in between. If you wish, decorate the centre of the bombe with a sprig of mint, some lemon-scented geranium leaves or some sweet cicely and take to the table. Cut and serve two slices of the bombe to each person with some of the melon and raspberries as accompaniment.

③

S U M M E R *M* E N U

GOAT CHEESE AND KIWI
IN FRESH THYME DRESSING ♦

~

SAUTÉ PROVENÇAL WITH COURGETTE FLOWERS ★

~

RED AND WHITE CURRANT PAVLOVA

~

This is a menu which doesn't require too much preparation since the starter is very quick to make, the filling for the courgette flowers may be made the day before and the Sauté Provençal is fairly speedy to cook; the pavlova may be made up to a few days in advance, provided it is kept in an airtight tin or box.

The starter may seem to have an unusual combination of ingredients but it is very refreshing and works extremely well. The main course has a contrast of textures as well as flavours. As it includes courgette flowers which are not widely used, their novelty should impress your guests. The pavlova, filled with white and red currants, is light and delicious.

GOAT CHEESE AND KIWI IN FRESH THYME DRESSING

SERVES 6

This starter consists of layers of green kiwi fruit and white goat cheese on a bed of mixed lettuce. The dish is then sprinkled with a fresh thyme and olive dressing to give it its character and delicious flavour. For the best results, choose a strong, mature goat cheese, and make sure that the dressing is chilled.

- *6 leaves* frisée *lettuce*
- *4 leaves radicchio lettuce*

- *250 g (9 oz) tubular mature goat cheese, chilled*
- *3 kiwi fruits, peeled*

<table>
<tr><td>FOR THE DRESSING</td><td>TO SERVE AND GARNISH</td></tr>
</table>

FOR THE DRESSING

- *1½ × 15 ml spoons (1½ tablespoons) fresh lemon juice*
- *2 × 15 ml spoons (2 tablespoons) white wine vinegar*
- *5 × 15 ml spoons (5 tablespoons) olive oil*
- *3 × 5 ml spoons (3 teaspoons) fresh chopped thyme*
- *salt and freshly ground black pepper*

TO SERVE AND GARNISH

- *1 punnet cress*
- *18 slices pink radishes, thinly sliced across*
- *2 × 5 ml spoons (2 teaspoons) fresh chopped thyme*
- *freshly ground black pepper*

First make the dressing by mixing all the ingredients together in a jam jar. Place in the refrigerator to chill and let the flavours develop while you prepare the rest of the ingredients.

Finely shred the *frisée* and radicchio leaves, and mix together in a mixing bowl.

Slice the goat cheese into 18 thin slices; you will find that it is easier to do this using a knife with a warm blade. Discard the top and bottom ends of the kiwi fruits and slice each in six slices, cutting across, so the fruit shows its seeds.

Pile a sixth of the lettuce over one half of each of six large starter plates. Place alternate slices of goat cheese and kiwi fruits over the other half, overlapping them as though forming a two-colour wheel; the first and last slices should lean slightly on the lettuce. Start with a slice of kiwi, then a slice of goat cheese, a slice of kiwi, a slice of goat cheese, a slice of kiwi and finish with a slice of goat cheese. Pour the dressing over all the plate but especially the goat cheese and kiwi mixture.

● **TO SERVE**

Place a little bouquet of cress in the centre of the lettuce and place three slices of radishes by its side to add colour. Sprinkle the extra fresh thyme and freshly ground black pepper over the kiwi and goat cheese and over the dressing and serve.

SAUTÉ PROVENÇAL WITH COURGETTE FLOWERS

SERVES 6

*C*ourgette flowers are available from your greengrocer in the heart of the summer; this filling is designed to contrast with the *Sauté Provençal* on to which it is served.

FOR THE SAUTÉ PROVENÇAL

- *1 × 15 ml spoon (1 tablespoon) olive oil*
- *1 Spanish onion, shredded*
- *2 cloves garlic, crushed*
- *6 stalks celery, sliced across*
- *4 small courgettes, sliced*
- *2 yellow peppers, de-seeded and chopped into strips*
- *450 ml (¾ pint) tomato passata*
- *1 × 15 ml spoon (1 tablespoon) tomato purée*
- *150 ml (¼ pint) water*
- *1 × 15 ml spoon (1 tablespoon) bouillon powder*
- *2 × 15 ml spoons (2 tablespoons) fresh chopped basil*
- *salt and freshly ground black pepper*

FOR THE COURGETTE FLOWER FILLING

- *75 g (3 oz) shelled, salted pistachio nuts*
- *75 g (3 oz) pine kernels*
- *4 eggs, beaten*
- *125 g (5 oz) white breadcrumbs*
- *salt and freshly ground black pepper*
- *12 courgette flowers*

TO GARNISH

- *6 sprigs fresh basil or 6 large basil leaves*

Heat the olive oil and fry the onion until tender. Add the garlic, celery and courgettes and cook for a further 10 minutes. Add the yellow peppers, tomato passata, tomato purée, water and bouillon powder; bring to the boil and simmer for 20 minutes. Add basil and seasoning.

● **MAKE THE FILLING FOR THE COURGETTE FLOWERS**

Mix the pistachio nuts and the pine kernels together. Place the beaten eggs in a mixing bowl, add the breadcrumbs, mixed nuts and seasoning and mix well. Make a slit on the side of each courgette flower. Divide the mixture into 12 portions and place approximately a tablespoon of mixture in each courgette flower. Steam in a steamer for 6–8 minutes or until the courgette stems attached to the flowers are tender.

● **TO SERVE**

Place some of the casserole on each plate; top with two filled and cooked courgette flowers and serve hot, garnished with some sprigs of fresh basil.

RED AND WHITE CURRANT PAVLOVA

SERVES 6–8

I have grown to dislike pavlovas filled with cream as I find them too rich but I like pavlovas filled with Greek yoghurt very much as it counterbalances the sweetness of the meringue. In this recipe I use red and white currants, dessert grapes (very tiny sweet grapes) and fresh raspberries as a filling because, as well as being sharp, these fruits look very pretty on top of the white Greek yoghurt. Other fruits may be used.

- *4 egg whites*
- *225 g (8 oz) white sugar*

FOR THE FILLING

- *350 g (12 oz) Greek yoghurt*
- *175 g (6 oz) mixture of red and white currants*

- *100 g (4 oz) dessert grapes*
- *175 g (6 oz) fresh raspberries*

TO DECORATE

- *a few extra fresh raspberries*
- *a few fresh mint, small nasturtium or sweet cicely leaves*

Preheat the oven to gas mark 3, 160°C (325°F).

Place the egg whites in a large bowl and whisk with an electric whisk until firm. Add the sugar, a tablespoon at a time, whisking well after each addition to make sure that all the sugar is incorporated in the mixture. Stop whisking when all the sugar has been added and the mixture looks shiny and very smooth.

Place a piece of baking parchment on a large, flat baking sheet. Spread the egg white mixture with a metallic or wooden spoon over it so it covers a circle of 23 cm (9 inches) in diameter. Hollow the centre a little (in the shape of a nest) because the sides of the meringues cook faster than the centre.

Place in the preheated oven for 1 hour 20 minutes (if the meringue starts to brown, turn the oven down); take out of the oven, leave to cool thoroughly and then peel off the base paper. If you keep it in an airtight tin, the meringue may be stored for a few days.

Line a sieve with muslin, add the Greek yoghurt and place the sieve over a bowl for 30 minutes to drain away excess juice. Discard the resulting liquid.

● **TO SERVE**

Place the meringue on a dish and fill with the Greek yoghurt. Do not do this more than 30–60 minutes before serving or the meringue will soften. Top with the fruits, displaying them in a decorative pattern. Place some bunches of whole red and white currants by the sides of the meringue. Decorate with a few fresh raspberries and fresh leaves and take to the table. Cut the pavlova into six or eight portions to serve.

❹ *SUMMER MENU*

MANGETOUT AND ARTICHOKE *VELOUTÉ* ♦

~

GINGER-BRAISED TOFU AND VEGETABLE
BROCHETTES WITH LIME AND SESAME SAUCE
AND FRAGRANT LEMON RICE TIMBALE ♦★

~

THREE-TIER PEACH AND APRICOT COCKTAIL ♦

~

This is a menu which will bring some 'ingenuity' to your dinner party as the main course has a strong far eastern influence. The starter is a delicious creamy bright green soup made with a combination of mangetouts and globe artichokes and is served with a little sour cream as an accompaniment. The main course is made with a combination of far eastern flavours all mingling together to produce a main course with plenty of strength. The last course is refreshing and made with a combination of fresh seasonal fruits, creamy yoghurt and crunchy toasted hazelnuts.

MANGETOUT AND ARTICHOKE *VELOUTÉ*

SERVES 6

The artichokes chosen should look fresh and plump. The mangetouts should be thin and small as the larger ones are not as sweet; to prepare the mangetouts, top and tail by hand, making sure that you remove the string attached as you do so.

6 globe artichokes
550 g (1¼ lb) small mangetouts
1 sprig fresh thyme
1½ vegetable stock cubes, crumbled
salt and freshly ground black pepper

TO SERVE

6 × 15 ml spoons (6 tablespoons)
sour cream
6 sprigs chervil

Trim the stalks from the globe artichokes and steam or boil them for 1 hour; after that time the leaves should come off easily from the heart of the artichoke. Drain well. Cool the artichokes and peel the leaves away until you get to the core of each artichoke; remove the fine hairs, then trim the base again so you are left with the artichoke bottom which is the base.

Top and tail the mangetouts and remove the strings, if any. Bring 900 ml (1½ pints) water to the boil, add the mangetouts, fresh thyme and stock cubes, and simmer for 10 minutes. Remove the thyme and cool a little. Place the mixture in a blender and blend until smooth. Add the artichoke bottoms and blend again. Transfer into a clean saucepan and season to taste. Reheat to boiling point.

● TO SERVE

Divide the soup between six bowls; garnish each bowl with a swirl of sour cream and a sprig of chervil.

GINGER-BRAISED TOFU AND VEGETABLE BROCHETTES
WITH LIME AND SESAME SAUCE
AND FRAGRANT LEMON RICE TIMBALE

SERVES 6

*T*he combination of the brochettes, the marinade, the sesame sauce and lemon timbale is refreshingly striking for the palate and provides a good combination of textures as well as colours and flavours.

The best tofu to use for these brochettes is fresh tofu which you will find in Chinese and Japanese supermarkets, where it is kept in water and sold by weight. Tofu is flavourless but picks up flavour from the marinade easily.

Tilda make a Thai fragrant rice which is the rice I use for the lemon and rice timbale; it is scented, has a delicious flavour and such a texture when cooked that it is suitable for shaping into timbales and turning out easily.

FOR THE BRAISED TOFU IN GINGER
MARINADE

- *300 g (11 oz) fresh plain regular tofu*
- *3 × 15 ml spoons (3 tablespoons) fresh ginger root, finely grated*
- *65 ml (2½ fl oz) shoyu*

- *2 × 5 ml spoons (2 teaspoons) toasted sesame oil*
- *3 cloves garlic, crushed*
- *2 × 15 ml spoons (2 tablespoons) rice vinegar*
- *4 spring onions, finely chopped*

VEGETABLES FOR THE BROCHETTES

- *6 wedges fresh lime*
- *24 button mushrooms*
- *12 pieces yellow pepper*
- *12 pieces orange pepper*
- *24 pieces small courgettes, chopped*
- *24 cherry tomatoes*

FOR THE ANISE, LIME AND SESAME

SAUCE

- *4 × 15 ml spoons (4 tablespoons) light tahini*
- *200 ml (7 fl oz) water*

- *juice of 3 limes*
- *2 × 15 ml spoons (2 tablespoons) ginger juice (see page 10)*
- *2 red chillies, de-seeded and very finely chopped*
- *2 whole star anise*

FOR THE LEMON RICE TIMBALE

- *450 g (1 lb) Thai fragrant rice*
- *6 slices lemon*

TO GARNISH

- *6 chilli flowers, see page 15*
- *6 leaves fresh coriander*

Cut the tofu into 36 pieces and leave to drain on kitchen paper while you make the ginger marinade. Squeeze the juice out of the ginger (see page 10) and place in a mixing bowl; add the shoyu, toasted sesame oil, garlic, rice vinegar and spring onions, and mix well.

Add the tofu to the marinade, stirring a little to make sure that all the tofu is coated and leave to stand for 2 hours. Stir again and leave to stand for another 2 hours.

Make the anise, lime and sesame sauce. Place the tahini in a mixing bowl and add the water, two tablespoons at a time; stir between each addition until the sauce becomes smooth. Add the lime juice, ginger juice, red chillies and, finally, the star anise. Leave the sauce to stand for 2 hours to let the flavour of the star anise develop.

Preheat the oven to gas mark 6, 400°F (200°C).

Place the tofu in a small tray with half its marinade and cook for 20 minutes in the preheated oven, turning it over half-way through. Cool the tofu and mix any marinade left over from baking with the other half of uncooked marinade. Thread the pieces of lime wedges, tofu and mixed vegetables on to 12 wooden skewers. Place on a tray and bake for another 10 minutes, basting the vegetables and tofu with the leftover marinade.

Meanwhile, bring 1.5 litres (2½ pints) of water to the boil in a large saucepan. Add the rice, bring back to the boil, turn the heat back down, cover and simmer until the rice is cooked and no water is left in the pan; this will take 12–15 minutes. Take the rice off the heat.

Line the base of 6 college pudding moulds 200 ml (⅓ pint) in capacity, with a slice of lemon; grease the sides of the moulds with butter or oil and fill each with the cooked rice; place in the hot oven for 8 minutes.

● **TO SERVE**

Place the cooked brochettes, crossing one another, on one side of a dinner plate; turn out the rice timbale next to it and place a coriander leaf over the slice of lemon as a garnish. Pour some of the anise, lime and sesame sauce over the brochettes, and pour the leftover marinade over this. Garnish each plate with a chilli flower and serve.

SUMMER MENU ④
right Mangetout and Artichoke Velouté *left* Ginger-braised Tofu and Vegetable Brochettes
with Lime and Sesame Sauce and Fragrant Rice Timbale *centre* Three-tier Peach and
Apricot Cocktail

THREE-TIER PEACH AND APRICOT COCKTAIL

SERVES 6

*T*his is a light dessert made principally of fresh apricots and peaches topped with delicious, lightly sweetened fromage frais and toasted hazelnuts which provide an excellent texture contrast to the base.

If apricot brandy is not available, use Drambuie or Cointreau instead.

* *750 g (1½ lb) fresh apricots, peeled, halved and stoned*
* *2 large peaches, peeled, halved and stoned*
* *300 ml (½ pint) fresh orange juice*
* *40 g (1½ oz) brown sugar*
* *30 ml (2 tablespoons) apricot brandy*
* *550 g (1¼ lb) fromage frais*
* *25 g (1 oz) brown sugar*

FOR THE TOPPING

* *50 g (2 oz) hazelnuts*

TO DECORATE

* *sprigs fresh mint*

Preheat the oven to gas mark 6, 400°F (200°C).

Place the apricots and peaches in a small saucepan with the orange juice and sugar; bring to the boil and cook for 15 minutes or until the fruits are well cooked. Remove from the heat and drain. Cut the fruit into slices, add the apricot brandy then cool thoroughly.

Mix the fromage frais with the sugar in a separate bowl and chill.

Place the hazelnuts on a tray and bake in the preheated oven for 10 minutes. If the hazelnuts have skins, rub them in a clean tea-towel to loosen the skins. Cool, remove the skins and finely chop the nuts.

Divide the fruit mixture between six sundae dishes or six tall glasses. Top with the fromage frais mixture and then add a top layer of chopped hazelnuts.

● **TO SERVE**

Place each sundae dish on a dessert plate and decorate the plates and the top of the glasses with sprigs of fresh mint.

⑤

ℐUMMER ℳENU

SPINACH PARCELS ON TOMATO COULIS ◆

~

TRIO OF ARTICHOKE, BABY VEGETABLES AND
HOLLANDAISE SAUCE *EN CHAPERONNE*

~

STRAWBERRY SORBET IN TUILE BASKETS
SERVED WITH ORANGE AND
STRAWBERRY SAUCE

~

*This is a light but rich summery menu which is colourful:
the green and white spinach parcels are served on a
brightly coloured and tasty coulis; the main course is rich and
golden; it is followed by a refreshing sorbet in a tangy sauce
which makes a tremendous finish to the meal.*

SPINACH PARCELS ON TOMATO COULIS

SERVES 6

These small spinach parcels are cut into slices to show their filling of white celeriac and red sun-dried tomatoes. Each plate is made from a combination of 9 slices shaped into a crown which looks very pretty. Celeriac is available in the shops from the end of the summer; if you want to make this recipe earlier in the summer, use floury potatoes instead. Sun-dried tomatoes are sold in jars in delicatessens.

- *18 medium, fresh spinach leaves*
- *350 g (12 oz) potatoes, peeled and chopped*
- *225 g (8 oz) celeriac, peeled and chopped*
- *¼ × 5 ml spoon (¼ teaspoon) garlic salt*
- *¼ × 5 ml spoon (¼ teaspoon) celery salt*
- *100 g (4 oz) Cheddar cheese, grated*
- *50 g (2 oz) ricotta cheese*
- *salt and black pepper*
- *6 sun-dried tomatoes*

FOR THE TOMATO COULIS

- *450 g (1 lb) ripe tomatoes, skinned and chopped*
- *150 ml (¼ pint) water*
- *2 × 5 ml spoons (2 teaspoons) bouillon powder*

- *pinch cayenne pepper*
- *40 g (1½ oz) sun-dried tomatoes*
- *salt and freshly ground black pepper*

TO SERVE

- *12–18 sprigs fresh parsley*
- *garlic pepper*

Wash the spinach leaves and steam for 2–4 minutes or until tender. Place the spinach leaves in a bowl of icy cold water then drain on a cooling rack or on a clean tea-towel while you make the filling.

Steam the potatoes for 6 minutes then add the celeriac to the steamer and steam for a further 8–10 minutes or until just tender. Place both in a mixing bowl, add the garlic and celery salt, Cheddar cheese, ricotta cheese and seasoning and mash with a potato masher. Cool thoroughly.

● MAKE THE COULIS

Place the tomatoes and water in a medium saucepan, bring to the boil, turn the heat down and cook, covered, until the tomatoes have broken down. Add the bouillon powder and cayenne pepper and cook for a further 5 minutes. Cool a little. Transfer into a blender, add the dried tomatoes and blend until completely smooth and silky. Season to taste and cool thoroughly.

● FILL THE SPINACH PARCELS

Take a steamed spinach leaf and place a tablespoon of the chilled potato mixture on it. Place a strip of dried tomato on top of the mixture and push it into the middle. Roll into a cylindrical shape, wrapping the spinach leaf around it. Make all 18 parcels in the same way.

● TO SERVE

Allow three spinach parcels per person and cut each one into three slices with a sharp knife. Pour some of the coulis on to each plate and place the spinach slices on top, arranging them so that they overlap one another and turn into a crown 9–10 cm (3½–4 inches) in diameter in the centre of the plate. Garnish the centre of the crown with some sprigs of parsley; sprinkle each crown with a few pinches of garlic pepper and serve.

TRIO OF ARTICHOKE, BABY VEGETABLES AND HOLLANDAISE SAUCE *EN CHAPERONNE*

SERVES 6

*T*his main course is not traditional in the sense that it is not served piping hot; all ingredients are served hot apart from the hollandaise which is served between warm and hot. The combination of ingredients works well because, although the hollandaise is very rich, the other ingredients have no fat used in their cooking; artichoke, asparagus, baby carrots, mangetouts and hollandaise sauce marry extremely well and are a pleasure to eat together.

6 globe artichokes

225 g (8 oz) dwarf carrots (no longer than 5cm/2 inches), topped and tailed

175 g (6 oz) mangetouts, topped and tailed, any strings removed

175 g (6 oz) extra-fine asparagus tips, trimmed at the top if necessary

75 g (3 oz) petits pois

FOR THE TOPS

15 slices thickly sliced white bread

FOR THE HOLLANDAISE SAUCE

100 g (4 oz) butter

3 × 15 ml spoons (3 tablespoons) water

3 egg yolks

salt

cayenne pepper

1 × 15 ml spoon (1 tablespoon) fresh lemon juice

150 ml (¼ pint) double cream

black pepper

TO GARNISH

6 sprigs fresh chervil or parsley

Bring 1.75 litres (3 pints) water to the boil in a large saucepan; add the artichokes and cook for 1 hour. Peel the leaves away and remove the fine hairs from the core to leave the artichoke hearts. Keep them warm.

● **MAKE THE FILLING**

Cut the carrots in half lengthways if they measure more than 1 cm (½ inch) in diameter. Steam the carrots for 3 minutes then add the mangetouts and asparagus and steam for 5 minutes; add the petits pois and steam for another 3 minutes. Keep the vegetables hot.

● **MAKE THE BREAD 'HATS'**

Toast the bread and cut out 12 round shapes using a 7.5 cm (3 inch) pastry cutter. Cut three of the rounds in half. Keep them warm.

● **MAKE THE HOLLANDAISE SAUCE**

Melt the butter on a low heat and keep aside. In a small, heavy-based saucepan, whisk the water and egg yolks with salt and cayenne pepper. Set over a low heat and whisk constantly until creamy, and the whisk leaves a trail on the base of the pan. This will take 2 minutes; do not try to hurry this process by turning the heat up. Take the pan off the heat and whisk in the butter, a few drops at a time. After 15 ml (1 tablespoon) has been added, the sauce will start to thicken and the butter can be added faster. Gently stir in the lemon juice, then the cream. Reheat to just below smoking point, stirring all the time. Keep the sauce hot in a pan of simmering water.

● **TO SERVE**

Mix together all the vegetables except the artichokes in a mixing bowl. Place one round of toast in the centre of each of six warmed plates and top with the warm artichoke bottoms. Place a sixth of the vegetable mixture over each artichoke heart letting the vegetables overflow on to the plate. Cover with a sixth of the hollandaise sauce and top with another round of toast. Finish by dipping the cut side of the half-rounds of toasts into any leftover hollandaise and stand each half-round up over the top round. Garnish with a sprig of chervil or parsley and serve immediately.

STRAWBERRY SORBET IN TUILE BASKETS SERVED WITH ORANGE AND STRAWBERRY SAUCE

SERVES 6

*T*his is such an impressive dessert that it is well worth all the effort; the sorbet is light but together with the biscuit and the syrup makes a satisfying dessert.

FOR THE STRAWBERRY SORBET

- *225–275 g (8–10 oz) white sugar*
- *200 ml (⅓ pint) water*
- *1.5 kg (3 lb) ripe strawberries, hulled and quartered*
- *few drops lemon juice*

FOR THE ORANGE AND STRAWBERRY SAUCE

- *100 g (4 oz) white sugar*
- *300 ml (½ pint) water*
- *175 g (6 oz) strawberries, hulled and quartered*

- *1 × 15 ml spoon (1 tablespoon) orange juice*

FOR THE TUILE BASKETS

- *40 g (1½ oz) plain white flour*
- *75 g (3 oz) caster sugar*
- *3 egg whites*
- *25 g (1 oz) butter, melted*

TO SERVE

- *12–18 wild strawberries with their hulls*
- *6 small leaves lemon balm*

● **MAKE THE STRAWBERRY SORBET**

Place the sugar and the water in a small to medium saucepan, slowly bring to the boil then boil fast for 5 minutes to make a sugar syrup. Take the pan off the heat and chill thoroughly. Blend the strawberries in a blender under completely smooth. Sieve through a fine sieve to remove any grittiness. Chill.

Mix the strawberry purée and the sugar syrup together in a mixing bowl, add the lemon juice and mix well. Transfer into an ice-cream maker and process until frozen but still soft. Keep in the freezer until required; if you leave the sorbet in the freezer for longer than 20 minutes you should allow 30–60 minutes thawing time in the refrigerator to re-soften before serving.

● **MAKE THE ORANGE AND STRAWBERRY SAUCE**

Place the sugar and water in a small saucepan and slowly bring to the boil then boil fast for 5 minutes, to make a sugar syrup. Take the pan off the heat and chill thoroughly. Blend the strawberries in a blender until completely smooth. Sieve through a fine sieve to remove any grittiness. Mix the strawberry purée with the sugar syrup and the orange juice and keep chilled.

● **MAKE THE TUILE BASKETS**

Preheat the oven to gas mark 6, 400°F (200°C). Mix the flour and sugar together in a mixing bowl, add the egg whites and melted butter and beat with a whisk until smooth. Cool a little. Grease and flour a non-stick, flat baking sheet. Beat the mixture once with a spoon and pour one dessertspoon of the mixture on one half of the baking sheet; spread the mixture so it makes a circle measuring at least 13 cm (5 inches) in diameter. Pour another dessertspoon of the mixture on to the other half of the baking sheet and spread out to the same size. Place the baking sheet in the preheated oven and bake for 4–5 minutes or until the edges are brown all around (I find that it usually takes 5 minutes but some ovens differ from others). Take out of the oven and carefully scrape the first biscuit off the baking sheet with a spatula or knife. Turn the biscuit over, then turn it back again to allow it to cool slightly, then right away place over an upturned college pudding mould and shape with your hands to make a wavy shaped biscuit. When doing so, make sure that you press the base only and not the sides or they might crack. Take the other biscuit off the baking sheet and, since it has had time to cool, place right away over an upturned college pudding mould and press the base to shape it as before. To accentuate the shape I often place another college pudding mould over each biscuit instead of keeping my hands pressed on the moulds. However, if the biscuits have cooked for long enough in the oven they will set more or less right away and keep their folded shape, so you won't need to press for long. Once cold, remove from the tins and keep in an airtight tin to preserve their crispness. Bake and make the other four baskets in the same way. The quantity allows for a few mistakes!

● **TO SERVE**

Place one basket on each plate and fill with 2 or 3 scoops of the sorbet. Pour a tablespoonful of orange and strawberry sauce next to the basket. Place 2 or 3 wild strawberries inside the basket, on top of the sorbet, and a leaf of lemon balm by the syrup.

6

SUMMER MENU

AUBERGINE AND HALLOUMI CHEESE TERRINE WITH CELERY LEAF AND TOMATO COULIS ♦

~

ARTICHOKE HEART PAELLA ♦★

~

INDIVIDUAL SUMMER PUDDINGS À MA FAÇON ♦

~

This combination of dishes makes a colourful summer menu: the cheese terrine with its coulis has wonderful, striking colours which make it a starter to remember; the paella has plenty of delicious vegetables of various textures and is flavoured with saffron which gives it a golden inviting colour; the puddings look most appealing on their bed of dazzled sauces.

AUBERGINE AND TOMATO TERRINE WITH CELERY LEAF AND TOMATO COULIS

SERVES 6

The colours of this light terrine are striking like those of a flag: it has alternating layers of purple steamed aubergine, white Greek halloumi cheese and red de-seeded tomato quarters. It is served on a bed of tomato coulis flavoured with a little balsamic vinegar.

- 450 g (1 lb) aubergine
- salt to taste
- 550 g (1¼ lb) large tomatoes
- 225 g (8 oz) Greek halloumi cheese

FOR THE CELERY LEAF
AND TOMATO COULIS

- 2 × 5 ml spoons (2 teaspoons) chopped celery leaves

- 3 × 5 ml spoons (3 teaspooons) balsamic vinegar
- ½ × 15 ml spoon (½ tablespoon) olive oil
- ½ × 15 ml spoon (½ tablespoon) sunflower oil
- salt and freshly ground black pepper

TO GARNISH

- 6 sprigs celery leaves

Trim the ends of the aubergine and cut each aubergine lengthwise into slices 7.5 mm ($\frac{1}{3}$ inch) thick. Place in a steamer and steam for 10 minutes until the slices are very tender. Drain on kitchen paper until cool and sprinkle a pinch of salt over the slices, or to taste. Bring 1.75 litres (3 pints) of water to the boil in a large saucepan; use a knife to criss-cross the tomatoes on their bases; add the tomatoes to the boiling water and boil for 15 seconds. Quickly remove them from the water and place in a bowl of cold water. Leave for 15 seconds then take them out and peel the skin away from the tomatoes. Cut each tomato into quarters then take out the seeds and the inner flesh of the tomatoes leaving just the 'shells'. Reserve the flesh and skins for making the coulis.

Cut the halloumi cheese into slices 3–5 mm ($\frac{1}{8}$–$\frac{1}{4}$ inch) thick. Dry-fry (without any oil) two slices at a time in a hot frying-pan on a medium heat until golden on both sides.

Line a 450 g (1 lb) loaf tin with food wrap. Arrange two slices of aubergines to cover the base of the tin. Cover with a layer of halloumi cheese, two slices should be enough. Cover this with a layer of tomato quarters neatly placed alongside one another across the tin and overlapping them slightly so that they cover the cheese. Cover with another layer of aubergine (which should, if needs be, fill the gaps so the terrine layers are flat), another layer of halloumi cheese, then tomatoes. Repeat the layers once more and finish with a layer of aubergines so you have three equal layers in total plus an extra layer of aubergines to finish. Cover with food wrap and place in the refrigerator overnight.

● MAKE THE CELERY LEAF AND TOMATO COULIS

Place the reserved inner flesh and skin of the tomatoes in a small saucepan, add 6 × 15 ml spoons (6 tablespoons) of water, bring to the boil and simmer, covered, for 10 minutes. Sieve the mixture to leave the tomato 'juice'. Add the celery leaves, cool thoroughly then add the balsamic vinegar, oils and seasoning. Just before serving turn the terrine out and delicately peel off the food wrap. Cut into 6 neat slices. You will need a sharp knife to do this (try a serrated knife) as there are many layers, each with a different texture.

● TO SERVE

Pour some of the coulis on each of six large white starter plates; place a slice of the terrine in the middle of each plate and garnish with a sprig of celery leaves on top.

ARTICHOKE HEART PAELLA

SERVES 6

*T*raditionally, all ingredients used in paellas are cooked in the same pan as the rice but with a vegetarian paella I find that if you do so the vegetables are overcooked. So I cook my rice and my sofrito – vegetables cooked with onions and tomatoes – separately.

This is a wonderful paella which is made with artichoke hearts, fennel, French green beans, baby and yellow courgettes, peas and, of course, tomatoes. Like any paella, it relies on the use of saffron to flavour the rice and stock which gives it a rich golden colour. Saffron is the dried stigmas of the crocus flower: to ensure that you have the real thing buy saffron in the form of strands rather than powder. Spanish saffron is best for this dish.

- *4 globe artichokes*
- *2 × 15 ml spoons (2 tablespoons) olive oil*
- *350 g (12 oz) long-grain wholemeal rice*
- *600 ml (1 pint) water*
- *1 onion, peeled and finely chopped*
- *½ × 5 ml spoon (½ teaspoon) saffron strands*
- *3 gloves garlic, crushed*
- *275 g (10 oz) fresh French green beans, cut into 2.5 cm (1 inch) pieces*
- *225 g (8 oz) fennel bulb, cut into thin slices across*
- *225 g (8 oz) small yellow courgettes, chopped into 2 cm (¾ inch) pieces*
- *450 g (1 lb) baby courgettes, chopped into 2 cm (¾ inch) pieces*
- *750 g (1½ lb) ripe plum tomatoes, peeled and chopped*

- *150 ml (¼ pint) white wine*
- *2 vegetable stock cubes, crumbled*
- *100 g (4 oz) garden peas*
- *1 × 15 ml spoon (1 tablespoon) tomato purée*
- *2 × 15 ml spoons (2 tablespoons) fresh chopped basil*
- *2 × 15 ml spoons (2 tablespoons) fresh chopped continental parsley*
- *salt and freshly ground black pepper*

TO GARNISH

- *16 kalamata large black olives*
- *6 slices plum tomatoes*
- *8 lemon wedges*
- *2 × 15 ml spoons (2 tablespoons) mixed coarsely chopped basil and continental parsley*

Trim the artichoke bases so you are left with just 1.25 cm (½ inch) stems. Remove the very small outside leaves, rinse the artichokes and steam for 50 minutes. Peel the outer leaves away until you get to the core. Remove the fine hairs then trim the base again so you are left with just the heart. Cut each artichoke heart into 6 pieces.

Heat ½ × 15 ml spoon (½ tablespoon) of the olive oil in a pan and fry the rice on a low to medium heat until it gives off a toasted aroma. Add the water, bring to the boil and simmer, covered, for 20 minutes. Turn the heat off, keep the lid on and leave aside.

Meanwhile, make the sofrito. Heat the rest of the oil in a large frying-pan and sweat the onion together with the saffron on a medium heat until the onion is translucent. Add the garlic, green beans, fennel and courgettes; cover and cook on a low heat for 10 minutes or until the vegetables are almost tender. Add the tomatoes, white wine, stock cubes, peas and tomato purée, and bring to the boil. Cook until the tomatoes have completely broken down, the mixture is golden and the vegetables look cooked and tasty. Add the cooked rice, basil, continental parsley, pieces of artichoke hearts and seasoning; mix well but lightly and cook for another 3 minutes, stirring once or twice. If the mixture seems dry, add a little tomato juice. Season again to taste.

● **TO SERVE**

Transfer on to a large platter or individual plates and arrange some of the artichoke hearts and other vegetables on top so the colours show up well. Garnish with black olives, slices of tomato, wedges of lemon and extra fresh herbs sprinkled liberally over the top.

INDIVIDUAL SUMMER PUDDINGS À MA FAÇON

SERVES 6

*T*here is nothing nicer than to have a pudding made from all the fresh summer fruits and eating it chilled straight from the refrigerator. These puddings should be shaped in college pudding moulds 200 ml (⅓ pint) in capacity. Prepare them the day before so that the bread is well soaked and the flavours have time to mingle.

750 g (1½ lb) mixed raspberries, strawberries, blackcurrants and redcurrants
100 g (4 oz) soft brown sugar
10–12 slices of medium sliced unbleached white bread
300 ml (½ pint) Greek yoghurt
25 g (1 oz) white sugar

TO SERVE AND DECORATE
300 ml (½ pint) Greek yoghurt
18 leaves fresh mint
6 small bunches blackcurrants
6 small bunches redcurrants

Place the fruits in a medium saucepan and add the soft brown sugar. Cook on a low heat for 8 minutes until the juice has run out of the fruit. Cool a little.

Cut the crusts off the bread and cut into triangular wedge shapes. Press against the sides of the moulds, overlapping the slices slightly. Almost fill the moulds with the fruit mixture (reserving a little juice), then wait for the juices to sink in. Mix the yoghurt with the white sugar. Press the fruit mixture against the sides then top with the yoghurt mixture. Cover with the ends of the triangles of bread and cover with more bread if necessary to seal the puddings. Place a plate over the moulds to help the juices be forced into the bread; leave to set in the refrigerator overnight.

● **TO SERVE**

Turn out the puddings on to dessert plates. Sieve the leftover fruit syrup and place some of the syrup on the plate next to the puddings then add the yoghurt. Feather out the mixture of the two juices (see page 17) and decorate each plate with three leaves of mint. Place a small bunch of blackcurrants and redcurrants on to each of the puddings and serve.

SUMMER MENU ⑥
top Aubergine and Halloumi Cheese Terrine with Celery Leaf and Tomato Coulis *right*
Artichoke Heart Paella *left* Individual Summer Pudding à Ma E

❼

$\mathscr{S}$ UMMER $\mathscr{M}$ ENU

FONDUE OF GARLIC AND TOMATO SERVED
WITH ICED MACEDOINE OF VEGETABLES ♦★

~

SMOKY SAFFRON AUBERGINES WITH A LIGHT
SPRING ONION PICKLE ♦

~

SWEET BLUEBERRY AND STRAWBERRY CASTLE
IN *CRÈME DE CASSIS* SYRUP ♦★

~

This is a cold menu suitable for a hot summer's day. The
chilled starter will cool you down and may be served
with crushed ice or on crushed ice; the main course is a further
refresher which should be served with a side salad; the dessert
is beautifully light and fruity and may be accompanied by
some biscuits or boudoirs.

FONDUE OF GARLIC AND TOMATO
SERVED WITH ICED MACEDOINE OF VEGETABLES

SERVES 6

This is a very simple chilled soup which contains breadcrumbs to thicken the soup a little and give it some 'body'; the cloves add a Mediterranean feel to a soup which – because of the use of so much raw garlic – can be nothing else but continental!

- *1 kg (2 lb) large ripe tomatoes, peeled and chopped*
- *2 whole cloves, crushed (with a pestle and mortar)*
- *3 cloves garlic, crushed*
- *40 g (1½ oz) wholewheat breadcrumbs*
- *2 × 5 ml spoons (2 teaspoons) clear honey*

TO SERVE AND GARNISH

- *225 g (8 oz) ripe tomatoes, diced*
- *½ small cucumber, diced*
- *6 small ice cubes*
- *1 × 15 ml spoon (1 tablespoon) fresh chopped mint*

Place the tomatoes, cloves, garlic, breadcrumbs and honey in a blender and blend until smooth. Transfer into a mixing bowl and leave to stand for 2 hours for the flavours to develop.

Pour the soup into soup bowls with underplates. Just before serving, place some tomatoes and cucumber around the edge and an ice cube in the middle of each bowl, and garnish with mint.

SMOKY SAFFRON AUBERGINES
WITH A LIGHT SPRING ONION PICKLE

SERVES 6

*T*hese aubergines have a smoky flavour due to the presence of smoked Cheddar cheese and because the aubergine skins have been baked a few times. If you dislike smoked flavours, use an ordinary Cheddar cheese. As this dish is served cold, the aubergines may be prepared and baked in advance, and sliced at the last minute on the plate.

- *225 g (8 oz) white basmati rice*
- *good pinch of saffron (use threads rather than powder)*
- *450 ml (¾ pint) water*
- *6 medium to large aubergines*
- *1 × 15 ml spoon (1 tablespoon) olive oil*
- *1 onion, peeled and finely chopped*
- *2 cloves garlic, crushed*
- *2 × 5 ml spoons (2 teaspoons) cumin seeds*
- *100 g (4 oz) pine kernels*
- *175 g (6 oz) smoked Cheddar cheese, grated*

- *salt and freshly ground black pepper*
- *40 g (1½ oz) sun-dried tomatoes, finely diced*

FOR THE SPRING ONION PICKLE

- *9 spring onions*
- *salt*
- *4 × 15 ml spoons (4 tablespoons) white wine vinegar*
- *2 × 15 ml spoons (2 tablespoons) olive oil*

TO GARNISH

- *30 leaves continental parsley or small sprigs fresh coriander*
- *15 thin slices tomatoes*

Preheat the oven to gas mark 6, 400°F (200°C).

Place the rice and saffron in a medium to large saucepan and cover with the water; leave to stand for 20 minutes. Turn the heat on and bring the contents of the pan to the boil; simmer on a low heat for 10 minutes, tightly covered.

Place the aubergines in the preheated oven and bake for 20–30 minutes or until they feel very heavy and soft. The majority of aubergines take 30 minutes. Cool for 10 minutes.

Place the aubergines on a chopping board and lay them on their sides. Make a lengthways incision from the hull of each aubergine straight through to the end, cutting through the top skin and the flesh but not the bottom skin (the aubergine should not break into two halves but should remain attached along one side). Open up the aubergines, remove and discard some of the seeds. Remove part of the flesh and save. Sprinkle a good pinch of salt over the remaining inside flesh of each aubergine, and place on a very lightly greased baking sheet, salted side down, spreading the skin out as much as possible without breaking it. Bake for 15 minutes. Turn the aubergine skins over, so the flesh dries out, and bake for a further 10 minutes. Take the aubergines out of the oven and leave to cool for 5 minutes. Scrape out and reserve the flesh from the aubergines, leaving more or less just the skin.

Heat the oil in a heavy based frying-pan and fry the onion until soft and golden. Chop all the cooked and uncooked reserved flesh of the aubergines. Add the garlic, chopped aubergine flesh and cumin seeds and fry on a medium heat for 10 minutes to brown the ingredients. Take the pan off the heat and add the cooked rice, pine kernels, cheese and seasoning. Mix well and leave to cool for 5 minutes.

Place the aubergine skins with the fleshy side upwards on a baking sheet; divide the rice mixture between each, spreading the skin as you do so to spread the filling over as wide a surface as possible. Sprinkle the diced sun-dried tomatoes over the rice and fold and roll each aubergine as though it were a Swiss roll, making sure that you don't break the skin. Leave a little of the flesh of the aubergine without filling at the top end of the roll, so you can 'stick' the purple aubergine flesh together. Place all the rolls on a lightly greased baking sheet, with the seam at the bottom, and bake in the preheated oven for 20 minutes. Cool thoroughly.

● **MAKE THE SPRING ONION PICKLE**

Cut off the bulbs of the spring onions and peel; cut each bulb in half and shred very finely. Place in a small mixing bowl and sprinkle a good pinch of salt over the onions. Leave to stand for 30 minutes, covered with food wrap, then stir in the vinegar and oil.

● **TO SERVE**

Place the aubergines on to a chopping board and, using a very sharp knife, trim the bottom ends off. Cut the main body of the aubergines into five round slices each 2 cm (¾ inch) wide and overlap those slices around one half of a large plate. Leave the top 3–4 cm (1¼–1½ inches) of the top of the aubergine uncut and place on the plate too. Cut the slices of garnishing tomatoes in half and place a slice of tomato on the outside of the aubergine slices, accentuating the curling effect of the aubergines. Pour the pickle over the tomato slices and part of the aubergine slices. Garnish further by placing a leaf of continental parsley or small sprig of coriander over each slice of tomato and serve. Accompany with a side salad.

INDIVIDUAL BLUEBERRY AND STRAWBERRY CASTLES IN *CRÈME DE CASSIS* SYRUP

SERVES 6

*T*hese turned-out moulds may be made with any summer fruits such as bilberries, raspberries or blackcurrants. However, do not make them with fruits such as peaches and pineapple because those fruits will affect the setting of the agar-agar. Agar-agar can be found in the form of powder which is very concentrated or in the form of flakes. Agar-agar powder takes only 2 minutes of simmering time to dissolve whereas the flakes take up to 10 minutes.

600 ml (1 pint) red grape juice

2½ × 5 ml spoons (2½ teaspoons) agar-agar powder or 7½ × 5 ml spoons (7½ teaspoons) agar-agar flakes

15 g (½ oz) white sugar

1 × 15 ml spoon (1 tablespoon) crème de cassis

225 g (8 oz) small ripe strawberries, hulled and halved

100 g (4 oz) blueberries

100 g (4 oz) redcurrants, destalked

FOR THE SYRUP

4–6 × 15 ml spoons (4–6 tablespoons) crème de cassis

4 × 15 ml spoons (4 tablespoons) red grape juice

TO DECORATE

450 ml (¾ pint) double cream

18 fresh mint leaves

● MAKE THE AGAR-AGAR JELLY

Place the grape juice in a small saucepan and add either the powder or the flakes. Add the sugar, bring to the boil and, if using the powder, simmer for 2 minutes; if using the flakes, simmer for 10 minutes, in a covered saucepan. Take the pan off the heat and add the *crème de cassis*. Leave aside to cool a little.

Divide the three fruits between six dariole moulds 150 ml (¼ pint) in capacity, and pour the agar-agar mixture over them. Do not fill them right to the top. Leave to cool for 15 minutes then place in a refrigerator to chill for two hours.

● TO SERVE

Take out of the refrigerator and dip them briefly in a pan of boiling water; loosen one side of the moulds with a small knife to allow air in and turn the moulds out on to a plate. Mix the *crème de cassis* and grape juice together, pour some of the mixture around each turned-out mould. Whip the cream stiffly and pipe a little over each mould. Decorate with 3 fresh mint leaves around each pudding just before serving.

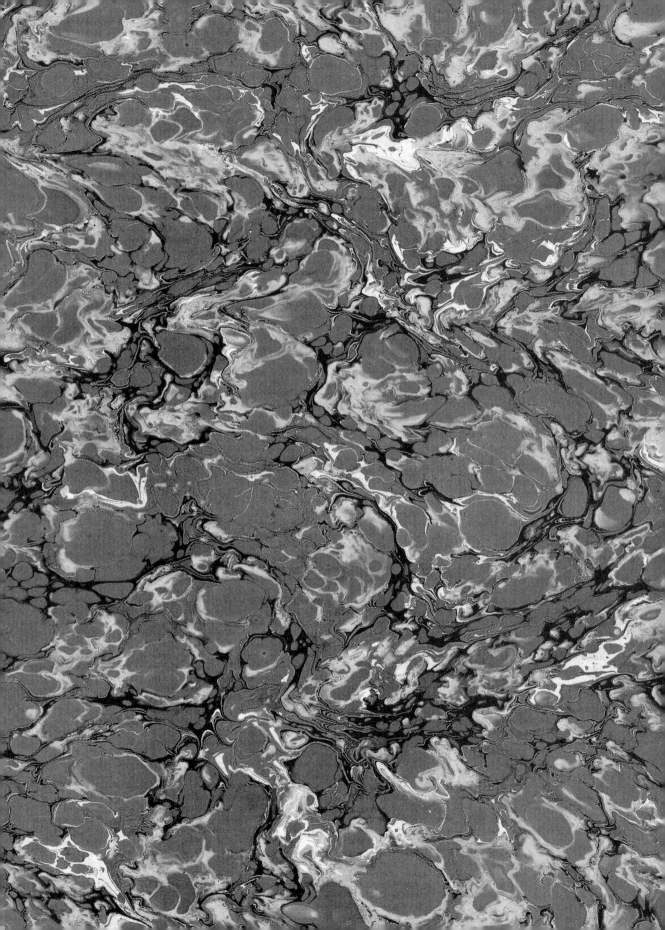

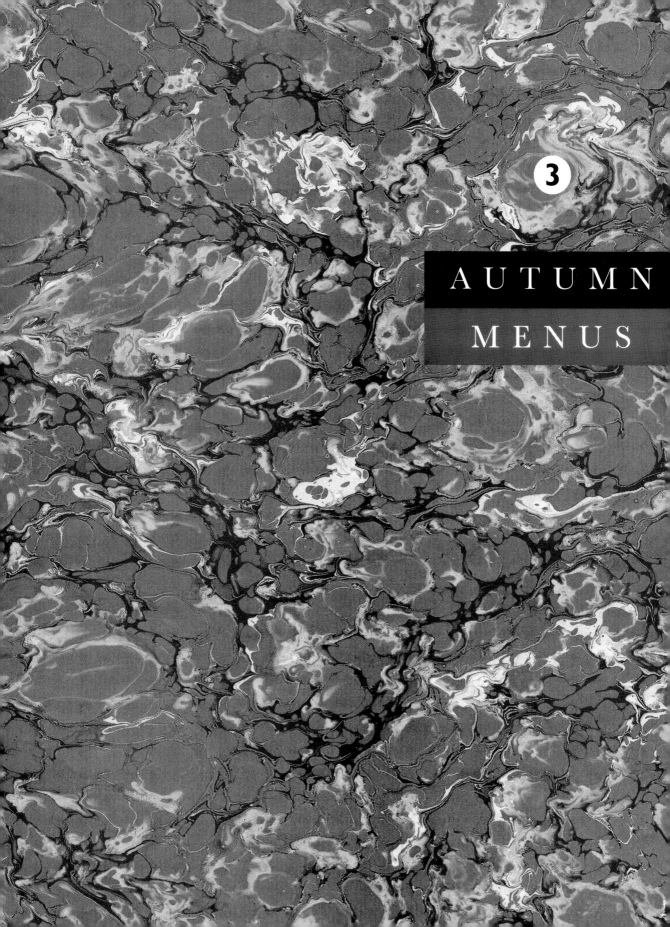

3

AUTUMN
MENUS

❶

𝒜 U T U M N 𝓜 E N U

FRESH THYME, GARLIC AND
GOAT CHEESE CROUSTADES ◆

~

WILD MUSHROOM STRUDEL SERVED WITH
GLACÉ-STYLE SHIITAKE AND SHALLOT SAUCE

~

PEARS NEW ENGLAND ◆★

~

This autumn menu has wonderful flavours and warm colours; the chaud-froid starter is light, fragrant and served on a bed of mixed leaves. The wild mushroom strudel takes you straight back to the autumnal forest and the poached pears dessert is a visual delight, served with a clear orange and cider sauce and decorated with all-year round strawberries. The starter takes little time to prepare, the main course may be prepared the day before and then cooked on the day and the pears may be cooked a few hours prior to the meal.

FRESH THYME, GARLIC AND
GOAT CHEESE CROUSTADES

SERVES 6

This is a very quick starter of goat cheese served on crisp toasted bread bases which are themselves served on a bed of mixed leaves. If you dislike goat cheese you may use a different cheese. What I like about this starter is the contrast of the warm, softening cheese with the cool and sharp vinaigrette.

FOR THE VINAIGRETTE

● *3 × 15 ml spoons (3 tablespoons) walnut oil*
● *2 × 15 ml spoons (2 tablespoons) garlic wine vinegar*

● *2 × 5 ml spoons (2 teaspoons) fresh chopped thyme*
● *salt and freshly ground black pepper*

FOR THE CROUSTADES

- 9 slices unbleached medium-sliced white bread
- 2 cloves garlic, peeled and cut in half across (not crushed)
- 250 g (9 oz) creamy goat cheese, preferably tubular in shape

TO SERVE AND GARNISH

- 6 leaves radicchio lettuce, shredded
- 6 leaves frisée lettuce, shredded
- 18 cherry tomatoes
- 1 × 5 ml spoon (1 teaspoon) fresh chopped thyme

Make the vinaigrette by shaking the walnut oil, garlic wine vinegar, fresh chopped thyme and seasoning in a jam jar. Leave to stand while you prepare the rest of this starter.

● PREPARE THE CROUSTADES

Toast the bread on both sides until golden, then cool the slices. Using a 5 cm (2 inch) unfluted round cutter, cut two rounds out of each slice. Rub the surface of each round with the cut side of the garlic cloves. Cut the goat cheese into 18 thin slices (using a knife with a hot blade makes this easier). Place a slice of cheese on each of the bread rounds and place the cheese croustades and the garnishing tomatoes on a large baking tray under a preheated moderately hot grill.

● TO SERVE

Mix the lettuces and divide equally between six large starter plates. Watch the grilling croustades carefully and when the cheese begins to soften, remove from the grill and place three rounds on each prepared plate. Pour some of the dressing over the lettuce and croustades and sprinkle chopped thyme over the warm goat cheese. Garnish the plates further by placing the partly baked cherry tomatoes in between the rounds and serve immediately.

WILD MUSHROOM STRUDEL SERVED WITH GLACÉ-STYLE SHIITAKE AND SHALLOT SAUCE

SERVES 6

*T*he filling for this strudel relies on the use of wild mushrooms: you should find fresh shiitake mushrooms in your supermarket but if not order them from your greengrocer (if you prefer use fresh oyster mushrooms instead); the flat mushrooms used are large field mushrooms. When preparing the mushrooms, do not wash them but just wipe them with a damp cloth. Serve this dish with the mushroom sauce given below, some buttered new potatoes and a hot side vegetable such as steamed broccoli or cauliflower. Make the mushroom sauce first and keep it warm while you prepare the strudel.

- 8 sheets fresh or frozen filo pastry
- 10 shiitake mushrooms (if the mushrooms are small use double the quantity)
- 65 g (2½ oz) butter
- 450 g (1 lb) leeks, finely shredded
- 350 g (12 oz) field mushrooms, chopped
- 65 g (2½ oz) finely chopped walnuts
- 2 × 5 ml spoons (2 teaspoons) fresh chopped oregano
- 1½ × 15 ml spoons (1½ tablespoons) tamari
- 225 g (8 oz) cooked long-grain whole-meal rice
- salt and freshly ground black pepper
- 1 beaten egg, to glaze
- 15 g (½ oz) sesame seeds

FOR THE SAUCE

- 15 g (½ oz) lightly salted butter
- 4 shallots, peeled and shredded
- 100 g (4 oz) shiitake mushrooms
- 100 g (4 oz) chestnut mushrooms, very thinly sliced
- 750 ml (1¼ pints) light stock (made with 1 × 5 ml spoon (1 teaspoon) bouillon powder mixed with hot water)
- 2 × 15 ml spoons (2 tablespoons) tamari
- 1 × 15 ml spoon (1 tablespoon) French brandy
- salt and freshly ground black pepper

TO GARNISH

- 6 tomato roses, see page 16
- 12 watercress leaves

If using frozen filo pastry, defrost at room temperature for two to three hours.

Preheat the oven to gas mark 6, 400°F (200°C). Prepare the shiitake mushrooms by chopping part of their hard stalks and shredding both the caps and the rest of the stalks.

Melt 25 g (1 oz) of the butter and fry the leeks on a medium to high heat until tender. Add all the mushrooms and stir-fry for another 8 minutes until soft. Add the walnuts, oregano, tamari, cooked rice and seasoning and mix well. Take the pan off the heat and leave aside to cool.

Place a clean tea-towel on your work surface; cover with a sheet of filo pastry. Melt the rest of the butter and brush the filo pastry liberally with it. Cover with another three sheets of filo pastry, each brushed with butter. Then spread half the mushroom filling across the pastry; make sure you spread the filling right to the outside edges. Helping yourself with the tea-towel underneath, wrap the pastry around the filling by rolling like a Swiss roll. Transfer the roll on to a lightly greased baking sheet, seam side down, and repeat the process with the other half of the filo pastry and the filling. Brush the beaten egg over both rolls and dust with the sesame seeds. Bake in the preheated oven for 25–30 minutes until the pastry is crisp and golden.

● MAKE THE SAUCE

It has no thickening agent so is left to reduce until thickened up. Melt the butter in a saucepan and fry the shallots until dark brown; keep the heat fairly high to darken the shallots in colour. Add the shiitake mushrooms and chestnut mushrooms and stir-fry for 5 minutes; then turn the heat down and cook for another 5 minutes. Add the stock, tamari and brandy and bring to the boil. Simmer, partly covered, for 25 minutes then season well and serve, as suggested above.

When the strudel is cooked remove it from the oven and let it stand for 5 minutes.

● **T O   S E R V E**

Cut each roll into three slices, at a slant, and serve on warm plates with the sauce poured by the
side. Garnish with a tomato rose and two watercress leaves, water-lily style, see page 16.

P E A R S   N E W   E N G L A N D

SERVES 6

*T*his marinated pear recipe is so simple, it is amazing that it tastes and looks so good. It
makes a light pudding which may be served with shortcake or other biscuits unless you
are planning to follow it with a cheeseboard, when it would be best to serve this dessert by itself.

450 ml (¾ pint) medium-sweet cider
*2 × 15 ml spoons (2 tablespoons) orange
curls, see page 15*
3 × 15 ml spoons (3 tablespoons) honey
6 Williams or Comice pears
3 × 5 ml spoons (3 teaspoons) arrowroot

TO DECORATE

18 strawberries, fanned out, see page 16
6 fresh mint leaves

Place the cider, orange curls and honey in a saucepan just big enough to take six pears standing
up; slowly bring to the boil.

Peel the pears but leave the stalks on, then core them with an apple corer. Place them in the
pan so they are standing up. Cover, bring back to the boil, turn the heat down and simmer for
10–20 minutes, until the pears are tender. Carefully lift the pears out, and drain them well. Sieve
the juice and save the orange curls for the decoration of the plates.

Place the arrowroot in a small saucepan and add the sieved juice, little by little, stirring after
each addition, until the arrowroot is completely dissolved; bring to the boil, stirring all the time
and simmer for 1 minute until the sauce clears and thickens. Cool.

● **T O   S E R V E**

Place the pears on individual large dessert plates; if they will not stand upright, cut part of the
base so they sit flat. Pour the sauce over them, letting any extra sauce fall on to the plate. Decorate
by placing three fanned-out strawberries at equal intervals around each pear, at the edge of the
sauce, and place the reserved orange curls in between the strawberries. Place a mint leaf on the
side of each pear, with the stalk of the mint at the pear stalk. Serve warm, cold or chilled.

2

Autumn Menu

Mixed Leaf Salad and Bundle of Asparagus
Tips in Raspberry Vinaigrette ♦★

~

Crown of Cabbage and Chestnut
Parcels on a Cream and Cider Sauce ♦

~

Bread Timbale on Dazzling
Blackcurrant Sauce

~

This menu starts with a light salad in an intriguing vinaigrette which sets off the taste buds gently; this is followed by an attractive and tasty main course which has plenty of contrasting textures and a deliciously smooth sauce. The dessert is sweet and 'puddingy' and colourful and is my idea of a great pudding!

Mixed Leaf Salad and Bundle of Asparagus Tips in Raspberry Vinaigrette

SERVES 6

This is a wonderful salad with a raspberry vinegar dressing which contrasts well with the more bitter continental lettuces and makes them seem sweeter. The asparagus used here is the extra fine asparagus tips which you can buy in 150 g (5 oz) packets or bundles which measure approximately 10 cm (4 inches) long.

- 1 yellow pepper
- 42 extra-fine asparagus weighing 150 g (5 oz) in total
- 4 leaves radicchio lettuce
- 1 little gem lettuce
- 1 endive

- 20 baby leaves spinach
- heart of 1 curly endive (approximately 50 g (2 oz))
- a few chives, chopped into pieces 1.25 cm (½ inch) long

FOR THE RASPBERRY VINAIGRETTE

- *2 × 15 ml spoons (2 tablespoons) raspberry vinegar*
- *1 × 15 ml spoon (1 tablespoon) red wine vinegar*
- *2 ×15 ml spoons (2 tablespoons) hazelnut oil*
- *3 ×15 ml spoons (3 tablespoons) sunflower oil*

- *1 × 5 ml spoon (1 teaspoon) wholegrain mustard*
- *salt and freshly ground black pepper*

TO GARNISH

- *6 'white' sprigs taken from the heart of the curly endive used in the salad*

Preheat the oven to gas mark 6, 400°F (200°C).

Place the yellow pepper on a baking sheet in the preheated oven for 25–30 minutes; turn the pepper over half-way through the cooking time to ensure that the pepper is blistered all over. Remove the pepper from the oven and cool, covered with a damp cloth, for 10 minutes. Peel the skin away from the pepper and take the core out; halve it and remove the seeds and the white pith. Cut 6 strips along the longest side. Cool further.

Steam the asparagus for 6 minutes or until tender; rinse in cold water then leave to cool.

Mix all the vinaigrette ingredients together and season to taste.

Shred all the lettuce and spinach finely. Cut the curly endive heart into pieces 4 cm (1½ inches) long and reserve 6 sprigs for garnishing. Add the chives and mix the salad well.

● TO SERVE

Tie the asparagus in bundles of 7 with the yellow pepper 'strings' (if you cannot manage to tie it just fold the pepper over the asparagus tips). Divide the lettuce between six plates and place the asparagus bundles to one side of the plates, looking outwards. Pour the dressing over the salad and the asparagus. Garnish with the reserved sprigs of curly endive on top of the mixed lettuces.

CROWN OF CABBAGE AND CHESTNUT PARCELS ON A CREAM AND CIDER SAUCE

SERVES 6

The nutty filling of the dill and chestnut parcels is based on a mixture of vegetables and nuts (chestnuts and walnuts); you will not need much of this to make a satisfying dish. Ready-prepared chestnuts can be found in tins or frozen; the tinned ones do not need extra cooking so I tend to use those.

This dish is excellent served with baby carrots, cut into fine matchsticks, steamed, buttered and placed in the centre of the inner ring. Sprinkle a little fresh chopped dill on top and serve.

- *1 small savoy cabbage, weighing
750 g (1¾ lb)*
- *225 g (8 oz) ready-prepared chestnuts*
- *25 g (1 oz) butter*
- *225 g (8 oz) leeks, finely chopped*
- *2 cloves garlic, crushed*
- *175 g (6 oz) mushrooms, finely chopped*
- *2 × 5 ml spoons (2 teaspoons) fresh
dill weed*
- *100 g (4 oz) finely-chopped walnuts*
- *2 × 15 ml spoons (2 tablespoons) shoyu*
- *salt and freshly ground black pepper*

FOR THE MARINADE

- *1 × 15 ml spoon (1 tablespoon) shoyu*
- *1 × 15 ml spoon (1 tablespoon) water*

FOR THE CREAM AND CIDER SAUCE

- *15 g (½ oz) butter*
- *1 medium to large onion, peeled and
finely chopped*
- *300 ml (½ pint) dry or medium cider*
- *1 × 15 ml spoon (1 tablespoon)
barley miso*
- *65 ml (2½ fl oz) single cream*
- *salt and freshly ground black pepper*
- *few drops fresh lemon juice*

Preheat the oven to gas mark 6, 400°F (200°C).

Remove 12 of the outside leaves of the cabbage and rinse. Remove part of the centre vein by making a 'V' cut at the base, 5–7.5 cm (2–3 inches) deep. Steam for 8–10 minutes until tender. Then turn the heat off, remove the lid but leave the leaves in the steamer to dry out.

Chop the remainder of the cabbage finely – you should be left with approximately 250 g (9 oz) of the heart. Coarsely chop the chestnuts by hand. Melt the butter in a frying-pan and fry the leeks until tender. Add the chopped cabbage and garlic and stir-fry for 2 minutes. Cover and cook for 5 minutes; add the mushrooms, stir-fry for 1 minute then cover and cook for another 5 minutes. Add the dill weed, walnuts, shoyu and season to taste.

Place 2 × 15 ml spoons (2 tablespoons) of the mixture in the centre of each steamed cabbage leaf. Fold the cut edges over the filling, then fold the sides over, roll up like a cigar and place in a deep dish 28 × 23 cm (11 × 9 inches). Repeat until all the leaves are filled and are placed side by side in the dish. Mix the marinade ingredients and pour over the leaves. Cover with foil and bake for 20 minutes. Take out of the oven and leave to stand for 8 minutes, covered.

● MAKE THE SAUCE

Melt the butter and fry the onion for about 10 minutes on a medium heat until golden brown. Add the cider, bring to a simmer and cook for 2–3 minutes. Cool a little, then blend in a blender with the miso until completely smooth. Place the cream in a clean saucepan and gradually stir in the blended sauce. Add salt and black pepper and stir well. Reheat gently, up to foaming point, stirring all the time. Add the lemon juice and serve hot.

● TO SERVE

Cut each leaf into 4 or 5 slices with a very sharp knife. Pour some of the sauce over 6 warmed plates and place overlapping cabbage slices in a circle in the centre of each plate.

BREAD TIMBALE ON DAZZLING BLACKCURRANT SAUCE

SERVES 8–10

*T*his pudding or cake is best eaten cold. If the white bread has dark crusts, remove them and replace by adding a few more breadcrumbs.

- *350 g (12 oz) sliced white bread*
- *1½ × 5 ml spoons (1½ teaspoons) agar-agar powder (or 4 × 5 ml spoons (4 teaspoons) agar-agar flakes*
- *600 ml (1 pint) milk*
- *90 g (3½ oz) soft light brown sugar*
- *3 eggs, beaten*
- *150 g (5 oz) frozen mixed redcurrants and blackcurrants*

FOR THE BLACKCURRANT COULIS

- *225–350 g (8–12 oz) blackcurrants*
- *50 g (2 oz) light brown or white sugar*

TO SERVE

- *a little single or double cream*
- *6 sprigs fresh mint*

Preheat the oven to gas mark 5, 375°F (190°C).

Cut the bread into pieces and process in a food processor until reduced to breadcrumbs.

Place the agar-agar in a pan and gradually add the milk, stirring the mixture with a hand whisk. Add the sugar and place the pan on a low heat. Bring to the boil, stirring all the time, and simmer, covered, for 1 minute if using the powder; for 8 minutes, if using the flakes.

Place the eggs in a large mixing bowl and gradually stir in the milk mixture. Fold in the breadcrumbs and mix well. Lastly, add the fruits, stirring the mixture gently. Pour the mixture into a lined and lightly greased 1.2 litre (2 pint) charlotte mould and level the top. Place on the middle shelf of the preheated oven and bake for 30–40 minutes or until set; do not overbake. Take the tin out of the oven and loosen the cake around the edges using a round-bladed knife. Leave the cake to cool thoroughly in the tin in the refrigerator for a few hours.

● MAKE THE COULIS

Place the blackcurrants and the sugar in a small saucepan and add 2–3 × 15 ml spoons (2–3 tablespoons) water. Bring to the boil and simmer for 6 minutes. Cool a little and pass the fruits through a sieve to the point where no pulp remains in the fruit. Cool thoroughly.

● TO SERVE

Place some of the coulis on dessert plates. Turn the cake out, cut into slices and place delicately on the coulis. Pour a little cream on each of the plates and streak with a knife to give a dazzling effect (see page 17). Decorate by placing a sprig of mint next to the cake.

❸

$\mathscr{A}$UTUMN $\mathscr{M}$ENU

PARSNIP AND LEMON POTAGE ♦

~

LEEK, FENNEL AND RED PEPPER CROUSTADE
WITH RED PEPPER SAUCE ♦

~

PEAR AND APPLE SOUFFLÉS
WITH BITTER CHOCOLATE SAUCE

~

This is a true autumn menu using the best of the seasonal produce. The starter is creamy, warming and refreshing with its hint of fresh lemon. The main course has a crunchy base, a creamy middle layer of leek and fennel purée, and a fresh topping of stir-fried leeks, fennel and red pepper, all providing good texture combinations and flavours. The delicious fruit soufflés are flavoured with pear eau de vie *and served on a base of chocolate sauce; they may be served with a crunchy biscuit.*

PARSNIP AND LEMON POTAGE

SERVES 6

*P*arsnip soups can sometimes be extremely heavy but this potage is lightened by the addition of apple and lemon which also make it a little fruity. The oatmeal thickens and enriches it. Serve this soup with buttered Italian or other continental bread.

- *40 g (1½ oz) butter*
- *5 sticks celery, chopped*
- *450 g (1 lb) parsnips, peeled and chopped*
- *900 ml (1½ pints) water*
- *25 g (1 oz) oatflakes*
- *2 green eating apples, peeled and chopped*

- *1½ × 15 ml spoons (1½ tablespoons) fresh lemon juice*
- *salt and freshly ground black pepper*

TO GARNISH

- *a few lemon curls, see page 15*
- *a few snipped chives or chopped chervil*

Melt the butter and fry the celery and parsnip for 10 minutes until golden, not brown. Blend the water and oatflakes together in a blender until completely smooth. Add this to the parsnip mixture and bring to the boil. Add the chopped apple and simmer for 10 minutes, covered, stirring from time to time. Cool a little and blend the soup, half at a time, until smooth.

● **TO SERVE**

Return the soup to a clean saucepan and reheat slowly. Add the lemon juice and seasoning, as required. Garnish with the lemon curls and fresh herbs and serve in warmed soup bowls.

LEEK, FENNEL AND RED PEPPER CROUSTADE
WITH RED PEPPER SAUCE

SERVES 6

*T*hese croustades are always very popular; they have three layers: a nutty base, a creamy middle layer and a topping of shredded vegetables stir-fried so they retain some crispness. The bases should remain crunchy to contrast with the top layers so do not pour the leek, fennel and red pepper purée on the croustade bases until they are ready to go into the oven.

FOR THE BASE

- 75 g (3 oz) cashews
- 75 g (3 oz) almonds
- 175 g (6 oz) white bread
- 2 × 5 ml spoons (2 teaspoons) fresh chopped marjoram
- 2 cloves garlic, crushed
- 1 × 5 ml spoon (1 teaspoon) wholegrain mustard
- 2 × 15 ml spoons (2 tablespoons) sunflower oil
- 175 g (6 oz) Cheddar cheese, grated
- 25 g (1 oz) hulled sesame seeds
- salt and freshly ground black pepper

FOR THE TOPPING

- 25 g (1 oz) butter
- 750 g (1½ lb) leeks, finely shredded
- 2 medium heads fennel, cored and finely shredded across
- 150 ml (¼ pint) water
- 1 vegetable stock cube, crumbled
- 3 red peppers
- salt and freshly ground black pepper

FOR THE RED PEPPER SAUCE

- 1 deep red pepper
- 15 g (½ oz) butter
- 100 g (4 oz) white of leek
- 1 × 400 g (14 oz) tin tomatoes
- 150 ml (¼ pint) water
- 1 vegetable stock cube, crumbled
- salt and freshly ground black pepper

TO GARNISH

- 6 sprigs fresh chervil

Preheat the oven to gas mark 6, 400°F (200°C).

● **MAKE THE BASE**

Place the cashews, almonds and bread in a food processor and process until the nuts are ground finely and the bread is reduced to breadcrumbs. Add the marjoram, garlic, mustard and oil and process again. Place the mixture in a mixing bowl, add the cheese, sesame seeds and seasoning.

Press and mould the mixture firmly into 6 rounds each 10 cm (4 inches) in diameter and 2.5 cm (1 inch) deep. Bake on the middle shelf of the oven for 20–25 minutes or until very crisp.

● **MAKE THE TOPPING**

Melt the butter and gently stir-fry the leeks and fennel until just tender; turn the heat off. Take a third of the mixture out of the pan and transfer into a small saucepan; add the water and stock cube, bring to the boil and simmer for 5 minutes. Season, cool a little and blend in a blender until completely smooth.

Remove the tops and bases from the red peppers, de-seed then cut into strips 2 cm (³/₄ in) wide, then shred across into pieces 5 mm (¹/₄ inch) wide. Reheat the original leek and fennel mixture and add the red pepper; stir-fry for 2 minutes. Season.

● **MAKE THE RED PEPPER SAUCE**

Place the red pepper in the preheated oven and bake for 30 minutes turning it over half-way through the cooking time to ensure that all sides are blistered. Take out of the oven and leave it to stand for 10 minutes, covered with a damp tea-towel. Remove the skin and de-seed. Melt the butter and fry the leek until tender; add the tin of tomatoes, water and stock cube and bring to the boil. Simmer, covered, for 10 minutes and cool a little. Blend the mixture until smooth in a blender and transfer into a pan, season well and reheat the sauce.

Pour the blended leek and fennel mixture over the cooked nut bases; top with the leek, fennel and red pepper mixture and place in the oven for 5–8 minutes to reheat through. Take the croustades out of the oven and place on warmed plates with a little of the red pepper sauce beside them. Garnish with sprigs of chervil.

PEAR AND APPLE SOUFFLÉS WITH BITTER CHOCOLATE SAUCE

SERVES 6

*T*hese wonderful soufflés are a variation of a recipe by the Roux brothers. I was attracted to this recipe because it is so light and unusual; this version uses more fruit and less sugar. These soufflés can be served warm or cold as they don't lose any volume once baked.

- 350 g (12 oz) cooking or eating apples, peeled and chopped
- 75 g (3 oz) soft brown sugar
- 50 ml (2 fl oz) water
- 1 × 15 ml spoon (1 tablespoon) arrowroot
- 2 × 15 ml spoons (2 tablespoons) pear eau de vie
- 2 ripe red Bart pears, left unpeeled but cored and chopped
- 4 egg whites

FOR THE CHOCOLATE SAUCE

- 25 g (1 oz) unsalted butter
- 2 egg yolks

- 1 × 15 ml spoon (1 tablespoon) cocoa powder
- 1 × 15 ml spoon(1 tablespoon) chocolate powder
- 3 × 15 ml spoons (3 tablespoons) maple syrup
- 4 × 15 ml spoons (4 tablespoons) orange juice
- 2 × 15 ml spoons (2 tablespoons) double cream, optional

TO SERVE

- 2 ripe red Bart pears, left unpeeled, cored and thinly sliced

Preheat the oven to gas mark 8, 450°F (230°C) and place a baking sheet in the oven to heat up.

Place the apples in a food processor and process until smooth. Transfer to a small saucepan and cook over a low heat for 20 minutes to dry the apple mixture.

Place 65 g (2½ oz) of the sugar and the water in another saucepan, bring to the boil and simmer for 2 minutes or until the mixture has reduced by a third; add to the apple mixture.

Mix the arrowroot with the pear *eau de vie* in a pan and stir until dissolved. Add the pear and syrup mixture, slowly bring to the boil and simmer for 2 minutes or until the arrowroot clears. Transfer into a mixing bowl, add the chopped pears and keep warm on one side.

Whisk the egg whites until stiff, then add the reserved 15 g (½ oz) sugar – this will soften the egg mixture. Fold ⅓ of the egg whites into the pear mixture and mix until completely amalgamated. Delicately fold in the rest of the egg whites. Fill 6 greased and lined ramekins (150 ml (¼ pint) in capacity) to the rim. Place the ramekins on the baking sheet in the preheated oven and bake for 3 minutes. Take out of the oven and leave to stand in a warm place.

● MAKE THE CHOCOLATE SAUCE

Melt the butter. Take the pan off the heat then add the egg yolks, the cocoa and chocolate powder and whisk until completely smooth. Place the pan back on the heat and warm through until the sauce thickens which should take no more than 3 minutes, whisking all the time – do not overheat. Add the maple syrup and orange juice and warm through, stirring all the time, until the sauce comes up to its first boil and thickens up again. Add the double cream, off the heat, if using.

● TO SERVE

Loosen the soufflés with a sharp knife around the edges and turn out on to plates. Pour some of the chocolate sauce around the soufflés and place 3 slices of the red pears above each one.

④

Autumn Menu

AVOCADO SALSA SERVED
WITH CHEESY NACHOS ◆

~

POTATO ROSTI WITH OKRA AND BLACK
BEAN FILLING AND CHILLI TOMATO SAUCE ◆

~

ORANGES IN ARMAGNAC NECTAR ◆★

~

This is a menu with a touch of Mexican influence. The salsa served with cheesy nachos has become quite a popular dish and it is still a favourite starter with me if home-made with lots of fresh coriander. The potato rosti is perfect for those who like to add a little spiciness to their meals. The final course is light orange slices in a brandy and redcurrant syrup; the nectar has an almost set texture and this pudding makes a colourful finish to the meal.

AVOCADO SALSA SERVED WITH CHEESY NACHOS

This avocado salsa is refreshing, tangy and delicious; the warm tortilla chips provide a good texture contrast and it is satisfying to dip the warm nachos in the very cool guacamole. It is fun to make your own tortilla chips but you may prefer to buy ready-made tortilla chips, in which case you will need 2 × 100 g (2 × 4 oz) packets. For the best contrast, the avocado salsa should be quite sharp and lemony.

FOR THE HOME-MADE NACHOS

- *350 g (12 oz) polenta*
- *1½ × 5 ml spoons (1½ teaspoons) salt*
- *5 × 15 ml spoons (5 tablespoons) corn oil*

FOR THE AVOCADO SALSA

- *3 very ripe avocados*
- *5 × 15 ml spoons (5 tablespoons) fresh lemon juice, or to taste*
- *5 × 15 ml spoons (5 tablespoons) fresh chopped coriander*

- *2 ×15 ml spoons (2 tablespoons) chopped continental parsley*
- *5 medium to large tomatoes, peeled and chopped*
- *½ × 5 ml spoon (½ teaspoon) Tabasco*
- *½–1 × 5 ml spoon (½–1 teaspoon) salt*

- *225 g (8 oz) Cheddar cheese, grated*
- *6 cherry tomatoes, halved*
- *6 large sprigs fresh coriander*

Preheat the oven to gas mark 5, 375°F (190°C).

● MAKE THE NACHOS

Mix the polenta and the salt together in a mixing bowl. Bring 300 ml (½ pint) water to the boil in a small covered saucepan. Pour the water over the polenta and add the oil; mix well and gather into a dough. Knead for 5 minutes and roll out the dough, half at a time, to a 3 mm (⅛ inch) thickness (keep the rest of the dough wrapped in food wrap). Do not worry if the dough seems patchy at first as the surface will even itself out as you roll it. Cut into triangles, the sides of which should be 6 cm (2½ inches) long. Leave to dry for 10 minutes and fry in batches in hot oil for 1 minute; drain on kitchen paper and keep warm in a tea-towel. In total, you will need 60–72 nachos.

● MAKE THE AVOCADO SALSA

Peel, halve and remove the stone from the avocado. Cut the flesh into chunks, place in a mixing bowl and mash until smooth. Add the lemon juice, coriander, parsley, tomatoes, Tabasco and salt and stir twice. The salsa should be fairly liquid and lemony; as it stands, the lemon flavour will become less accentuated. Cover.

Place the tortilla chips on ovenproof individual plates, in a circle measuring approximately 14 cm (5½ inches) wide and overlapping each one over one another as though forming a crown. Sprinkle the grated cheese over each crown and place in the preheated oven until the cheese has melted. Take out of the oven and pour the avocado salsa in the centre.

● TO SERVE

Place two halves of cherry tomatoes over the salsa and garnish with a sprig of coriander.

POTATO ROSTI WITH OKRA AND BLACK BEAN FILLING AND CHILLI TOMATO SAUCE

SERVES 6

*T*his consists of light Edam rosti 'sandwiched' and filled with a spicy black bean, aubergine and sweetcorn mixture. The rostis should be cooked in advance and kept warm. You can, if you prefer, reheat them in the oven for 10 minutes at gas mark 5, 375°F (190°C).

- *1.25 kg (2½ lb) romano potatoes*
- *1½ × 5 ml spoons (1½ teaspoons) salt*
- *350 g (12 oz) Edam cheese, grated*
- *6 × 15 ml spoons (6 tablespoons) sunflower oil to cook the rosti*

FOR THE OKRA AND BLACK BEAN FILLING

- *50 g (2 oz) black-eyed beans*
- *3 × 15 ml spoons (3 tablespoons) corn oil*
- *1 large aubergine, diced*
- *225 g (8 oz) leeks, chopped*
- *2 large cloves garlic, crushed*
- *125 g (5 oz) baby sweetcorn, sliced into pieces 2 cm (¾ inch) long*
- *225 g (8 oz) okra, topped and tailed and sliced into pieces 1 cm (½ inch) long*
- *1½ × 5 ml spoons (1½ teaspoons) ground cumin*
- *½ × 5 ml spoons (½ teaspoon) garam masala*
- *1 × 5 ml spoon (1 teaspoon) whole cumin seeds*

- *2 red or green dwarf chillies, de-seeded and very finely chopped*
- *450 g (1 lb) ripe tomatoes, peeled and chopped*
- *5 × 15 ml spoons (5 tablespoons) tomato purée*
- *salt and freshly ground black pepper*

FOR THE CHILLI TOMATO SAUCE

- *1 × 15 ml spoon (1 tablespoon) corn oil*
- *750 g (1½ lb) ripe tomatoes, skinned and chopped*
- *2 × 15 ml spoons (2 tablespoons) tomato purée*
- *2 × 5 ml spoons (2 teaspoons) bouillon powder*
- *¼ × 5 ml spoon (¼ teaspoon) chilli powder*
- *300 ml (½ pint) water*
- *salt and freshly ground black pepper*

TO GARNISH

- *2 medium tomatoes, each cut into 9 wedges*
- *6 sprigs continental parsley*

● **PREPARE THE POTATO ROSTI**

Peel the potatoes and grate with the coarse grate of a food processor. Transfer into a sieve, add the salt and leave to stand for 30 minutes. The potatoes will lose some of their moisture.

● **PREPARE THE OKRA AND BLACK BEAN FILLING**

Place the black-eyed beans in a saucepan, cover with 2.5 cm (1 inch) water, bring to the boil and boil fast for 10 minutes; turn the heat down to a simmer and cook for a further 25 minutes; drain. Heat 2 × 15 ml spoons (2 tablespoons) of the oil and fry the aubergines until tender; take the aubergines out of the pan and keep aside. Heat the rest of the oil and fry the leeks until tender, on a low heat. Add the garlic and baby sweetcorn and fry for another 3 minutes. Add the okra, ground cumin, garam masala, cumin seeds and chillies, cover the pan and cook for another 3 minutes. Add the tomatoes, tomato purée and cooked black-eyed beans, bring to the boil and cook, covered, for 10 minutes. Add the cooked aubergine, season well and leave aside.

● **MAKE THE CHILLI TOMATO SAUCE**

Heat the oil and cook the tomatoes in a covered saucepan until tender. Add the tomato purée, bouillon powder, chilli powder and water, bring to the boil, cover and simmer for 10 minutes. Cool a little and blend in a blender until completely smooth. Season and reheat.

● **COOK THE POTATO ROSTI**

Transfer the potato mixture into a mixing bowl and add the grated cheese. Take a twelfth of the potato mixture and pat in a tea-towel to remove excess moisture. Heat $\frac{1}{2}$ × 15 ml spoon ($\frac{1}{2}$ tablespoon) sunflower oil in a heavy-based frying-pan; place a 10 cm (4 inch) crumpet ring mould in the centre of the preheated pan and place the potato mixture inside it. Level with a metallic spoon and cook on a low to medium heat for 6 minutes. Carefully loosen the mixture with the help of a sharp knife and remove the ring. Turn the rosti over and cook for a further 4 minutes. Drain on kitchen paper and keep warm. Repeat with the rest of the mixture. Note: if you have a large frying-pan, you will be able to cook four at a time.

● **TO SERVE**

Place a rosti on the centre of each plate; top with a sixth of the okra and black bean filling and top with another rosti. Garnish the top with 3 slices of tomatoes and sprig of continental parsley. Serve the sauce separately so each guest may pour it over the rosti.

Oranges in Armagnac Nectar

SERVES 6

*T*his is a simple dessert, and I think all that is needed after a main course that is filling and rather cheesey. The oranges are cooling and colourfully arranged in the centre of the plate, in a ring shape. The nectar is softly set and lightly sweetened.

8 large oranges

FOR THE NECTAR

300 ml (½ pint) orange juice
300 ml (½ pint) water
5 × 15 ml spoons (5 tablespoons) redcurrant jelly
6 cloves
¾ × 5 ml spoon (¾ teaspoon) gelozone or 1½ × 5 ml spoons (1½ teaspoons) agar-agar powder

2 × 15 ml spoons (2 tablespoons) orange curls (made with an orange zester)
2 × 15 ml spoons (2 tablespoons) honey
2 × 15 ml spoons (2 tablespoons) Armagnac or good brandy

TO DECORATE

175 g (6 oz) frozen redcurrants or raspberries

Remove the skin and pith of the orange as though cutting into segments, see page 15. Cut each orange across into 8 slices, so each slice looks like a star with segments.

● **MAKE THE NECTAR**

Mix the orange juice, water, redcurrant jelly, cloves and gelozone and orange curls in a small saucepan. Whisk until the gelozone is amalgamated and the redcurrant jelly is fairly smooth. Bring the mixture to boiling point, whisking and stirring from time to time so that the liquid is completely smooth. If using gelozone, take the pan off the heat just before boiling point; if using agar-agar powder, simmer for 2 minutes. Remove from the heat, sieve to extract the orange curls and cloves and add the honey and Armagnac to the liquid.

Arrange the slices of orange overlapping in a wheel shape in the centre of individual dessert plates. Pour the nectar mixture over each plate, arrange some curls over the oranges in a decorative manner and leave to cool and set for 30 minutes. The setting should be very soft.

● **TO SERVE**

Arrange a redcurrant or raspberry in the centre of each slice of orange.

⑤

AUTUMN MENU

WARM MOZZARELLA SALAD ♦

~

ARBORIO PASTA SHELLS
ON CHUNKY PASSATA

~

HAZELNUT *SABLÉS* WITH CALVADOS APPLES
AND *CRÈME CHANTILLY*

~

This colourful menu provides an array of contrasting textures. It begins with a warm mozzarella salad served with a light side salad. The main course consists of large pasta shells filled with arborio rice, placed over a chunky, sieved, tomato-based sauce and topped with a cheese sauce. The dessert makes use of autumn apples cooked with a touch of Angostura Bitters and Calvados to give them an edge. It is served with hazelnut biscuits and a lightly whipped and sweetened crème chantilly.

WARM MOZZARELLA SALAD

SERVES 6

This salad is made from marinated mozzarella cheese and tomatoes both popped in the oven just before serving so the cheese is warm and about to melt. The rest of the accompanying salad is based on avocado and mixed Italian lettuces which make a good crunchy side dish.

- *350 g (12 oz) mozzarella cheese*
- *3 large beef tomatoes*
- *3 × 5 ml spoons (3 teaspoons) dried basil*
- *½ × 5 ml spoon (½ teaspoon) dried oregano*
- *½ × 5 ml spoon (½ teaspoon) dried thyme*
- *½ × 5 ml spoon (½ teaspoon) salt*
- *½ × 5 ml spoon (½ teaspoon) coarsely ground black pepper*

FOR THE SIDE SALAD

- *2 ripe avocados*
- *12 sprigs frisée lettuce*
- *6 small leaves radicchio lettuce, cut in half through the centre*
- *salt and black pepper*

TO GARNISH

- *3 × 15 ml spoons (3 tablespoons) fresh shredded basil*
- *salt and black pepper*

Preheat the oven to gas mark 6, 400°F (200°C).

Discard the ends of each round of mozzarella cheese and cut the rest into 5 mm (¼ inch) slices; you should have 18 slices. Cut the ends off the tomatoes and cut each into 8 slices from top to bottom. Place the cheese and tomato slices in a large mixing bowl, add the herbs and seasoning and mix carefully. Cover with food wrap and leave to marinate for 30 minutes.

● MAKE THE SALAD GARNISH

Peel and halve the avocados, remove the stone and cut the flesh into slices across. Mix all the ingredients together in a mixing bowl and season to taste.

Place the mozzarella and the tomato slices on individual plates overlapping them in a slight semi-circle to one side of the plate (reserve the marinade). Place in the preheated oven for 4–5 minutes or until the cheese looks glossy and is starting to melt. Take out of the oven and pour the marinade over each plate. Sprinkle the garnish of fresh basil and black pepper over. Place the side salad on the other side of the plates and serve.

ARBORIO PASTA SHELLS ON CHUNKY PASSATA

SERVES 6

*T*hese filled pasta shells are served on a tomato sauce which contains plenty of sharp ingredients such as olives and capers, and provides a good colour and texture contrast to the rice, pasta and white sauce topping.

FOR THE CHUNKY PASSATA

- *1 × 15 ml spoon (1 tablespoon) olive oil*
- *1.5 kg (3 lb) ripe tomatoes, peeled and chopped*
- *3 × 15 ml spoons (3 tablespoons) tomato purée*

- *2 × 5 ml spoons (2 teaspoons) bouillon powder*
- *1 fresh bouquet garni*
- *450 g (1 lb) courgettes, finely diced*
- *2 cloves garlic, crushed*
- *100 g (4 oz) pitted black olives*

- 50 g (2 oz) small gherkins, finely diced
- 50 g (2 oz) capers
- salt and freshly ground black pepper

FOR THE PASTA SHELLS

- 1 × 15 ml spoon (1 tablespoon) olive oil
- 1 onion, peeled and finely chopped
- 250 g (9 oz) arborio rice
- 750 ml (1¼ pints) water
- 2 × 5 ml spoons (2 teaspoons) bouillon powder
- 1 fresh bouquet garni
- 1½ × 15 ml spoons (1½ tablespoons) tomato purée

- 100 g (4 oz) pine kernels
- salt and freshly ground black pepper
- 30 large dried pasta shells

FOR THE CHEESE SAUCE

- 40 g (1½ oz) butter
- 25 g (1 oz) white flour
- 450 ml (¾ pint) milk
- 75 g (3 oz) Cheddar cheese, grated
- salt and freshly ground black pepper

TO GARNISH

- 25 g (1 oz) Cheddar cheese, grated
- 6 sprigs fresh parsley

● **MAKE THE CHUNKY PASSATA**

Heat the oil in a medium to large saucepan and fry the tomatoes until they break down. Cool a little and blend in a blender until fairly smooth. Transfer back into the pan and add the tomato purée, bouillon powder, bouquet garni, courgettes and garlic and cook for 15 minutes, covered, on a low heat. Finely chop the olives. Add the olives, gherkins, capers and seasoning and cook for another 10 minutes. Keep hot.

● **MAKE THE FILLING FOR THE PASTA SHELLS**

Heat the oil and fry the onion until soft. Add the rice, water, bouillon powder and bouquet garni, bring to the boil and simmer on a low heat for 20 minutes. Add the tomato purée and pine kernels and cook for a further 3 minutes. Season and keep warm.

● **COOK THE PASTA SHELLS**

Bring 1.5 litres (2½ pints) of water to the boil in a saucepan; add the pasta and cook until *al dente*. Drain and keep hot.

● **MAKE THE CHEESE SAUCE**

Melt the butter in a small saucepan and add the flour, stirring well to make a roux. Cook the roux on a low heat for 2 minutes. Take the pan off the heat and gradually add the milk, stirring well after each addition to make the texture of the sauce smooth again. When all the milk is incorporated, place the pan back on the heat and bring to the boil, stirring all the time. When boiling, turn the heat down and simmer for 5 minutes. Turn the heat off and stir in the cheese and seasoning; keep hot.

● **TO SERVE**

Fill the pasta shells with the rice mixture and keep warm. Pour some of the chunky passata sauce on each of the warmed plates and place the pasta shells on it. Pour the cheese sauce in the centre of the plates and over part of the pasta shells – leaving half the surface of the shells uncovered. Garnish with a sprinkling of grated cheese over the sauce and a sprig of parsley in the centre of the plate.

HAZELNUT *SABLÉS* WITH CALVADOS APPLES AND *CRÈME CHANTILLY*

SERVES 6

*T*his consists of lightly cooked Bramley apples sandwiched between hazelnut sablés, and served with lightly whipped *crème fraîche*.

FOR THE HAZELNUT *SABLÉS*

● *15 g (½ oz) ground hazelnuts*
● *150 g (5 oz) plain white flour*
● *40 g (1½ oz) soft brown sugar*
● *75 g (3 oz) butter*
● *2 egg yolks*

FOR THE CALVADOS APPLES

● *1.25 kg (2 lb) Bramley apples*
● *25 g (1 oz) unsalted butter*
● *65 g (2½ oz) soft brown sugar*
● *2 drops Angostura Bitters*

● MAKE THE CALVADOS APPLE FILLING

Peel, quarter and core the apples; slice across into 5 mm ($\frac{1}{4}$ inch) slices. Melt the butter and cook the apples, uncovered, for 5 minutes, stirring from time to time. Add 2×15 ml spoons (2 tablespoons) water, cover and cook for a further 10 minutes or until the apple slices are tender. Add the sugar, Angostura Bitters and Calvados and cook for a further 3 minutes. Cool a little.

● MAKE THE CRÈME CHANTILLY

Place the *crème fraîche* and the sugar in a mixing bowl and whisk until it has doubled in size and is fairly stiff; do not whisk too much or it will turn into butter. Keep in a cool place.

Prepare the pistachio nuts for decoration. Place them in boiling water and leave for 2 minutes. Take the skin off and chop into small pieces.

● TO SERVE

Place 2×15 ml spoons (2 tablespoons) of the apple mixture in the centre of each serving plate; top with a *sablé* then top with another 2×15 ml spoons (2 tablespoons) of apple mixture. Top with another *sablé*. Rain some icing sugar through a sieve over the *sablé* and around each plate, sprinkle a little of the pistachio nuts around the *sablés*, and scatter some of the orange curls at random in between the pistachio nuts. Serve with the *crème chantilly*.

❻

A U T U M N *M* E N U

LIGHT SHIITAKE AND ARAMÉ CONSOMMÉ ♦★

~

INDIVIDUAL THREE-LAYER BAKE ♦

~

SUNCREST PEACHES IN
GLAZED WHITE WINE SYRUP ♦★

~

*This menu starts with a very light consommé which is
based on tamari, miso and aramé seaweed. Aramé is
found in good wholefood shops and imparts a delicate flavour of
the sea; the shiitake mushrooms are the more dominant flavour
in this tasty starter. The individual three-layer bake never
ceases to amaze me and guests; it is so simple yet so impressive
. . . The dessert peaches are set on a light pink syrup which
should be sweetened according to the wine in which the peaches
are poached. All three courses may be served hot.*

LIGHT SHIITAKE AND ARAMÉ CONSOMMÉ

SERVES 6

This soup is made with dried shiitake mushrooms and dried aramé seaweed; aramé looks
like black spaghettini and is very soft and tender. The stock is made with shoyu sauce
and nothing can replace the wonderful flavours that these ingredients bring. For added interest,
colour and flavour, the carrots are cut into very thin flower shapes (see page 14) and the mooli
(also called daikon or white radish) is cut into very thin half-moon shapes. The soup is finished
by the addition of cream sherry and smoked tofu, all imparting their strong flavours to produce
a delicious and very suitable clear autumn consommé.

- *1.5 litres (2½ pints) water*
- *6 dried shiitake mushrooms*
- *10 g (¼ oz) aramé seaweed*

- *2 × 15 ml spoons (2 tablespoons)
  sunflower oil*
- *1 × 5 ml spoon (1 teaspoon) toasted
  sesame oil*

- *150 g (5 oz) carrot, peeled and cut into thin flower shapes, see page 14*
- *100 g (4 oz) mooli, peeled and cut into half-moons*
- *75 g (3 oz) button mushrooms, thinly sliced*
- *3 × 15 ml spoons (3 tablespoons) shoyu*

- *1½ × 15 ml spoons (1½ tablespoons) cream sherry*
- *65 g (2½ oz) smoked tofu*
- *salt and freshly ground black pepper*
- *2 small spring onions (including the green tops), finely shredded*

Place the water in a mixing bowl, add the whole shiitake mushrooms and the aramé seaweed. Leave to stand overnight, covered.

Heat the sunflower and toasted sesame oil together in a medium to large saucepan and fry the carrots for 5 minutes. Add the mooli and fry for a further 5 minutes. Add the button mushrooms and cook for a further 4 minutes; stir the mixture from time to time but do not hesitate to brown the ingredients. Drain the mushrooms and aramé away from their soaking water and reserve the soaking juice. Discard the stalks from the shiitake mushrooms and thinly shred the caps; add the caps to the saucepan and cook for 2 minutes. Add the reserved soaking juice and the aramé to the saucepan and bring to the boil. When simmering add the shoyu, sherry, tofu and seasoning. Cook for a further 5 minutes. Finally, add the spring onions, turn the heat off and serve in warm soup bowls.

INDIVIDUAL THREE-LAYER BAKE

SERVES 6

*T*his easy terrine consists of three different layers, each having a different consistency which makes this dish very successful and interesting. The base is made of rice which is cooked *al dente* and, since it is cooked in little water, retains some crunchiness. The middle layer has plenty of vegetables and colour; the topping of yoghurt with a little ground cumin is both unusual and delicious. The portions look a little large at first glance but it is a dish which requires only a side salad or one or two steamed green vegetables such as green beans to accompany it.

FOR THE RICE LAYER

- *750 ml (1¼ pints) water*
- *salt and freshly ground black pepper*
- *400 g (14 oz) easy-cook American rice*
- *175 g (6 oz) Cheddar cheese, grated*

FOR THE YOGHURT LAYER

- *600 ml (1 pint) set plain natural yoghurt*
- *150 g (5 oz) Cheddar cheese, grated*
- *1 × 5 ml spoon (1 teaspoon) ground cumin*

FOR THE COURGETTE
AND TOMATO LAYER

- *2 × 15 ml spoons (2 tablespoons) olive oil*
- *750 g (1½ lb) courgettes*
- *2 red peppers, de-seeded and diced into 2 cm (¾ inch) squares*
- *2 green peppers, de-seeded and diced into 2 cm (¾ inch) squares*
- *4 large cloves garlic*
- *4 medium to large tomatoes, peeled and chopped*
- *3 × 15 ml spoons (3 tablespoons) tomato purée*
- *10 × 15 ml spoons (10 level tablespoons) fresh chopped parsley (not too fine)*

- *½ × 5 ml spoon (½ teaspoon) fresh chopped thyme*
- *salt and freshly ground black pepper*

FOR THE CUMIN
AND TOMATO COULIS

- *750 g (1½ lb) fresh ripe tomatoes, peeled and chopped*
- *¼ × 5 ml spoon (¼ teaspoon) freshly ground cumin, preferably made from freshly roasted cumin seeds*
- *1½ × 5 ml spoons (1½ teaspoons) bouillon powder*
- *salt and freshly ground black pepper*

TO GARNISH

- *6 tomato triangles (see page 16)*
- *6 sprigs fresh parsley*

Preheat the oven to gas mark 5, 375°F (190°C).

● MAKE THE RICE LAYER

Bring the water to the boil in a medium to large covered saucepan; when boiling, add salt and rice and simmer for 15 minutes. Do not take the lid off or stir the rice during this time. Remove from the heat and leave to stand for 5 minutes in the covered pan then add the cheese and season to taste. Press the rice mixture firmly into six crumpet ring moulds 10 cm (4 inch) in diameter and 2.5 cm (1 inch) deep and bake in the preheated oven for 12 minutes. Remove from the oven but leave the rounds on the baking sheet and keep warm.

● MAKE THE COURGETTE AND TOMATO LAYER

Heat the oil and fry the courgettes for 7 minutes. Add the red and green peppers and garlic and cook on a medium heat for another 6 minutes, stirring from time to time. Add the tomatoes, tomato purée, parsley, thyme and seasoning and cook in a partly covered pan for 10 minutes. Take the lid off and cook for another 2 minutes to dry out the mixture a little. Check the seasoning.

● MAKE THE YOGHURT LAYER

Mix the cheese and the yoghurt together in a mixing bowl.

● PUT THE THREE-LAYER BAKE TOGETHER

Place six other rings over the existing rings to give the full height of the bakes. Spoon 2 × 15 ml spoons (2 tablespoons) of the yoghurt mixture over the rice then carefully spoon 3–4 × 15 ml spoons (3–4 tablespoons) of the pepper mixture over it; top with another 2½ × 15 ml spoons (2½ tablespoons) of the yoghurt mixture and sprinkle a sixth of the ground cumin over each ring. Bake in the preheated oven for 30 minutes.

● MAKE THE CUMIN AND TOMATO COULIS

Place the tomatoes, ground cumin, bouillon powder and seasoning in a medium to large saucepan and cook together for 25 minutes. Cool a little then blend in a blender until completely smooth. Check the seasoning and reheat.

● TO SERVE

Take the bakes out of the oven and leave to stand for 8 minutes. Carefully slide a small vegetable knife around the edges and lift one ring at a time on to warmed plates and surround with some cumin and tomato coulis. Place a tomato triangle over the bake and garnish further with a sprig of fresh parsley 'shooting off' the triangle.

right Warm Oyster and Spinach Leaf Salad in Black Pepper Sauce *centre* Light Seitan Bourguignon with Individual Couscous Timbale and Brassica *left* Grand Marnier and Orange Pancakes

SUNCREST PEACHES IN GLAZED WHITE WINE SYRUP

SERVES 6

*M*y favourite peaches for making this dessert are the suncrest peaches which are not too big and have a nice deep yellow colour when cooked; however, any yellow peach will do. The wine used for the syrup should be very sweet such as a Monbazillac, Moscatel de Valencia or a sweet German wine – the sweeter the better. Peaches are usually available until October, so make this dessert in the early part of the autumn. Boudoirs biscuits (see page 201) may be served with this dessert.

9 ripe yellow peaches
200 ml (7 fl oz) sweet white wine
200 ml (7 fl oz) water
75 g (3 oz) white sugar

TO DECORATE

50 g (2 oz) pistachio nuts
15 g (½ oz) icing sugar
12 × 5 ml spoons (12 teaspoons) crème de framboise
18 Cape gooseberries

Preheat the oven to gas mark 6, 400°F (200°C).

Skin the peaches (place in boiling water for 30 seconds first) and cut around their circumference; loosen the peach halves away from the stone and remove the stone. Place the wine, water and sugar in a large saucepan and bring to the boil. Carefully add the peaches and simmer, covered, for 10–15 minutes or until tender and just beginning to soften. The cooking liquid should have taken on a pink tint. Lift the peaches out of the cooking water and place on the serving plates, cup side up, three halves to a plate. The peaches should hold their shapes. Pour the lightly thickened juice around the peaches and leave to cool.

Place the pistachio nuts in water that has just boiled and leave for 2 minutes then skin the nuts and chop finely. Place the chopped nuts on a baking sheet in the preheated oven and toast for 5–6 minutes, stirring quickly every 2 minutes. Take the nuts out of the oven and sprinkle with icing sugar. Cool a little then sprinkle around the peaches over the syrup.

● **TO SERVE**

Pour 2 × 5 ml spoons (2 teaspoons) *crème de framboise* on each plate over the three halves of peaches. Fan out the Cape gooseberries (see page 16) and place upright, as though flowers, where the stone of the peaches should be.

❼

A UTUMN *M* ENU

WARM OYSTER AND SPINACH LEAF SALAD IN BLACK PEPPER SAUCE ♦

~

LIGHT SEITAN BOURGUIGNON WITH INDIVIDUAL COUSCOUS TIMBALE AND BRASSICA ♦

~

GRAND MARNIER AND ORANGE PANCAKES

~

This menu is perfect for the autumn as all the dishes may be served hot. The starter consists of oyster mushrooms cooked in a cream sauce and served with plain spinach to counterbalance the richness. The main course is light yet very warming; and the dessert pancakes are sweet and refreshing.

WARM OYSTER AND SPINACH LEAF SALAD IN BLACK PEPPER SAUCE

SERVES 6

*T*his is a very seasonal starter of oyster mushrooms in a cream and black pepper sauce, which is quite rich but delicious. It should be well seasoned to your liking. The oyster mushrooms for this salad need to be the freshest; for best results, pick the smaller mushrooms as these are more tender and are sweeter than the larger ones.

- 75 g (3 oz) butter
- 9 shallots, finely shredded
- 350 g (12 oz) oyster mushrooms, left whole
- 175 ml (6 fl oz) crème fraîche
- 2 × 15 ml spoons (2 tablespoons) double cream
- 4 × 15 ml spoons (4 tablespoons) water
- ½ × 5 ml spoon (½ teaspoon) coarsely ground black pepper

- salt
- 1½ × 15 ml spoons (1½ tablespoons) cream sherry
- 2 × 15 ml spoons (2 tablespoons) chopped chives
- 1 kg (2 lb) fresh spinach

TO GARNISH

- 18 tomato triangles, see page 16
- 18 sprigs fresh chervil

● **MAKE THE BLACK PEPPER SAUCE**

Melt the butter in a large frying-pan, add the shallots and cook on a medium heat until tender. Add the oyster mushrooms, with the underside of the caps face down and cook in an open pan for 8 minutes. Take the pan off the heat and add the *crème fraîche*, double cream, water, black pepper, salt to taste and sherry, without disturbing the mushrooms. Place the pan back on a low heat, cover tightly, and bring to a low boil; simmer for another 5 minutes. Add the chives and simmer for another 2 minutes. Thin down with extra water if necessary.

Steam the spinach for 4 minutes or until just tender.

● **TO SERVE**

Divide the spinach between 6 plates, placing it in a half-moon shape in the centre of each plate. Place the mushrooms and cooking juices on the opposite side, as though to form a whole circle, and garnish each plate with three tomato triangles, at equal intervals around the mushrooms and spinach. Add the sprigs of chervil at the side of the tomato triangles.

LIGHT SEITAN BOURGUIGNON WITH INDIVIDUAL COUSCOUS TIMBALE AND BRASSICA

SERVES 6

*T*his is a delicious and light bourguignon with a good selection of vegetables in the casserole. It is served with a castle of couscous turned out in the centre of the plate.

● *1 × 15 ml spoon (1 tablespoon) sunflower oil*
● *25 g (1 oz) butter*
● *175 g (6 oz) leeks, chopped*
● *175 g (6 oz) seitan, drained, rinsed well and chopped into 1 cm (½ inch) squares*
● *175 g (6 oz) carrots, sliced at a slant*
● *175 g (6 oz) green kohlrabi, peeled and chopped into 1 cm (½ inch) squares*
● *600 ml (1 pint) water*
● *2 × 5 ml spoons (2 teaspoons) bouillon powder*
● *2 × 15 ml spoons (2 tablespoons) shoyu*
● *1 × 5 ml spoon (1 teaspoon) barley miso*

● *4 tomatoes, peeled and chopped*
● *salt and freshly ground black pepper*

FOR THE COUSCOUS TIMBALES

● *275 g (10 oz) couscous*
● *750 ml (1¼ pint) boiling water*
● *½ × 5 ml spoon (½ teaspoon) salt*
● *50 g (2 oz) salted butter*

TO SERVE

● *225 g (8 oz) spring cabbage, very finely shredded*
● *275 g (10 oz) broccoli*
● *225 g (8 oz) Brussels sprouts, halved*

Heat the oil and butter together in a large saucepan and fry the leeks and seitan on a medium heat for 8 minutes, stirring from time to time. Add the carrots and cook for another 5 minutes, stirring occasionally. Add the kohlrabi and cook for a further 5 minutes, covered. Add the water, bouillon powder, shoyu, miso (try to dissolve it in the water as you add it) and the tomatoes. Season, bring to the boil and simmer for 30 minutes, covered.

Preheat the oven to gas mark 3, 325°F (160°C).

● MAKE THE COUSCOUS TIMBALES

Place the couscous in a small mixing bowl and pour the boiling water over it. Cover and leave to stand for 15 minutes. Add the salt and butter, mix well and pack into 6 dariole moulds (150 ml (¼ pint) in capacity), pressing down the mixture well. Place in the preheated oven for 15 minutes to reheat the couscous through.

Steam the brassicas in a steamer which has three compartments or in a Chinese steamer. The cabbage will take 10 minutes, the broccoli (cut it into medium florets) 8–10 minutes and the Brussels sprouts 10–12 minutes. Note: you may make your own compartments yourself by separating the vegetables with a triple layer of foil; first add the vegetables that take the longest to cook, then the second, then those that take the least time.

● TO SERVE

Turn out the couscous moulds and place in the centre of the plates. Spoon the bourguignon around the timbales and either serve each brassica in 'pockets', at equal intervals around the bourguignon or serve in a separate side dish.

GRAND MARNIER AND ORANGE PANCAKES

SERVES 6

*T*his pancake dessert has colour added by its accompaniment of strawberries or Chinese gooseberries. The crêpe batter should not be whisked too much or it activates the gluten in the flour and makes it tough. For this dessert, the pancakes should be light and thin. The batter makes at least 12 pancakes using a 18 cm (7 inch) pancake pan. The orange filling is thin but makes a good contrast to the pancakes.

FOR THE BATTER

- *100 g (4 oz) plain white flour*
- *pinch of salt*
- *1 × 15 ml spoon (1 tablespoon) sugar*
- *3 eggs*
- *300 ml (½ pint) milk*
- *25 g (1 oz) melted butter*

FOR THE FILLING

- *3 × 5 ml spoons (3 teaspoons) arrowroot*
- *200 ml (7 fl oz) orange juice*

- *40–50 g (1½–2 oz) white sugar, to taste*
- *8 oranges, segmented, see page 15*
- *3 × 15 ml spoons (3 tablespoons) Grand Marnier*
- *50 g (2 oz) butter to fry the pancakes*

TO DECORATE

- *350 ml (12 fl oz) Greek strained yoghurt*
- *15 g (½ oz) toasted poppy seeds*
- *12 fanned-out strawberries, see page 16, or Chinese gooseberries*

● **MAKE THE BATTER**

Mix the flour in a bowl with the salt and the sugar. Make a well in the centre, break the eggs into the well and whisk until they are thoroughly mixed. Add half the milk and melted butter in a steady stream and whisk, gradually drawing in the flour to make a smooth paste. Add the rest of the milk and leave to stand for 1 hour.

● MAKE THE FILLING

Mix the arrowroot with the orange juice and sugar until the mixture is smooth. Transfer into a small saucepan and bring to the boil, stirring all the time. Simmer for 2 minutes. Take the pan off the heat and add the orange segments and Grand Marnier.

● MAKE THE PANCAKES

Fry the crêpes in a little butter over a medium to high heat until set on top and brown underneath. Do not touch the pancake as it is cooking, just loosen it with a spatula when it starts looking golden on the edges, then flip it over. Keep the cooked pancakes warm while you cook the whole batch. Place some of the filling (the orange segments mainly) into each pancake then fold it in half then in half again to obtain a triangular shape.

● TO SERVE

Place one of the triangles on one side of the plate, then another on the opposite side so that the pointed edges face one another. Sieve the orange syrup and pour on the side of the pancakes so they sit on a bed of syrup. Push the segments to the outside so they show when the pancakes are folded. Spoon a tablespoon of Greek yoghurt over the pointed edges of the pancakes and sprinkle the poppy seeds over the yoghurt and pancakes. Finish decorating the plate with the strawberries or Chinese gooseberries and serve warm.

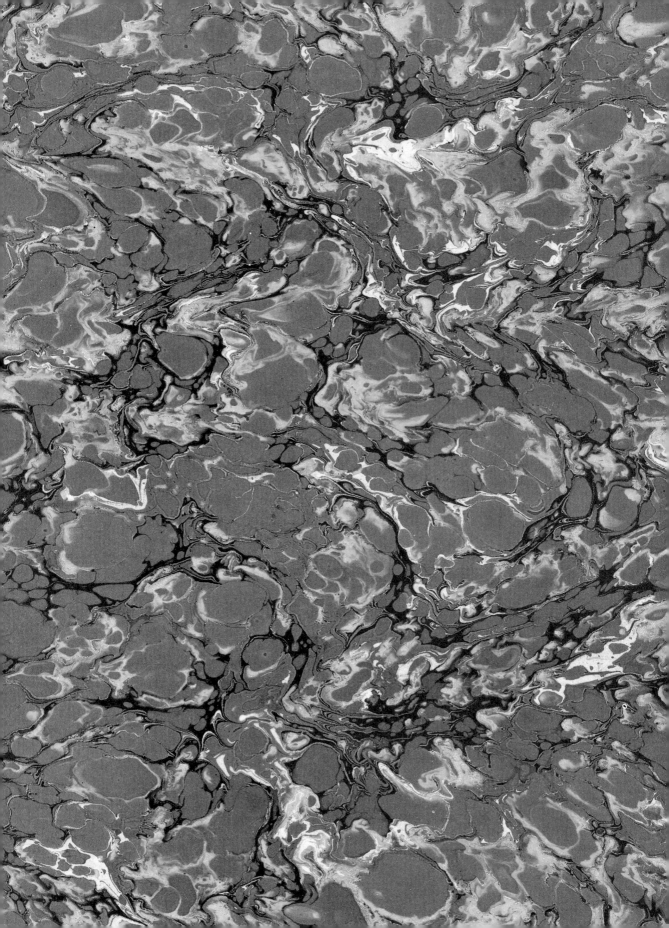

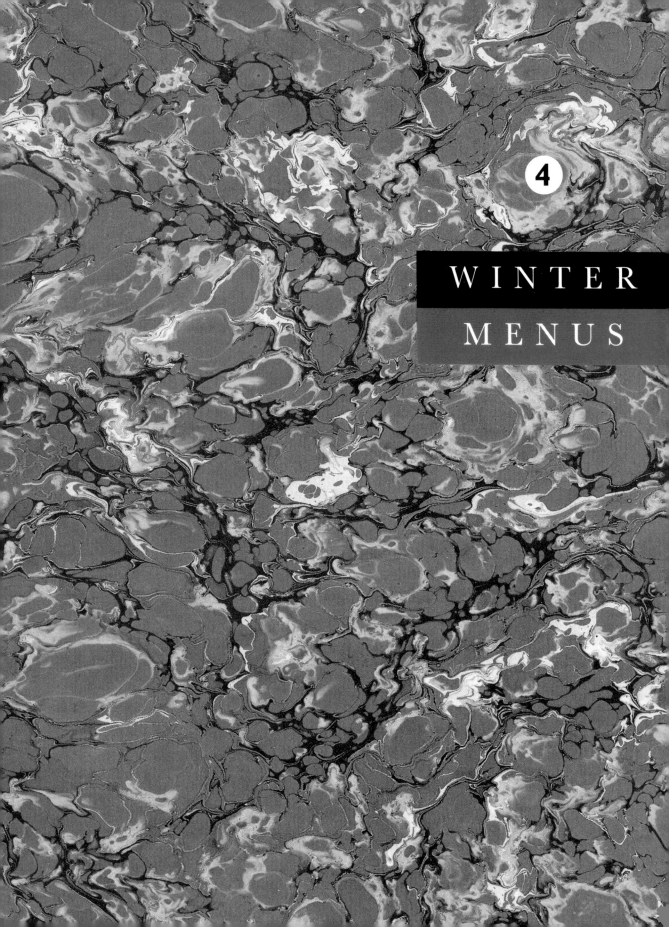

4

WINTER

MENUS

❶ *W*INTER *M*ENU

CARROT AND DILL *CHAUD-FROID* RAMEKINS
IN NORI OVERCOAT

~

BRAISED TEMPEH ON A POTATO GALETTE
WITH A TOPPING OF TRELLIS OF
MIXED VEGETABLES ♦★

~

PEAR AND ORANGE PUDDING WITH LIGHT
GINGER SAUCE

~

This menu makes use of two unusual ingredients, nori seaweed and tempeh, a high-protein soya bean by-product, which add some interesting flavours and textures. The starter has a delicious filling based on creamed carrots, pickled dill cucumber, cream and fresh dill tops. The main course is easy to prepare, looks wonderful on the plate and could be a whole meal in itself. The pudding is full of flavour and provides a satisfying finish to the meal. Altogether, this menu is not for the faint-hearted as it has strong flavours throughout.

CARROT AND DILL *CHAUD-FROID* RAMEKINS IN NORI OVERCOAT

SERVES 6

The colour contrast between the orange of the carrot, the pickled dill cucumber filling and the black wrapping of nori seaweed looks stunning. These ramekins are served warm on a bed of cold fresh dill vinaigrette to give them their *chaud-froid* appeal. Don't overbake the terrines or the egg in the filling will overcook and the texture will not be so pleasant. Nori seaweed is available in dark square flat sheets which can be bought from good wholefood shops. Here it imparts a specific and wonderful flavour to the dish, which you cannot get from any other vegetarian source. This starter should be served alone, with no bread or other accompaniment.

- *450 g (1 lb) carrots, peeled and finely diced*
- *6 sheets nori seaweed*
- *6 × 15 ml spoons (6 tablespoons) double cream*
- *175 g (6 oz) pickled dill cucumber, very finely diced*
- *3 eggs, beaten*
- *1½ × 5 ml spoons (1½ teaspoons) fresh chopped dill weed*
- *salt and freshly ground black pepper*

FOR THE DRESSING

- *3 × 15 ml spoons (3 tablespoons) white wine vinegar*
- *4½ × 15 ml spoons (4½ tablespoons) sunflower oil*
- *3 × 5 ml spoons (3 teaspoons) fresh dill weed tops*
- *salt and freshly ground black pepper*

TO GARNISH

- *18 very thin slices of carrot, cut at a slant, steamed for 5 minutes*
- *18 cocktail gherkins, fanned, see page 16*

Preheat the oven to gas mark 6, 400°F (200°C).

Place the carrots in a saucepan, cover with water and bring to the boil. Cook until tender, this will take 15–20 minutes.

Lightly grease six ramekins each 150 ml (¼ pint) in capacity.

Cut and shape the square ends of the nori sheets so they become rounded then dip them in a bowl of water, lightly shake off the excess water and line the ramekins with the sheets. Take care not to break the seaweed but if you do, patch the hole with excess seaweed. The nori sheets should come over the rim of the dishes.

Drain the carrots and mash them with a potato masher. Add the cream, pickled dill cucumber, eggs and dill. Mix well and season to taste. Fill the ramekins with the mixture and fold the seaweed over the filling. Place the ramekins on a baking sheet and bake in the preheated oven for 10 minutes or until set.

● MAKE THE DRESSING

Mix all the ingredients together in a jam jar and shake well. When the ramekins are cooked, leave them to cool for 8–10 minutes then loosen the edges and turn out on to six white plates.

● TO SERVE

Pour some of the vinaigrette over and around the nori timbale; garnish each plate with three slices of carrot placed at equal intervals around the timbale and top each with a small fanned-out gherkin, looking outwards.

Braised Tempeh on a Potato Galette with a Topping of Trellis of Mixed Vegetables

SERVES 6

*T*his main course looks impressive and needs no other vegetable accompaniment. You can buy frozen tempeh from good wholefood shops; it may be kept in the freezer for quite a long time but once defrosted it should be used at once. My favourite beansprouts are the thinner ones which I get from my greengrocer. They have a nicer texture and flavour when cooked than the thicker shoots which one finds in almost any supermarket.

FOR THE POTATO GALETTE

- *6 large old potatoes, each weighing 250 g (9 oz)*
- *2 × 15 ml spoons (2 tablespoons) sunflower oil*

FOR THE BRAISED TEMPEH

- *3 × 15 ml (3 tablespoons) sunflower oil*
- *4 cloves garlic, crushed*
- *275 g (10 oz) frozen tempeh, defrosted overnight in the refrigerator, sliced*
- *½ × 5 ml spoon (½ teaspoon) ready-made English mustard*
- *3 × 15 ml spoons (3 tablespoons) tamari*
- *300 ml (½ pint) water*
- *2 × 5 ml spoons (2 teaspoons) arrowroot mixed with 4 × 15 ml spoons (4 table-spoons) water*

- *salt and freshly ground black pepper*

FOR THE TRELLIS OF MIXED VEGETABLES

- *1 × 15 ml spoon (1 tablespoon) oil*
- *1 yellow pepper, de-seeded and cut into fine strips*
- *1 red pepper, de-seeded and cut into fine strips*
- *225 g (8 oz) beansprouts*
- *225 g (8 oz) spring cabbage, finely shredded*
- *salt and freshly ground black pepper*

TO GARNISH

- *6 sprigs parsley*

Preheat the oven to gas mark 6, 400°F (200°C).

● MAKE THE POTATO GALETTE

Wash but do not peel the potatoes and discard approximately 2.5 cm (1 inch) of the ends. Cut them into thin slices across, 3–5 mm (⅛–¼ inch) thick. You should have approximately 20–22 slices per potato. Lightly grease a baking sheet and overlap the larger potato slices on it in a circle so that when you have placed 15 slices on the baking sheet you have a circle 16 cm (6½ inches) in diameter with a hole in the centre approximately 5–6 cm (2–2½ inches) wide. Make another smaller wheel to one side of the larger one, using 6 of the remaining smaller slices. The second circle should measure 9 cm (3½ inches) wide and have hardly any gap in the middle. Brush both circles with oil and bake in the preheated oven for 20–25 minutes or until the potatoes are golden brown on the edges and their texture is soft and cooked. Repeat the same process with the other potatoes, keeping the cooked rings hot by loosely covering with foil and placing at the bottom of the oven. They may be made in advance and reheated in the oven for 10–15 minutes at gas mark 5, 375°F (190°C).

● MAKE THE BRAISED TEMPEH

Heat the oil in a large frying-pan and fry the garlic on a low heat until golden brown. Scrape the pan to unstick the garlic, add the tempeh slices and fry on a medium heat until crisp underneath – do not stir – then carefully turn the slices over and fry on a low heat until crisp. When golden brown, add the mustard, tamari and water and bring to the boil. Cover, reduce the heat to a simmer and cook for 5 minutes. Add the arrowroot mixture and bring back to the boil, stirring. Season to taste, simmer for 1 minute then leave aside, keeping it warm.

● MAKE THE TRELLIS OF MIXED VEGETABLES

Heat the oil and stir-fry the pepper strips on a high heat for 1 minute. Add the beansprouts and cook for another minute, stirring all the time. Add the cabbage and stir-fry for another minute or so. The vegetables should now be bright in colour and tender. Quickly reheat the tempeh in the pan and add the juice to the stir-fry, season to taste, mix well, then turn the heat off.

● TO SERVE

Transfer the potato galettes on to warmed, large flat plates. Place 8 pieces of tempeh in the centre of each of the rings and top the tempeh with a sixth of the vegetable mixture, making sure that the vegetables are fairly levelled on the top and that they are placed in a circular shape. Top with the second potato ring. Garnish with a sprig of parsley placed in the centre of the small ring.

PEAR AND ORANGE PUDDING
WITH LIGHT GINGER SAUCE

SERVES 6

This is a delicious pudding made with cooked basmati rice and flavoured with orange and cardamom; the pears help to keep it moist and light. It is served with a ginger and orange sauce which complements it beautifully and strengthens the ginger flavour. The pudding should be served warm in slices; the sauce is served cold.

- 175 g (6 oz) basmati rice
- 450 ml (¾ pint) water
- 75 g (3 oz) butter
- 3 eggs, beaten
- 40 g (1½ oz) stem ginger, very finely chopped
- 50 g (2 oz) soft brown sugar
- 2 × 5 ml spoons (2 teaspoons) grated orange rind

- good pinch ground cardamom seeds
- 2 ripe pears, peeled, cored and chopped

FOR THE LIGHT GINGER SAUCE

- 15 g (½ oz) stem ginger
- 40 g (1½ oz) sugar
- 450 ml (¾ pint) orange juice
- 2 × 5 ml spoons (2 teaspoons) arrowroot

TO DECORATE

- 18 strawberries, fanned out, see page 16

Place the rice and the water in a small saucepan, bring to the boil, cover and simmer for 20 minutes until the rice is very soft.

Add the butter, then process in a food processor until the rice is very fine. Transfer the contents into a mixing bowl. Cool a little and add the eggs, stem ginger, sugar, orange rind, cardamom seeds and pears.

Place the mixture in a 1.2 litre (2 pint) pudding bowl, the base of which should be lined with greaseproof paper. Steam for 1¼ hours.

● MAKE THE SAUCE

Place the stem ginger, sugar and orange juice in a blender and blend until completely smooth. Place the arrowroot in a small saucepan, gradually add the blended liquid and stir until the arrowroot is dissolved. Bring to the boil, stirring all the time, cover and simmer for 1 minute or until the sauce clears. Cool thoroughly.

Leave the steamed pudding to stand for 15 minutes then turn out on to a flat dish.

● TO SERVE

Cut into slices and serve with a little of the ginger sauce poured around in a semi-circle. Decorate each plate with three fanned-out strawberries placed at the point where the sauce meets the plate.

②

WINTER MENU

ROULÉ CHEESE CRESCENTS SERVED WITH
SPICED APPLE AND TOMATO CHUTNEY ♦

~

MUSHROOM AND RED WINE CROUSTADES

~

RUM FLAMBÉ PEARS FILLED WITH HOME-
MADE RUM AND RAISIN ICE-CREAM ♦★

~

This is a simple and delicious menu, very suitable for cold winter nights. The starter is a great warming dish; the croustades are filling and satisfying; and the meal ends with another warming dish which has a lightly alcoholised finish to make you feel quite 'cosy'!

Both the chutney and the crescents for the starter may be prepared the day before; the filling for the croustades may also be prepared the day before and reheated slowly, covered, so that you don't lose any moisture. The pears should be cooked on the day they are served or they lose their colour from the centre; the ice-cream is best made and eaten on the same day.

ROULÉ CHEESE CRESCENTS SERVED WITH SPICED APPLE AND TOMATO CHUTNEY

I love the spiced chutney which accompanies the cheese crescents and they make good companions. It should be very moist; if it seems dry, add a little water before serving. To make the cheese crescents, use a French white baguette for the breadcrumbs. The outer coating becomes very crisp when shallow-fried and this provides a good texture contrast to the chutney. No bread accompaniment is needed with this starter.

FOR THE CHEESE CRESCENTS

- *90 g (3½ oz) white baguette*
- *225 g (8 oz) garlic and herb roulé*
- *salt and freshly ground black pepper*

FOR THE COATING

- *6 × 15 ml spoons (6 tablespoons) milk*
- *25 g (1 oz) white baguette*

FOR THE SPICED APPLE
AND TOMATO CHUTNEY

- *1 × 15 ml spoon (1 tablespoon) sunflower oil*
- *1 onion, peeled and finely chopped*
- *1 × 5 ml spoon (1 teaspoon) garam masala*
- *1 × 5 ml spoon (1 teaspoon) ground cumin*
- *1 × 5 ml spoon (1 teaspoon) ground coriander*
- *1 × 5 ml spoon (1 teaspoon) curry powder*
- *450 g (1 lb) fresh ripe tomatoes, peeled, de-seeded and chopped*
- *1 Bramley cooking apple, chopped (not peeled)*
- *4 × 15 ml spoons (4 tablespoons) water*
- *salt and freshly ground black pepper*
- *2 × 15 ml spoons (2 tablespoons) fresh chopped coriander*

TO SERVE

- *2 × 15 ml spoons (2 tablespoons) sunflower oil*
- *6 small leaves lettuce, from the heart of a round lettuce*
- *18 sprigs fresh coriander*

● MAKE THE CHEESE CRESCENTS

Chop the baguette into small pieces and process in a food processor until completely fine. Add the cheese and seasoning and process until both are amalgamated. Take the mixture out and flatten into a circle measuring 20 cm (8 inches) in diameter; the thickness should be no more than 1 cm (½ inch). Using a crescent-shaped cutter, shape into 18 crescents; dip into milk and breadcrumbs to coat the crescents and leave to cool in the refrigerator.

● MAKE THE SPICED APPLE AND TOMATO CHUTNEY

Heat the oil in a small saucepan and fry the onion until soft and translucent. Add the spices and fry gently for 3–4 minutes. Add the tomatoes, apple and water and bring to the boil. Break up the tomatoes, cover, reduce the heat and simmer for 20 minutes. Season to taste, add the fresh coriander and leave to cool thoroughly.

● TO SERVE

Heat 1 × 15 ml spoon (1 tablespoon) of the oil and fry 9 crescents until golden brown underneath. Turn the crescents over and fry for another minute or so until crisp and golden. Keep them warm while you repeat the process. Arrange the crescents side by side on one side of each plate and place the chutney in a small lettuce leaf on the opposite side of the plate. Overlap the crescents slightly so they are raised a little and look more attractive. Garnish the plate with some fresh coriander sprigs.

MUSHROOM AND RED WINE CROUSTADES

SERVES 6

A croustade is a dish which has a very crisp base, usually in the shape of a flan base, which is filled with a creamy filling. Here my base is made of puff pastry, baked over upturned small brioche moulds to make a nest shape. The filling of thinly sliced mushrooms has a strong flavour and is tasty and light. Serve with small new potatoes and a colourful side vegetable.

450 g (1 lb) puff pastry

FOR THE FILLING

15 g (½ oz) butter
100 g (4 oz) leeks, finely chopped
225 g (8 oz) large button mushrooms, thinly sliced
225 g (8 oz) chestnut mushrooms, thinly sliced
2½ × 5 ml spoons (2½ teaspoons) cornflour mixed with 600 ml (1 pint) water
2 × 5 ml spoons (2 teaspoons) bouillon powder

2½ × 15 ml spoons (2½ tablespoons) shoyu
2 × 15 ml spoons (2 tablespoons) red wine
2 × 15 ml spoons (2 tablespoons) finely chopped fresh chives
salt and freshly ground black pepper

TO GARNISH

6 tomato roses, see page 16
12 sprigs chervil

Preheat the oven to gas mark 7, 425°F (220°C).

● **MAKE THE CROUSTADE BASES**

Roll out half the puff pastry to a rectangle measuring 13 × 38 cm (5 × 15 inches). Divide the pastry equally into three squares and then, with the help of some sharp scissors, cut each square into a circle. Turn over 3 individual brioche moulds (each measuring 9 cm (3½ inches) wide and 2.5 cm (1 inch) deep), and place them on a baking sheet. Place the puff pastry over the tins, so their entire surface is covered with pastry and press down hard so it takes the shape of the tin. Repeat the process with the other half of the pastry. Bake in the preheated oven for 15 minutes; take out of the oven and leave to cool for 5–8 minutes. Turn the pastry back over and carefully remove the brioche mould. Prick the shells and place on the middle shelf of the oven to dry out the centre and cook for a further 5 minutes.

● MAKE THE FILLING

Melt the butter and fry the leeks until tender. Add both kinds of mushrooms and quickly stir-fry. When the mushrooms look tender, have changed colour and are beginning to shrink, stir in the cornflour and water mixture, vegetable bouillon, shoyu and red wine; bring to the boil and simmer for 10 minutes. Add the chives, cook for a further 2 minutes and season to taste.

● TO SERVE

Take the croustades out of the oven, fill each with the mushroom mixture. Collect some extra juice from the pan and pour over the filling and overflow on to the plate. Garnish the plate with a tomato rose placed next to the croustade and two sprigs of chervil on either side of the tomato.

RUM FLAMBÉ PEARS FILLED WITH HOME-MADE RUM AND RAISIN ICE-CREAM

SERVES 6

*T*his is a delicious dessert of a creamy home-made rum and raisin ice-cream, presented *'sous cloche'* under a poached pear. Provided soya milk is used the ice-cream is completely dairy free; its creamy texture is derived from the use of tofu and ground cashews.

FOR THE RUM AND RAISIN ICE-CREAM

- *4 × 15 ml spoons (4 tablespoons) dark rum*
- *175 g (6 oz) raisins*
- *450 g (1 lb) silken tofu, diced*
- *4 × 15 ml spoons (4 tablespoons) maple syrup*
- *4 × 15 ml spoons (4 tablespoons) sunflower oil*
- *4 × 15 ml spoons (4 tablespoons) soya milk or dairy milk*
- *50 g (2 oz) cashews (broken or whole)*
- *2 × 5 ml spoons (2 teaspoons) orange rind*
- *2 × 5 ml spoons (2 teaspoons) lemon juice*
- *1 × 5 ml spoon (1 teaspoon) vanilla essence*

TO POACH THE PEARS

- *6 Comice or Williams pears*
- *450 ml (¾ pint) orange juice*
- *3 × 15 ml spoons (3 tablespoons) maple syrup*

FOR THE ORANGE SAUCE

● *3 × 5 ml spoons (3 teaspoons) arrowroot*

TO DECORATE

● *12 nasturtium flowers*
● *extra rum to flambé, optional*

● MAKE THE RUM AND RAISIN ICE-CREAM

Warm the rum to smoking point and pour it over the raisins. Leave to stand, covered, for 1 hour so the raisins plump up and become moist and sweet. Stir from time to time to coat the raisins with alcohol. Blend the tofu in a blender with the maple syrup, sunflower oil and milk until completely smooth. Grind the cashews in a coffee grinder until they are almost a paste; add this to the tofu and blend again until smooth. Take the mixture out of the blender and place it in a mixing bowl. Add the orange rind, lemon juice, vanilla essence and finally the rum and raisins. Mix well and place in the freezer until frozen; this will take 3–4 hours. Stir well once or twice during the freezing process. Take the ice-cream out of the freezer 20 minutes before serving.

● PREPARE THE POACHED PEARS

Peel the pears but leave the stalks on, then core them from the base. Place the pears in a medium saucepan and cover them with the orange juice and maple syrup. Bring to the boil and simmer for 10–20 minutes or until just tender. Drain and leave to cool. Reserve the poaching liquid.

● MAKE THE ORANGE SAUCE

Place the arrowroot in a small saucepan and gradually add 250 ml (8 fl oz) of the reserved liquid from the poaching of the pears and mix well. Bring to the boil and simmer for 1–2 minutes or until clear. Remove more of the core of the pears and make four cuts from half-way down the pear to their base (so that when placed on the plates the pears open up to show the ice-cream positioned where the core was).

● TO SERVE

Pour the orange sauce on to plates and place a scoop of ice-cream on top; cover the ice-cream with the pear and decorate each plate with two nasturtium flowers. Serve with almond biscuits, if liked. Flambé the pears at the table for a grand finish: warm up some rum in a ladle over a flame, such as a candle. Pour over the pears and set alight straightaway.

❸

W I N T E R *M* E N U

CREAM OF CHEESE AND CELERY WITH
TORTILLA DUMPLINGS ◆

~

ACORN SQUASH BOATSHELL FILLED WITH
SPICY WATER CHESTNUT RICE SERVED WITH
KUMQUAT AND ONION SAUCE AND TWO
VEGETABLE PURÉES ◆

~

CRÈME AND PEARS *RENVERSÉES*

~

This is a surprisingly light menu with a 'warmingly' spicy main course. The tasty starter is accompanied by tortilla chips to provide a good texture contrast. The main course is an excellent combination of flavours and textures; there are crunchy and smooth ingredients, and spicy and cooling mixtures. The dessert may be served cool or warm and has a soft texture.

CREAM OF CHEESE AND CELERY WITH TORTILLA DUMPLINGS

SERVES 6

This soup benefits from a good flavour from the celery, richness from the cheese, texture from the tortilla chips and sharpness from the parsley. Overall, it is an excellent and warming starter. For the best flavour, choose white celery. For the ingredients and method for home-made tortilla chips (nachos) see page 110. For spicy tortilla chips, add ½ × 5 ml spoon (½ teaspoon) chilli powder to the dough.

- *25 g (1 oz) butter*
- *1½ heads celery, roughly chopped*
- *1.2 litres (2 pints) water*

- *4 × 5 ml spoons (4 teaspoons) bouillon powder*
- *100 g (4 oz) cheese, grated*
- *salt and freshly ground black pepper*

● *18 spicy tortilla chips, see page 110*

TO SERVE

● *2½ × 15 ml spoons (2½ tablespoons)*
fresh chopped parsley

● *40 g (1½ oz) Cheddar cheese, grated*

Melt the butter in a large saucepan and fry the celery for 15 minutes, stirring from time to time. Add the water and bouillon powder, bring to the boil and simmer for another 10 minutes. Cool the soup a little. Place half the soup in a blender and blend until completely smooth then place it in a clean pan. Place the other half in the blender and blend until the celery is left a little chunky. Add this to the pan and reheat to boiling point. Take the pan off the heat, add the cheese and season to taste.

● **TO SERVE**

Pour the soup into warmed bowls and sprinkle the chopped parsley on top. Place 3 tortilla chips over the parsley and sprinkle some cheese over the tortilla chips. Serve straightaway.

ACORN SQUASH BOATSHELL FILLED WITH SPICY WATER CHESTNUT RICE SERVED WITH KUMQUAT AND ONION SAUCE AND TWO VEGETABLE PURÉES

SERVES 6

*T*his dish consists of a baked and stuffed acorn squash, served with an onion sauce and side vegetables of two very colourful purées of sweet potato and courgette. The filling for the acorn squash is truly delicious and nutty as it contains water chestnuts. The onion sauce is sweet and sour as it is made with a few sliced kumquats and a little lemon. The overall dish is colourful and an intriguing blend of flavours. No other vegetables are needed to accompany this.

The quantities of the rice filling given make enough for 6 or 12 halves of squash; if you decide to make just half a large acorn squash per person (which should be enough) then you may have a little of the filling left over, which you can freeze. Choose acorn squashes which are still green in colour for the best effect when cooked. If red chillies are not available use green chillies instead.

● *3 small or 6 fairly large acorn squashes*

FOR THE FILLING

● *350 g (12 oz) white basmati rice*
● *2 good pinches Spanish saffron*

● *4 × 15 ml spoons (4 tablespoons)*
groundnut oil
● *4 × 5 ml spoons (4 teaspoons) paprika*
● *6 green cardamom pods*
● *8 whole cloves*

- 2 × 5 ml spoons (2 teaspoons) whole cumin seeds
- 2 small red chillies (not dwarf chillies, they are too hot for this dish), de-seeded and finely chopped
- 450 g (1 lb) open cup mushrooms
- 24 water chestnuts, sliced
- 4 × 5 ml spoons (4 teaspoons) bouillon powder
- salt and freshly ground black pepper
- 1 × 15 ml spoon (1 tablespoon) fresh lemon juice
- 6 spring onions, finely chopped

FOR THE COURGETTE
AND GREEN PEPPER PURÉE

- 1 green pepper
- 750 g (1½ lb) courgettes, topped and tailed and cut into chunks
- 25 g (1 oz) butter
- salt and freshly ground black pepper

FOR THE SWEET POTATO
AND RED PEPPER PURÉE

- 1 red pepper
- 25 g (1 oz) butter
- 1 × 5 ml spoon (1 teaspoon) bouillon powder

- 450 g (1 lb) orange sweet potatoes, peeled and chopped
- salt and freshly ground black pepper

FOR THE OKRA
AND TOMATO CASSEROLE

- 250 g (9 oz) okra, topped and tailed and sliced into pieces 1 cm (½ inch) long
- 2 large beef tomatoes, peeled and chopped
- salt and freshly ground black pepper

FOR THE ONION SAUCE

- 1 × 15 ml spoon (1 tablespoon) groundnut oil
- 1 onion, shredded
- 450 ml (¾ pint) water
- 2 × 15 ml spoons (2 tablespoons) rice miso
- 2 × 15 ml spoons (2 tablespoons) tamari
- 2 kumquats, topped and tailed, then each sliced into six
- 1 thin slice lemon
- salt and freshly ground black pepper

TO GARNISH

- 18 ends of chives, each measuring 5 cm (2 inches) long

Preheat the oven to gas mark 6, 400°F (200°F).

Place the whole acorn squashes on the middle shelf of the oven and bake for 40 minutes or until tender; the squashes should give when pressed with your finger.

- **MAKE THE FILLING**

Place the rice together with the saffron in a medium to large saucepan; add 900 ml (1½ pints) of water and leave to stand for 30 minutes. Place over heat, bring to the boil and simmer on a low heat for 10 minutes, covered with a tight lid. Heat the oil and gently fry the paprika for 3 minutes in a large frying-pan. Meanwhile grind the whole cardamoms, cloves and cumin seeds in a coffee grinder until completely fine; the best way to do this is to let the coffee grinder start and stop a few times, so the blade picks up any coarse pieces left. Add the ground spices to the frying-pan and cook for another 2 minutes; add the chillies, mushrooms and water chestnuts and cook for approximately 10 minutes on a medium heat or until the mushrooms are tender.

Cut the cooked squashes in half to make 'boatshells' and scoop out most of the flesh, leaving 5 mm (¼ inch). Chop the flesh and add to the pan together with the bouillon powder, cooked rice and seasoning; you will need to add two good pinches of salt. Cook, covered, for 8–10 minutes. Add the lemon juice and spring onions and check the seasoning. Fill the shells with the rice mixture and reheat in the oven, covered with foil, 15 minutes before serving.

● MAKE THE COURGETTE AND GREEN PEPPER PURÉE

Place the green pepper on a baking sheet and bake in the preheated oven for 30 minutes, turning it once during its cooking time so all sides are blistered. Remove from the oven, cover with a damp tea-towel and leave to cool for 10 minutes. Peel the skin away from the pepper, take the core out, de-seed, and chop the flesh. Steam the courgettes for 15 minutes or until soft. Place them in a food processor, add the green pepper and process until the purée is smooth but still has a little texture. Transfer into a small frying-pan, add the butter and plenty of seasoning and simmer in the open pan for 15 minutes to dry out the purée.

● MAKE THE SWEET POTATO AND RED PEPPER PURÉE

Place the red pepper on a baking sheet and bake in the preheated oven for 30 minutes, turning it once during its cooking time so all sides are blistered. Cover with a damp tea-towel and leave to cool for 10 minutes. Peel the skin away from the pepper, take the core out, de-seed, and chop the flesh. Steam the sweet potatoes for 15 minutes or until soft. Place them in a food processor, add the red pepper and process until the purée is completely smooth. Transfer into a small frying-pan, add the butter, 25 ml (1 fl oz) of water and the bouillon powder and bring to the boil. Simmer for 10 minutes, covered.

● MAKE THE OKRA AND TOMATO CASSEROLE

Place the okra and tomatoes in a small to medium saucepan, bring to the boil and simmer for 15 minutes, covered. Season generously.

● MAKE THE ONION SAUCE

Heat the oil and brown the onion. Add the water, miso and tamari and bring to the boil, stirring all the time. Add the kumquats, lemon and seasoning and simmer for 8 minutes, partly covered.

● TO SERVE

Reheat the filled acorn squash as instructed above. Pour some of the onion sauce (including some of the onion shreds) on to plates; place the acorn squash on one side of the plate with the core looking outwards. Using an ice-cream scoop, place one scoop of the green purée opposite the shell and a scoop of the red purée on the side of the green purée. Garnish the plate with a ring of kumquat (taken from the onion sauce) threaded with a few chives, next to the acorn squash. Serve the okra and tomato casserole in a separate warmed side dish.

CRÈME AND PEARS RENVERSÉES

SERVES 6

his is a light and sweet dessert which makes use of colourful red Bartlett pears; if none is available use ripe green pears instead. This dish consists of layers of pears cooked in a light custard until set and then turned out. The dessert has a soft texture but the pears should retain a little of their crispness. The *crème renversées* are served on a bed of light syrup made from the cooking of the pears in a sugar syrup. If you want more sauce, add a little pear liqueur and water to this mixture. This dessert may be served warm or cold.

* 4 ripe red Bartlett pears

FOR THE SYRUP

* 50 g (2 oz) white or light soft brown sugar
* 4 × 15 ml spoons (4 tablespoons) water

FOR THE CRÈME RENVERSÉE

* 600 ml (1 pint) milk

* 2.5 cm (1 inch) vanilla pod
* 2 eggs
* 4 egg yolks
* 65 g (2½ oz) light soft brown sugar

TO DECORATE

* 2 pears, quartered, cored and sliced
* 6 sprigs fresh mint

Preheat the oven to gas mark 6, 400°F (200°C). Place a bain-marie to preheat in the oven.

● **PREPARE THE PEARS**

Quarter and core each pear (do not peel) and cut each quarter across into slices 5 mm (¼ inch) thick. Cook the pear slices in a large dry frying-pan over a medium heat for 2–3 minutes until tender.

- **MAKE THE SUGAR SYRUP**

Place the sugar in another small saucepan, add the water and bring to the boil, stirring once or twice. Simmer for 2 minutes, uncovered. Add the sugar syrup to the pears and mix delicately; leave aside.

- **MAKE THE CRÈME RENVERSÉE**

Bring the milk to boiling point and add the vanilla pod. Whisk the eggs, egg yolks and sugar together in a mixing bowl. Gradually whisk in the milk and remove the vanilla pod.

Line and grease 6 ramekin dishes each 250 ml (8 fl oz) in capacity. Divide the cooked pear mixture between the dishes, reserving the sugar syrup. Pour the egg and milk custard over the top of the pears and place the ramekins in the hot bain-marie. Bake in the preheated oven for 40 minutes or until set. Take the bain-marie and ramekins out of the oven carefully; leave the ramekins to cool in the water in which they have cooked for 1 hour. If you are in a hurry, place in cold water and leave to cool for 30 minutes.

- **TO SERVE**

Carefully ease the custard away from the edges with a knife and turn out on to individual plates. Serve with a little of the reserved sugar syrup. Decorate with 3 thin slices of fanned-out pears and add a sprig of mint at the point where the pear slices gather.

❹

$\mathscr{W}$ I N T E R $\mathscr{M}$ E N U

MARBLED RED AND YELLOW PEPPER
MOUSSES ON ROSEMARY LEAVES

~

INDIVIDUAL NUT ROASTS SERVED
WITH ROASTED SHALLOTS
AND TURNED VEGETABLES ◆

~

APPLE AND BLACKBERRY *AUMONIÈRES* ON
MIXED BERRY COULIS

~

The starter is a very colourful and extremely successful combination of flavours. The main course looks wonderful and needs no other side vegetables. The pretty dessert is made of fruits wrapped in pancake parcels and served on a coulis of mixed berries.

MARBLED RED AND YELLOW PEPPER MOUSSES ON ROSEMARY LEAVES

SERVES 6

This is a combination that I find excellent as the rosemary revives the dull flavour of the peppers and sharpens their rounded taste. If your friends find it odd to be served whole leaves of rosemary, do reassure them that they do not have to eat them; they are just there on the plate for flavouring! Serve this starter with a French baguette to mop up the dressing.

- *2 red peppers*
- *2 yellow peppers*
- *4 × 15 ml spoons (4 tablespoons) double cream*
- *salt and freshly ground black pepper*
- *3 eggs, separated*

FOR THE ROSEMARY MARINADE

- *3 × 15 ml spoons (3 tablespoons) rosemary leaves*
- *2 × 15 ml spoons (2 tablespoons) red wine vinegar*

● *3 × 15 ml spoons (3 tablespoons)
sunflower oil*
● *salt and freshly ground black pepper*

● *6 × 15 ml spoons (6 tablespoons)
rosemary leaves*

Preheat the oven to gas mark 6, 400°F (200°C). Line the base of 6 small college pudding moulds (150 ml (¼ pint) in capacity) with greaseproof paper.

Place the peppers on a baking sheet and bake in the preheated oven for 35 minutes turning the peppers over half-way through the cooking time to ensure that the skin is blistered all round. Take the peppers out of the oven, cover with a damp cloth and leave to cool for 20 minutes. Remove the skin and seeds and collect the juices that will run from the peppers. Place the flesh on kitchen paper for 15 seconds on each side to drain any moisture. Place the red pepper flesh in a blender and blend until thoroughly smooth. Take out and place in a mixing bowl. Blend the yellow pepper flesh in a blender in the same manner, and place in a separate mixing bowl. Add 2 × 15 ml spoons (2 tablespoons) of double cream and half the egg yolks to each of the mixtures, add seasoning and mix well.

Whip the egg whites in a clean mixing bowl to the point where they don't slide in the bowl. Fold half the whipped egg whites into red pepper mixture using a metal spoon; and half the egg whites into the yellow pepper mixture, using a clean spoon. Mix in until completely incorporated. Fill the moulds carefully as follows. Pour 1 × 15 ml spoon (1 tablespoon) of the red pepper mixture first into one side of the moulds, tilt the mould slightly over to that side, then pour 1 × 15 ml spoon (1 tablespoon) of the yellow pepper mixture on the other side; add more red pepper mixture and more yellow pepper mixture in the same way, so that the mould is filled with the red pepper mixture on one side and the yellow pepper mixture on the other side. Place on a baking sheet and bake in the preheated oven for 20 minutes.

Check the pepper mousses after 20 minutes in the oven; the mixture should feel set. Take out of the oven, leave to stand for 8 minutes then loosen the edges with a small palette knife.

● **MAKE THE ROSEMARY MARINADE**

Mix all the ingredients together until smooth and leave to stand while the mousses are baking.

● **TO SERVE**

Turn the mousses out on to large white plates and pour the marinade all around. Arrange the rosemary leaves by hand so they form a pretty pattern around the mousses.

INDIVIDUAL NUT ROASTS SERVED
WITH ROASTED SHALLOTS AND TURNED VEGETABLES

SERVES 6

*T*he nut roasts are cooked in dariole moulds, each with a capacity of 150 ml (¼ pint). Each nut roast is served surrounded by the selection of colourful vegetables. The sauce in which the vegetables are cooked has no thickening agent, but thickens by reduction.

FOR THE INDIVIDUAL NUT ROASTS

- *15 g (½ oz) butter*
- *1 small onion, peeled and finely chopped*
- *100 g (4 oz) mushrooms, chopped*
- *2 large tomatoes, peeled and chopped*
- *150 ml (¼ pint) water*
- *1½ × 5 ml spoons (1½ teaspoons) Marmite*
- *salt and freshly ground black pepper*
- *150 g (5 oz) almonds*
- *150 g (5 oz) cashew nuts*
- *150 g (5 oz) wholemeal bread*
- *6 baby spinach leaves, approximately 5 cm (2 inches) in diameter*

FOR THE VEGETABLES IN THE SAUCE

- *6 medium to large carrots, each cut into 5 pieces*
- *6 large potatoes, each cut into 5 pieces*
- *4 large turnips, each cut into 6 pieces*
- *40 g (1½ oz) butter*
- *12 small shallots, peeled and left whole*
- *6 slim, medium to large courgettes, each vandyked (see page 15) and chopped into pieces 3 cm (1¼ inch) long*
- *100 g (4 oz) mangetouts, topped and tailed*
- *750 ml (1¼ pints) water*
- *2 × 5 ml spoons (2 teaspoons) Marmite*
- *2½ × 15 ml spoons (2½ tablespoons) shoyu*
- *salt and freshly ground black pepper*

Preheat the oven to gas mark 6, 400°F (200°C).

● PREPARE THE NUT ROASTS

Melt the butter and fry the onion until soft and a little browned. Add the mushrooms and fry until tender. Add the tomatoes and cook until they have nearly all broken down. Add the water, Marmite and seasoning and cook, covered, for 3 minutes.

Place the almonds, cashews and bread in a food processor and process until fine and the bread reduced to fine breadcrumbs. Transfer into a mixing bowl and pour the vegetable mixture on to it. Mix thoroughly. Grease, then line 6 dariole moulds with a spinach leaf each. Divide the mixture between the moulds, place in the preheated oven and bake for 20–25 minutes.

● **PREPARE THE VEGETABLES IN THE SAUCE**

Turn the carrots, potatoes and turnips (see page 14). Melt the butter in a large frying-pan and add the shallots and carrots. Cook, covered, for 5 minutes on a low to medium heat. Add the potatoes and turnips and cook, covered, for a further 5 minutes. Add the courgettes, mangetouts, water, Marmite, shoyu and seasoning and cook, uncovered, for 8–10 minutes or until the liquid has reduced by one-third and the mangetouts and other vegetables are cooked.

● **TO SERVE**

Take the nut roasts out of the oven and leave to stand for 5 minutes. Turn them out on to serving plates and surround each by a selection of the cooked vegetables.

APPLE AND BLACKBERRY *AUMONIÈRES* ## ON MIXED BERRY COULIS

SERVES 6

*T*hese *aumonières* look pretty on the plate. The filling may be varied but it should not be too wet. The pancakes should be made as thin as possible and tied up with a thin strip of lightly blanched orange rind (see page 17). If you cannot find fresh or frozen blackberries, use tinned blackberries in fruit juice instead. Prepare the pancakes (see page 130 for ingredients and method) first and then the filling and coulis. Serve cold.

* *12 thin pancakes 18 cm (7 inch) in diameter (see page 130 for recipe)*
* *3 Bramley cooking apples, peeled, cored and sliced*
* *100 g (4 oz) soft brown sugar*
* *225 g (8 oz) fresh or frozen blackberries*

FOR THE MIXED BERRY COULIS

* *175 g (6 oz) blackberries*
* *350 g (12 oz) fresh or frozen raspberries*
* *75 g (3 oz) soft brown sugar*

TO SERVE

* *100 g (4 oz) slices of cooked apples, cooked in a little sugar*
* *a few extra cooked blackberries*
* *40 g (1½ oz) icing sugar*

● MAKE THE PANCAKES

Follow the method on pages 130–1.

● MAKE THE APPLE AND BLACKBERRY FILLING

Place the apples, sugar and blackberries in a saucepan and cook on a low to medium heat for 15 minutes or until the fruits are soft, taking the lid off towards the end of the cooking time to dry the mixture. Cool.

● MAKE THE COULIS

Place the blackberries and the raspberries in a saucepan with 8 × 15 ml spoons (8 tablespoons) water. Bring to the boil, cook for a few minutes then add the sugar. Cook, covered, for another 10 minutes and then take the pan off the heat. Sieve the mixture to extract the pips. If the coulis seems a little thick, add a little extra water. Chill thoroughly.

● TO SERVE

Place 2 × 15 ml spoons (2 tablespoons) of the prepared filling in the centre of each pancake and wrap the pancake around it, making sure that you lift the edges of the pancake as you do so, and gather it on top, in a pretty curly pattern. Tie each *aumonière* with a blanched orange strip and fold the tops back over slightly to make a pretty purse.

Spoon some of the coulis on to each of the six plates and place two *aumonières* on top. Rain some icing sugar through a sieve over the plates, coulis and *aumonières*. Decorate the plates by placing three cooked apple slices, overlapping, and a few cooked berries on the side of the *aumonières*.

⑤

𝒲INTER 𝑀ENU

TOASTED TOMATOES IN A FRESH HERB AND OLIVE VINAIGRETTE ♦★

~

GOAT CHEESE AND BRUSSELS SPROUT SOUFFLÉ SERVED WITH LEEK, MUSTARD AND WATERCRESS SAUCE

~

'FRAISIER-STYLE' CHOCOLATE AND STRAWBERRY CAKE

~

This menu begins with a light starter which may be served hot or cold. The main course is an unusual but delicious soufflé served with a tangy sauce; this soufflé may be served with new potatoes and other side vegetables. The pudding is an inviting layered square cake with a banana, ricotta, crème fraîche and strawberry filling.

TOASTED TOMATOES IN A FRESH HERB AND OLIVE OIL VINAIGRETTE

SERVES 6

*I*n order to make this starter successfully, obtain the walnuts from a supplier who can assure you that they have been harvested in the same year; good wholefood shops usually have fresh nuts in store. If slicing tomatoes are not available, use beef tomatoes instead.

- *6 slicing tomatoes*

FOR THE VINAIGRETTE

- *1 × 15 ml spoon (1 tablespoon) walnut oil*
- *4 × 15 ml spoons (4 tablespoons) olive oil*
- *3 × 15 ml spoons (3 tablespoons) red wine vinegar*

- *1 × 5 ml spoon (1 teaspoon) garlic vinegar*
- *salt and freshly ground black pepper*
- *18 leaves continental parsley*
- *2 × 15 ml spoons (2 tablespoons) chives, chopped into pieces 2.5 cm (1 inch) long*

FOR THE TOMATO TOPPING

- *50 g (2 oz) white bread*
- *100 g (4 oz) fresh walnuts*
- *1 clove garlic*

- *1 × 15 ml spoon (1 tablespoon) finely chopped stalks continental parsley*

TO SERVE

- *1 clove garlic, cut in half*

Preheat the oven to gas mark 7, 425°F (220°C).

● MAKE THE VINAIGRETTE

Place the walnut oil, olive oil, red wine vinegar, garlic vinegar, salt and black pepper in a mixing bowl and stir until smooth. Add the fresh herbs and leave to stand.

● MAKE THE TOMATO TOPPING

Place the bread, walnuts and garlic in the food processor and process until the nuts are chopped but not finely milled. Transfer into a mixing bowl and add the parsley.

Slice all the tomatoes into 3 slices, north to south; the slices should be between 1 and 2 cm (½ and ¾ inch) thick. Place the tomato slices on a baking sheet; top each slice of tomato with 1 × 15 ml spoon (1 tablespoon) of the walnut nut mixture and level the top. Place on the top shelf of the preheated oven and cook for 10 minutes, until the topping is crisp.

● TO SERVE

Rub the cut side of the garlic clove on six plates. Place the slices of tomatoes on to the plates and pour the vinaigrette next to (not over) the slices. Arrange the fresh herb leaves on the top of the vinaigrette.

GOAT CHEESE AND BRUSSELS SPROUT SOUFFLÉ SERVED WITH LEEK, MUSTARD AND WATERCRESS SAUCE

SERVES 6

*T*here are many types of goat cheese available, some are mild and others are strong. I find that this dish is best made with a strong goat cheese. Serve these impressive soufflés as soon as they are cooked as they sink quite readily.

- *350 g (12 oz) Brussels sprouts*
- *40 g (1½ oz) butter*
- *40 g (1½ oz) wholewheat flour*
- *1 × 5 ml spoon (1 teaspoon) Dijon mustard*
- *450 ml (¾ pint) milk*
- *75 g (3 oz) strong goat cheese, chopped*
- *6 eggs, separated*
- *salt and freshly ground black pepper*
- *1 egg white*

FOR THE SAUCE

- *15 g (½ oz) butter*
- *225 g (8 oz) leeks, chopped*
- *100 g (4 oz) watercress, chopped*
- *600 ml (1 pint) water*
- *2 × 5 ml spoons (2 teaspoons) bouillon powder*
- *4 × 15 ml spoons (4 tablespoons) double cream*
- *1 × 5 ml spoon (1 teaspoon) Dijon mustard*
- *salt and freshly ground black pepper*

Preheat the oven to gas mark 6, 400°F (200°C). Lightly grease 6 ramekins each 300 ml (½ pint) in capacity. Place a large baking sheet in the oven so it heats up.

Peel the Brussels sprouts and cut into their base so this dense part cooks at the same rate as the leaves. Steam for 10–12 minutes or until tender. Melt the butter in a small to medium saucepan and add the flour and mustard, stirring well to make a roux. Cook the roux for 2 minutes on a low heat. Take the pan off the heat and gradually add the milk, stirring after each addition until the texture of the sauce is smooth again. Return the pan to the heat and bring to the boil, stirring all the time. Turn the heat down and simmer, uncovered, for 5 minutes. Cool.

Place the cooked Brussels sprouts in a food processor and process until fairly fine. Add the goat cheese and process again. Transfer into a large mixing bowl, add the egg yolks and white sauce and season generously.

Whip the 7 egg whites until they stand in peaks. Add 2 × 15 ml spoons (2 tablespoons) of egg whites to the Brussels sprout mixture and stir lightly with a whisk. This lightens the mixture and will make it easier to fold in the rest of the egg whites. Fold in the rest of the egg whites, using a large metallic spoon. Pour into the prepared ramekin dishes and bake on the heated baking sheet in the oven for 20–25 minutes.

● MAKE THE LEEK, MUSTARD AND WATERCRESS SAUCE

Melt the butter and fry the leeks until tender. Add the watercress, water and bouillon powder; bring to the boil and simmer for 5 minutes then cool a little. Blend until smooth in a blender and return the sauce to the pan over a gentle heat. Add the cream and mustard, reheat and season to taste.

● TO SERVE

Take the soufflés out of the oven and serve straightaway on warmed plates with new potatoes, side vegetables and the sauce served separately.

'FRAISIER-STYLE' CHOCOLATE AND STRAWBERRY CAKE

SERVES 6

*T*his is an enticing dessert which is made of a very light chocolate cake base and topping; a delicious filling of whole strawberries in a ricotta cheese, banana and *crème fraîche* base is sandwiched in between the chocolate cakes; and then topped with a plain chocolate icing. This is ideal for the chocoholic!

Note: 2 × 5 ml spoons (2 teaspoons) Cointreau, Grand Marnier or banana liqueur may be sprinkled over the chocolate cake before spreading the ricotta and banana filling.

- *6 × 15 ml spoons (6 tablespoons) chocolate powder*
- *1 × 15 ml spoon (1 tablespoon) cocoa powder*
- *150 ml (¼ pint) milk*
- *5 eggs, separated*
- *150 g (5 oz) white caster sugar or soft brown sugar*
- *few drops vanilla essence*

FOR THE FILLING

- *2 ripe bananas, mashed*
- *225 g (8 oz) ricotta cheese*
- *4 × 15 ml spoons (4 tablespoons) chilled* crème fraîche
- *50 g (2 oz) caster sugar*
- *350 g (12 oz) small strawberries, hulled and left whole*

FOR THE ICING

- *225 g (8 oz) good-qaulity milk chocolate*
- *25 g (1 oz) butter*

TO DECORATE

- *6 whole strawberries with their hulls left on*
- *300 ml (½ pint)* crème chantilly: *(300 ml (½ pint) crème fraîche lightly whisked with 2 × 15 ml spoons (2 tablespoons) caster sugar)*
- *15 g (½ oz) icing sugar*

Preheat the oven to gas mark 6, 400°F (200°C). Line a large Swiss roll tin 39.5 × 26.5 cm (15½ × 10½ inches) with greased baking parchment.

● **MAKE THE CAKE**

Place the chocolate powder and cocoa powder in a small saucepan and gradually add the milk, whisking all the time. Place the pan on a medium heat and bring to the boil; simmer, uncovered, for 5 minutes then cool thoroughly.

Whisk the egg yolks and the sugar together with an electric whisk in a large mixing bowl until thick and creamy. Add the vanilla essence then the cooled chocolate mixture.

Whisk the egg whites in a clean bowl until stiff but not dry. Using a hand whisk, fold in 2 × 15 ml spoons (2 tablespoons) of the egg whites into the cold chocolate mixture. Delicately fold the rest of the egg whites into the chocolate mixture, using a large metallic spoon. Pour the cake mixture into the prepared tin, level with a spatula and bake on the middle shelf of the preheated oven for 22 minutes. Take out of the oven and cool for 5 minutes. Turn the cake out on to a cooling rack and leave to cool thoroughly. When the cake is cold, trim the edges neatly with a sharp knife and cut the cake into two parts across.

● **MAKE THE FILLING**

Mash the bananas with the ricotta cheese in a mixing bowl until smooth. Whip the *crème fraîche* until soft, add the sugar and whip again lightly; fold into the banana mixture and chill.

● **MAKE THE ICING**

Break the chocolate into pieces and place in a small mixing bowl over a pan of simmering water. Wait for the chocolate to melt, add the butter and stir; the mixture will thicken. Remove the bowl from the heat; add 2–3 × 15 ml spoons (2–3 tablespoons) cold water or as much as it takes to make the mixture smooth and runny. Pour over one half of the cake, spreading with a warm blade, if necessary. Leave to cool.

Place the other half of the cake on a dessert tray and spread the banana filling over. Press the hulled whole strawberries lightly into the filling at random (if you have very large strawberries, cut them in half). Carefully place the iced cake over the strawberry filling and leave to set in a cool place.

● **TO SERVE**

Using a warm blade and a very sharp knife, cut the cake into six portions. You will have to cut through the strawberries and this looks extremely attractive on the plate. Top each slice with a whole strawberry and serve with a dusting of icing sugar sprinkled through a sieve, and extra *crème chantilly*, served separately.

⑥
WINTER MENU

PETITES COURGETTE TIMBALES ON
CHAMPAGNE VINAIGRETTE ♦

~

INDIVIDUAL BRIOCHES FILLED WITH
ROASTED GARLIC, BUTTON MUSHROOMS AND
PORTO SAUCE

~

GRAND-STYLE MERINGUES ON A DUET OF
KIWI AND RASPBERRY COULIS

~

This is an extremely impressive dinner party menu: it sounds grand and looks grand. The courgette timbales are a delight to eat, chilled, and the champagne vinaigrette adds something pétillant to this starter. The main course is savoury and light; make your own brioches because there is no real alternative to good old home-made brioches. The dessert looks really impressive as it makes use of two different coloured coulis; it is, however, surprisingly straightforward.

The brioches may be made one day in advance and the meringues may be made up to two days in advance provided you keep both (separately) in airtight tins. The sauce for the brioches may be made up to one day in advance, provided you take care not to allow the sauce to reduce further on reheating.

The courgette timbales and the vinaigrette may also be prepared up to one day in advance, provided both are stored in the refrigerator.

PETITES COURGETTE TIMBALES ON CHAMPAGNE VINAIGRETTE

SERVES 6

Don't be daunted by the fact that these courgette timbales need turning out because they come out of the ramekins extremely easily. The filling, which sets on cooling in the refrigerator, is crunchy and creamy at the same time because it contains a mixture of various cheeses and some finely diced courgettes. Serve well chilled.

- *500 g (1 lb 2 oz) fresh spinach leaves*
- *1½ × 15 ml spoons (1½ tablespoons) grapeseed oil*
- *500 g (1 lb 2 oz) baby or small courgettes, finely diced*
- *salt*
- *5 spring onions, very finely chopped*
- *120 g (4½ oz) ricotta cheese*
- *165 g (5½ oz) curd cheese*
- *3 × 5 ml spoons (3 teaspoons) fresh thyme, finely chopped*

FOR THE CHAMPAGNE VINAIGRETTE

- *4½ × 15 ml spoons (4½ tablespoons) grapeseed oil*
- *3 × 15 ml spoons (3 tablespoons) champagne vinegar*
- *3 × 5 ml spoons (3 teaspoons) thyme, very finely chopped*
- *salt and freshly ground black pepper*

TO GARNISH

- *18 sprigs fresh chervil*
- *6 yellow pepper triangles (see page 16), steamed for 1½ minutes then chilled*

Take 175 g (6 oz) of the best spinach leaves, remove their stems, wash them thoroughly and steam for 2 minutes. Plunge them straightaway into a mixing bowl already filled with icy cold water and leave to cool. When cold, drain on a tea-towel.

Wash and remove the stems from the rest of the spinach leaves and steam for 6 minutes. Drain thoroughly in a sieve and chop finely.

Heat the oil and fry the courgettes in an open pan for a few minutes until almost tender. Add a good pinch of salt, cover and cook for a further 2–3 minutes. Add the spring onions and cook for another minute. Remove the pan from the heat and leave to cool. Meanwhile, sieve the ricotta cheese and mix with the curd cheese. Add this to the courgette mixture then add the spinach (reserving the 175 g (6 oz) leaves) and fresh thyme. Mix well and season to taste.

Line the inside of six ramekin dishes 150 ml (¼ pint) in capacity with the reserved spinach leaves, overlapping the leaves so there are no gaps. Fill the ramekins to the rim with the courgette mixture. Fold the spinach leaves over the mixture and place the terrines in the refrigerator to cool and set.

Make the champagne vinaigrette by whisking all the ingredients together and stir it again just before serving.

● **T O   S E R V E**

Pour the vinaigrette on to plates, turn the terrines out on to a chopping board and delicately transfer them, with the help of a palette knife, on to each plate. Arrange them slightly to one side and garnish each plate with the sprigs of chervil, placed at equal intervals on the opposite side. Place a yellow pepper triangle over the terrine.

INDIVIDUAL BRIOCHES FILLED WITH ROASTED GARLIC, BUTTON MUSHROOMS AND PORTO SAUCE

SERVES 6

*T*his recipe makes rich, well risen, savoury, French-style, impressive brioches, hollowed out and filled with a light mushroom filling which moistens the brioche.

The brioches may be baked a day in advance and kept fresh wrapped in a tea-towel (or in the freezer) until the day of use; they can then be microwaved or warmed through and filled with the piping hot filling.

Serve these brioches with small parsley potatoes, matchstick carrots, green beans and/or other colourful vegetables.

- *7 g (¼ oz) fresh yeast*
- *75 ml (2½ fl oz) warm milk*
- *1 × 5 ml spoon (1 teaspoon) salt*
- *4 eggs, beaten*
- *350 g (12 oz) strong white flour*
- *175 g (6 oz) butter, softened*
- *25 g (1 oz) extra strong white flour (for the kneading of the brioche)*

TO GLAZE

- *1 egg yolk, beaten and mixed with 1 × 15 ml spoon (1 tablespoon) milk*

FOR THE FILLING

- *25 g (1 oz) butter*
- *12 large cloves garlic, peeled (not crushed), and halved lengthwise*
- *6 baby leeks, peeled and chopped into pieces 1.25 cm (½ inch) long*
- *450 g (1 lb) celeriac, peeled and chopped into pieces 1.25 cm (½ inch) square and 5 mm (¼ inch) thick*
- *750 g (1½ lb) button mushrooms, sliced*
- *25 g (1 oz) white flour*
- *450 ml (¾ pint) water*
- *2–3 × 15 ml spoons (2–3 tablespoons) shoyu or to taste*
- *2 × 15 ml spoons (2 tablespoons) port*
- *salt and freshly ground black pepper*

TO GARNISH

- *6 × 5 ml spoons (6 teaspoons) fresh thyme, chopped*
- *6 sprigs fresh thyme*

● **MAKE THE BRIOCHES**

Place the yeast and the warm milk in a small bowl and whisk until the yeast is dissolved and the mixture creamy. Add the salt and mix again. Add the eggs and flour and mix well. Transfer into a mixer with a dough hook and process for 10 minutes. Alternatively, knead by hand for 15 minutes, until the dough is shiny and elastic. You may need to add some of the extra flour on the kneading board at this point.

Then add the butter gradually and process in a mixer for another 5 minutes. If you are mixing by hand this will take another 8–10 minutes (or until the dough is smooth and glossy). You may need to add the rest of the extra flour to the dough at this point.

Place the dough in a mixing bowl, cover with a tea-towel and leave to stand in a warm place for approximately 2½ hours or until the dough has doubled in size. Then knock the air out of the dough by beating it lightly with your fingertips for 15 seconds.

Divide and shape the dough into six 75 g (3 oz) balls. Lightly grease six 3½ fl oz (100 ml) small individual brioche moulds. Placing the seam underneath (and flattening the brioches slightly), drop the dough balls into the brioche moulds. Take another 6 pieces of dough each weighing 40 g (1½ oz). Shape each one into an elongated egg shape. Make a deep hole in the centre of the large brioche bases with your fingertips; press the narrow end of the egg-shaped dough into the hole, making sure that the 'hats' are sitting straight. Leave to rise in a fairly warm place for approximately 1 hour or until the dough has almost doubled in size. Meanwhile, preheat the oven to gas mark 7, 425°F (220°C).

Glaze with the egg and milk mixture, making sure that no liquid drips in between the brioches and the moulds. Place them on a large baking sheet and bake on the middle shelf of the preheated oven for 10 minutes. Turn the oven down to gas mark 6, 400°F (200°C) and bake for another 20–25 minutes or until golden. Take the brioches out of the tins; they should sound hollow when tapped underneath. Leave to cool on a cooling rack.

● MAKE THE FILLING

Melt the butter and fry the halved garlic cloves on a low to medium heat for 5–7 minutes or until golden. Add the leeks and celeriac and fry for another 7 minutes. Add the sliced mushrooms and cook until tender. Sprinkle the flour over the vegetables and cook on a low heat for 2 minutes, stirring from time to time. Take the pan off the heat and gradually add the water, stirring well between each addition. When all the water is added, place the pan back on the heat and bring the mixture up to the boil, stirring slowly all the time. Simmer for 5 minutes. Add the shoyu and port, season with salt and black pepper, and simmer for another 5 minutes.

● TO SERVE

Cut the lids off the brioches by making a straight horizontal cut. Scoop out the inside of the brioches with a teaspoon, leaving a shell 1.25 cm (½ inch) thick, all around. Reheat the brioches in the oven for 8 minutes at gas mark 6, 400°F (200°C). Place each on to warmed plates and fill with the piping hot mushroom filling, letting some of the filling overflow on one side in a decorative manner. Place the lids over the filling, slightly slanted, and sprinkle the fresh thyme over the overflowing filling. Garnish the plate with a sprig of fresh thyme and (if liked) a tomato rose (see page 16) and serve hot with colourful vegetables to accompany.

left Marbled Red and Yellow Pepper Mousse on Rosemary Leaves *centre* Individual Nut Roast served with Roasted Shallots and Turned Vegetables *right* Apple and Blackberry Aumonières on Mixed Berry Coulis

❼ WINTER MENU

MARINATED TRICOLOUR PEPPERS IN A FRESH
BASIL MARINADE ♦★

~

CASHEW AND ALMOND ROULÉ FILLED WITH
BRANDIED CHESTNUTS AND SMALL ONIONS
AND SERVED WITH MUSHROOM AND
BRANDY SAUCE ♦

~

INDIVIDUAL CREAM AND BLACKCURRANT
CHARLOTTES ♦

~

This successful menu consists of a brightly coloured pepper starter, a satisfying cashew and almond roulé, and small delicious charlottes served on a bed of redcurrant and black-currant coulis; the pudding is very straightforward but none the less colourful and impressive. Both the starter and the pudding can be prepared the day before.

MARINATED TRICOLOUR PEPPERS IN A FRESH BASIL MARINADE

SERVES 6

This dish is based on three different coloured peppers, a green, a red and a yellow, partly baked, skinned and marinated in a fresh basil marinade. It makes a colourful starter which is made even tastier with the addition of pesto (a fresh basil sauce). Since the recipe calls for such a small quantity, I use a ready-made pesto sauce.

You should be able to buy ready-made pastry cups from delicatessens or good supermarkets. If you cannot find them, however, either bake your own (using a maximum of 50 g (2 oz) ready-made shortcrust pastry for all cups, roll out thinly to line the bases of 6 bun tins and bake in a preheated oven at gas mark 6, 400°F (200°C) for 4–6 minutes); or use large fresh basil leaves as a recipient for the pesto sauce.

This starter may be made up to two days in advance and kept refrigerated until the day of use. Serve with a warm French baguette or garlic bread.

- 1 green pepper
- 2 red peppers
- 2 yellow peppers

FOR THE MARINADE

- 3 × 15 ml spoons (3 tablespoons) sunflower oil
- 1½ × 15 ml spoons (1½ tablespoons) olive oil
- 3 × 15 ml spoons (3 tablespoons) white wine vinegar
- 2 × 5 ml spoons (2 teaspoons) wholegrain mustard

- 1½ × 15 ml spoons (1½ tablespoons) fresh chopped basil
- ¼ × 5 ml spoon (¼ teaspoon) dried oregano
- salt and freshly ground black pepper

TO SERVE

- 6 ready-made pastry cups, 4 cm (1½ inches) in diameter or 6 fairly large basil leaves
- 6 × 5 ml spoons (6 teaspoons) pesto sauce
- 18 small sprigs fresh oregano or 18 small basil leaves
- warm French baguette or garlic bread

Preheat the oven to gas mark 6, 400°F (200°C).

Place the whole peppers on a baking sheet on the middle shelf of the oven and bake for 25–30 minutes, turning them over twice, every ten minutes, so that all sides are cooked, blistered and rather brown/black. Take the peppers out, cover them with a slightly damp tea-towel and leave to cool for 10 minutes; as well as allowing the peppers to cool down, this will make the peeling of the skin away from the peppers easier.

Meanwhile make the marinade by mixing all the ingredients together in a mixing bowl and season to taste.

Peel the skin away from the peppers and discard their seeds and stalks. Cut the flesh into thin slices about 2.5 cm (1 inch) long and 5 mm (¼ inch) wide. Stir the strips into the marinade and leave to stand for 2–3 hours or overnight for the flavours to develop.

● TO SERVE

Divide the mixture between six plates; each plate should have in its centre a colourful mound of peppers. Pour the marinade around, just so that it covers the base of each plate and place the pastry cups, each filled with 1 × 5 ml spoon (1 level teaspoon) of pesto sauce over the peppers. Garnish each plate with three sprigs of fresh oregano delicately placed at equal intervals over the marinade. Serve with a warm French baguette or garlic bread.

left Marinated Tricolour Peppers in a Fresh Basil Marinade *centre* Cashew and Almond Roulé
Filled with Brandied Chestnuts and Small Onions and served with Mushroom and Brandy Sauce
right Individual Cream and Blackcurrant Charlotte

CASHEW AND ALMOND ROULÉ FILLED WITH BRANDIED CHESTNUTS AND SMALL ONIONS AND SERVED WITH MUSHROOM AND BRANDY SAUCE

SERVES 6

*I*f you dislike mushrooms you may add courgettes to the nut mixture or you may vary the nuts; in fact the variations are endless. The filling too may be changed but I like this one as it makes use of chestnuts, an ingredient rarely used other than at Christmas, and because it makes use of a great flavouring, namely Armagnac! If small pickling onions are not available, use shallots instead.

If you have a fish kettle, it will prove ideal to steam this dish; otherwise use a large steamer – the old-fashioned ones are the largest.

This dish can be prepared the day before up to the point where it needs cooking; it should, however, be cooked the day it is eaten. The sauce can be made the day before, stored in the refrigerator and reheated gently.

- 15 g (½ oz) butter
- 1 onion, peeled and finely chopped
- 100 g (4 oz) mushrooms, chopped
- 2 tomatoes, peeled and chopped
- 150 ml (¼ pint) water
- 1 × 5 ml spoon (1 rounded teaspoon) Marmite
- 175 g (6 oz) ground almonds
- 175 g (6 oz) ground cashew nuts
- 175 g (6 oz) white breadcrumbs
- salt and freshly ground black pepper

FOR THE FILLING

- 175 g (6 oz) frozen or tinned chestnuts
- 15 g (½ oz) butter or margarine
- 12 small pickling onions, peeled and halved
- 175 g (6 oz) button mushrooms, halved
- 2 cloves garlic, crushed
- 2 × 15 ml spoons (2 tablespoons) chopped parsley
- 2 × 15 ml spoons (2 tablespoons) Armagnac or brandy
- salt and freshly ground black pepper

FOR THE MUSHROOM AND BRANDY
SAUCE

- 25 g (1 oz) butter or margarine
- 225 g (8 oz) open cap mushrooms (not
  field), chopped
- 1 bayleaf
- 1 × 15 ml spoon (1 tablespoon)
  Armagnac or brandy

- 65 ml (2½ fl oz) red wine
- 300 ml (½ pint) dark stock (e.g. made
  with 1 × 5 ml spoon (1 level teaspoon)
  Marmite and water)
- 2½ × 15 ml spoons (2½ tablespoons)
  shoyu
- good pinch thyme
- salt and freshly ground black pepper

Melt the butter and fry the onion and mushroom until soft. Add the tomatoes and cook until they are soft. Add the water and Marmite and simmer, covered, for 5 minutes. Meanwhile mix the almonds, cashews and breadcrumbs together in a mixing bowl. Pour the wet mixture over the dry ingredients and mix well. Season to taste.

● **MAKE THE FILLING**

Cook the chestnuts as indicated on the packet (if frozen) or drain if canned. Chop the chestnuts in half. Melt the butter and brown the onions thoroughly on a medium to high heat. Add the mushrooms and cook for another 5–8 minutes then turn the heat down. Add the garlic and chestnuts and cook for 2 or 3 minutes. Add the parsley, brandy and seasoning to taste, and cook to reduce the liquid to the point where no liquid remains in the pan. Take the pan off the heat.

● **COOK THE ROULÉS**

Place two damp 18 × 18 cm (7 × 7 inch) pieces of muslin or cheesecloths on a chopping board. Spread half the nut and breadcrumb mixture evenly on to each one, spreading it to the edges, then place half the chestnut filling on top of each of the squares. Note: if using a fish kettle use a larger piece of muslin, measuring 36 × 18 cm (14 × 7 inch) and make only one roulé (twice as long). Helping yourself with the piece of muslin, roll the nut and breadcrumb mixture over once so the chestnuts are in the centre of the roulés. The shape should be cylindrical and the nut mixture should meet. Gather the ends as neatly as possible so that the seam will not split while cooking. Place both roulés in a steamer and cook for 45 minutes. Then turn the heat off and leave for a further 10 minutes and remove from the steamer. Cool for 5 minutes, wrapped loosely in a tea-towel on the chopping board; then remove the muslin and cut into slices no more than 2 cm (¾ inch) thick.

● **MAKE THE SAUCE**

Meanwhile, melt the butter and gently fry the mushrooms and bayleaf together until soft. Add the Armagnac, red wine, stock, shoyu and thyme. Bring to the boil and simmer, uncovered, for 20 minutes. Remove the bayleaf and blend the sauce in a blender until very smooth. Season to taste. Return the sauce to the pan and reheat gently.

● **TO SERVE**

Arrange two slices of the roulé on each plate on a bed of mushroom and brandy sauce and accompany with roast potatoes and seasonal vegetables.

INDIVIDUAL CREAM
AND BLACKCURRANT CHARLOTTES

MAKES 6 CHARLOTTES

*T*hese charlottes have an attractive red and white topping and look very appealing when turned out on the plate. They are quite simple to make as all you need to do is layer currants, cream and biscuits. They are best prepared the day before so are an ideal recipe when entertaining.

● *175 g (6 oz) mixed frozen redcurrants and blackcurrants, defrosted*
● *200 ml (7 fl oz) double cream, chilled*
● *275 g (10 oz) vine fruit or currant biscuits*
● *200 ml (7 fl oz) white grape juice*

FOR THE COULIS

● *175 g (6 oz) mixed frozen blackcurrants and redcurrants*
● *75 g (3 oz) soft light brown or white sugar*

TO DECORATE

● *6 sprigs fresh mint*

Line the base of six ramekin dishes, each 150 ml ($\frac{1}{4}$ pint) in capacity, with greaseproof paper.

● **MAKE THE CHARLOTTES**

Drain the blackcurrants and redcurrants and keep the juice aside. Whip the cream until firm. Place the biscuits in a mixing bowl, pour the grape juice over and mash with a fork until the mixture is smooth and crumbly. Divide the fruit mixture between the six ramekins, place the whipped cream over them and level the layer. Top with the crushed biscuits and level. Place in the coolest part of the refrigerator overnight.

● **MAKE THE COULIS**

Place the currants in a saucepan with 4 × 15 ml spoons (4 tablespoons) of water, the reserved juice and the sugar, bring to the boil and simmer, covered, for 5 minutes. Leave to cool a little then sieve to remove the seeds. Leave the coulis to cool thoroughly. Chill well.

● **TO SERVE**

Neatly slide a knife around the edges of the ramekin dishes to loosen the edges. Turn the ramekins out on to a plate, shaking them a little if necessary. Pour a little coulis around each charlotte and decorate with a sprig of mint.

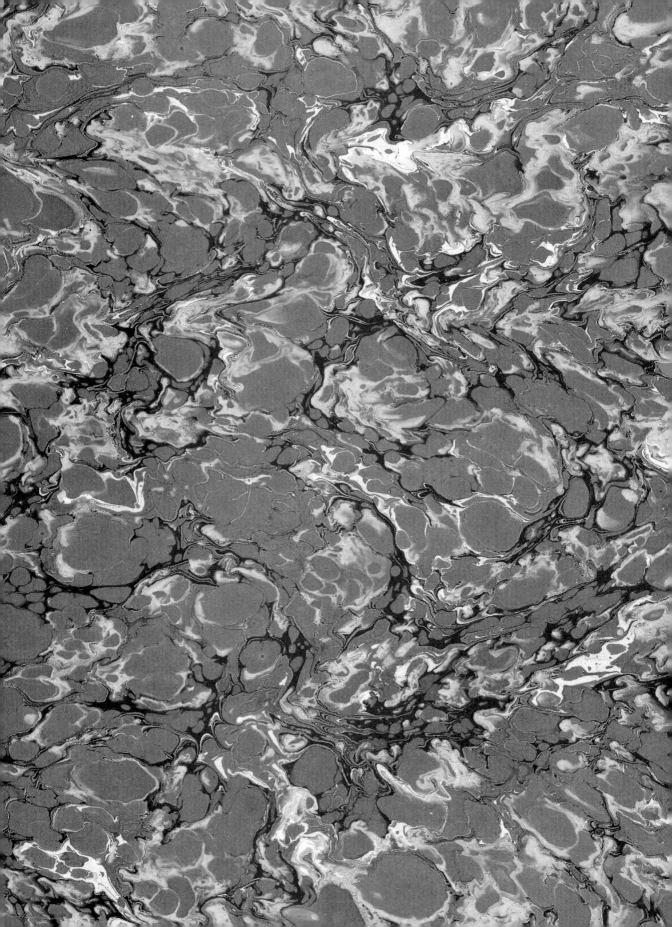

5

SPECIAL

OCCASIONS

E ASY

E NTERTAINING

LEEKS IN MIXED PEPPERCORN VINAIGRETTE ♦★

~

WALNUT ROULADE SERVED WITH BRAISED
FENNEL AND TOMATO *CONCASSÉE*

~

ORANGE, APRICOT AND TOFU WHIP WITH
COINTREAU AND ORANGE TOPPING ♦★

~

*This is a light and easy supper menu which may be
served as an ending to an evening or before you go
out. All the dishes may be prepared in advance.*

LEEKS IN MIXED PEPPERCORN VINAIGRETTE

SERVES 6

I love this effective and tasty starter, flavoured with black, green and pink peppercorns, mixed with a green peppercorn vinaigrette. If you have a fish kettle (I use mine for vegetables), this is perfect for steaming leeks, as they often do not fit in an ordinary steamer. If you do not own one, use the largest steamer you have, and bend the leeks in half. Do keep most of the green tops on the leeks, as this is their tastiest part.

- *6 young medium leeks, each approximately 100 g (4 oz)*
- *18 steamed carrot batons, see page 14*

FOR THE VINAIGRETTE

- *5 × 15 ml spoons (5 tablespoons) sunflower oil*
- *3 × 15 ml spoons (3 tablespoons) white wine vinegar*

- *1 × 5 ml spoon (1 teaspoon) green peppercorn wholegrain mustard*
- *1 × 5 ml spoon (1 teaspoon) mixed black, green and pink peppercorns, finely ground*
- *salt*

TO SERVE

- *6 sprigs chervil*

● **PREPARE THE LEEKS**

Trim off the tops and base of the leeks; cut them in half lengthways from almost the base to the tops to open them up and wash thoroughly. Steam the leeks whole for 10–12 minutes, depending on their thickness, drain.

Make the vinaigrette by mixing all the ingredients together. Add the leeks and the carrot batons to the vinaigrette and leave to marinate until required.

● **TO SERVE**

Place the leeks, folded, on each plate and pour a little marinade over. Arrange the carrot batons, side by side in a fanned-out pattern shape next to the leeks then garnish with a sprig of chervil. Serve with a warm baguette or white Italian bread.

WALNUT ROULADE SERVED WITH BRAISED FENNEL AND TOMATO *CONCASSÉE*

SERVES 6

*T*his roulade is unusual because it is made with ground walnuts to give it a savoury flavour. It may be made the day before and served cold either with mixed salad or with hot side dishes such as braised fennel and buttered new potatoes. If you are serving this meal as an after-theatre supper, just reheat the fennel (adding a little water, if necessary), with some ready-cooked potatoes in butter, in a covered pan, while you are eating the starter.

FOR THE WALNUT ROULADE

- *6 eggs, separated*
- *120 g (4½ oz) walnuts, finely ground*
- *3 × 5 ml spoons (3 teaspoons) tamari*
- *6 × 15 ml spoons (6 tablespoons) fromage frais*
- *salt and freshly ground black pepper*
- *65 g (2½ oz) extra ground walnuts*

FOR THE FILLING

- *350 g (12 oz) fresh spinach*
- *1 × 15 ml spoon (1 tablespoon) white wine vinegar*
- *300 ml (½ pint) fromage frais*
- *salt and freshly ground black pepper*

FOR THE FENNEL AND TOMATO CONCASSÉE

- *2 heads fennel, quartered, cored and tops trimmed*
- *1½ × 15 ml spoons (1½ tablespoons) olive oil*
- *1 kg (2 lb) ripe tomatoes, peeled, de-seeded and chopped*
- *1½ × 15 ml spoons (1½ tablespoons) tomato purée*
- *rind ½ orange*
- *juice 1 orange*
- *3 × 15 ml spoons (3 tablespoons) fresh chopped basil*
- *salt and freshly ground black pepper*

Preheat the oven to gas mark 5, 375°F (190°C). Grease and line a 39 × 26 cm (15½ × 10½ inches) Swiss roll tray with greased baking parchment.

Mix the egg yolks together with 120 g (4½ oz) walnuts, tamari, fromage frais and seasoning.

Whisk the egg whites until they stand in peaks (and, when tilting the bowl sideways, they do not slide). Using a large metallic spoon, fold the egg whites into the walnut mixture making sure that you keep as much air as possible in the mixture. Quickly transfer it into the prepared tin. Bake on the middle shelf of the preheated oven for 15–18 minutes until cooked: the roulade should spring back to the touch.

● MAKE THE FILLING

Wash the spinach, adding a little white wine vinegar to the water to help get rid of impurities. Remove the toughest stalks, place the leaves in a heavy saucepan and cook, covered, over a low heat for 10 minutes or until tender. When cooked, place the spinach in a sieve and press as much water out as possible then chop it very finely. Mix with the fromage frais and season well.

When the roulade is cooked, flip it over on to a second sheet of baking parchment, dusted with the extra ground walnuts. Spread the spinach filling over the roulade, leaving 1.25 cm (½ inch) clear at the top and at the sides of the roulade, then roll it up loosely like a Swiss roll, along its longest side. Allow to cool and serve cold.

● MAKE THE FENNEL AND TOMATO CONCASSÉE

Steam the fennel quarters for 10 minutes. Heat the oil in a medium pan and stir-fry the tomatoes for a few minutes until reduced to a pulp. Add the tomato purée, orange rind, orange juice, steamed fennel, basil and seasoning and cook, covered, for 15 minutes. Serve hot or cold as an accompaniment to the roulade.

ORANGE, APRICOT AND TOFU WHIP
WITH COINTREAU AND ORANGE TOPPING

SERVES 6

*T*his is a two-layer dessert which has a base of apricot and tofu with an apricot and orange topping of a lighter texture but a darker colour, giving this dessert a pretty appearance. It may be made a few hours in advance or the day before and kept in the refrigerator.

FOR THE APRICOT AND TOFU WHIP

- *350 g (12 oz) dried apricots*
- *1 × 5 ml spoon (1 teaspoon) orange rind*
- *1 × 300 g (10 oz) packet of silken tofu, chopped*
- *1–2 × 15 ml spoons (1–2 tablespoons) honey, or to taste*

FOR THE COINTREAU
AND ORANGE TOPPING

- *2 × 15 ml spoons (2 tablespoons) Cointreau*

TO DECORATE

- *6 fanned-out strawberries, see page 16*
- *few orange curls, see page 15*
- *6 sprigs fresh mint*

● **MAKE THE APRICOT AND TOFU WHIP**

Place the apricots and orange rind in a medium saucepan and cook in 600 ml (1 pint) water until soft; this will take approximately 30–40 minutes, depending on how soft the apricots are. Reserve 175 g (6 oz) of the cooked apricots and the cooking juice to one side. Blend the other apricots with 200 ml (7 fl oz) of the cooking juice (still reserve the rest). Add the tofu and blend again; add honey to taste and cool. Rinse the blender and blend the reserved apricots with 100 ml (3½ fl oz) of the remaining cooking juice until completely smooth. Add the Cointreau and mix well.

● **TO SERVE**

Divide the apricot and tofu whip between 6 slim sundae dishes or wine glasses and level the top. Slowly pour the Cointreau and orange topping over the apricot and tofu whip. Place each glass on a plate; decorate the top of the glass with a fanned-out strawberry and decorate the plate with a few orange curls and a sprig of mint. Chill and serve.

EXOTIC
FINGER BUFFET

NORI SUSHI ROLL WITH
PICKLED GINGER AND TAMARI ◆★

~

WILD MUSHROOM AND CORIANDER
CROÛSTADES

~

MINIATURE MARINATED TOFU AND MIXED
VEGETABLE BROCHETTES ◆★

~

GINGER SPICY FILO TRIANGLES ◆

~

PINEAPPLE AND MALIBU GRANITA
SERVED IN EXOTIC ICE BOWL ◆★

~

CHIFFON MACADAMIA AND PISTACHIO FILO
PASTRIES ◆

~

This light buffet is full of strong flavours from some unusual ingredients used. Personally, I love discovering new flavours and varying the combinations of ingredients, so I hope you will try many of these dishes. The quantities given make enough for 20 people as part of this buffet.

NORI SUSHI ROLL
WITH PICKLED GINGER AND TAMARI

MAKES 40 ROUNDS

*N*ori is a seaweed which comes in large sheets. In Japan, seaweed is used to wrap all sorts of fillings; various pieces of sushi rolls are taken for packed lunches and rice always seems to be used. Here the sushi is cut into thin slices to be served as part of a buffet.

Note: sushi nori is nori which has already been toasted over a flame; if you cannot find sushi nori buy ordinary shushi, then toast the sheet of seaweed on both sides over a naked flame until it changes colour to green. Do not overheat or it will crack.

- *350 g (12 oz) white basmati rice*
- *900 ml (1½ pints) water*
- *4 sheets sushi nori*
- *2 × 15 ml spoons (2 tablespoons) tamari*
- *16 carrot batons, see page 14, cooked* al dente

- *8 green beans, cooked until tender*
- *16 cucumber batons, see page 14*
- *2 × 15 ml spoons (2 tablespoons) rice vinegar*
- *16 pieces pickled ginger shavings (obtainable from a wholefood shop)*

Place the rice, a good pinch of salt and water in a saucepan and leave it to stand for 20 minutes. Bring to the boil and cook for 10 minutes or until soft in a pan with a tight-fitting lid.

Place a sushi nori sheet on a bamboo sushi mat or your work surface; cover with an even layer of cooked rice 1 cm (½ inch) thick, leaving 2 cm (¾ inch) clear at the top of the nori sheet. Sprinkle the rice with a little tamari. Dip the vegetables in rice vinegar and lay the strips of lightly cooked carrot and green beans and raw cucumber across the centre. Add the pickled ginger shavings to one side of the vegetables. Roll up the sushi fairly tightly. Wet the end of the nori which is clear of rice to form a tight self-seal. Serve freshly rolled with each roll sliced into at least 10 rounds. Accompany with a side dish of tamari mixed with a little rice vinegar for people to dip the sushi in.

WILD MUSHROOM AND CORIANDER CROUSTADES

SERVES 20

FOR THE PASTRY

- *350 g (12 oz) plain white flour*
- *200 g (7 oz) butter, cut into small pieces*
- *salt*

FOR THE FILLING

- *6 dried shiitake mushrooms, soaked in 200 ml (7 fl oz) water*
- *25 g (1 oz) butter*
- *175 g (6 oz) field mushrooms, caps and stalks finely shredded*
- *175 g (6 oz) open cup mushrooms, caps and stalks finely shredded*

- *20 g (¾ oz) white flour*
- *150 ml (¼ pint) water*
- *150 ml (¼ pint) soaking water from the mushrooms*
- *2 × 15 ml spoons (2 tablespoons) shoyu*
- *2 × 15 ml spoons (2 tablespoons) port*
- *2 × 15 ml spoons (2 tablespoons) fresh chopped coriander*
- *salt and freshly ground black pepper*

TO GARNISH

- *sprigs of fresh coriander*

● MAKE THE PASTRY

Preheat the oven to gas mark 6, 400°F (200°C). Rub the butter into the flour with a good pinch of salt until it resembles fine breadcrumbs. Add a little water and mix into a smooth dough. Chill for 30 minutes then roll out and cut out 40 rounds 7.5 cm (3 inches) in diameter. Line 40 greased deep bun tins, prick with a fork and bake blind in the oven for 8 minutes.

● MAKE THE FILLING

Drain the shiitake mushrooms and reserve the soaking liquid. Shred the caps of shiitake mushrooms and discard the hard stalks. Melt the butter and fry all the mushrooms on a medium heat for 5 minutes or until tender. Stir in the flour and mix well to form a roux. Cook the roux for 3 minutes on a very low heat, stirring all the time. Take the pan off the heat and gradually add the water and some of the soaking liquid, stirring well after each addition. Place the pan back on the heat and bring to the boil. Add the shoyu and port and simmer for 5 minutes. Add the coriander, season to taste, simmer for 1 minute and take the pan off the heat.

Fill the pastry cups with the mixture and serve warm, each cup garnished with a sprig of coriander.

MINIATURE MARINATED TOFU AND MIXED VEGETABLE BROCHETTES

SERVES 20

*T*he marinade for these brochettes is savoury and delicious; if you have some left, it is worth keeping it to use as an accompaniment to rice.

FOR THE MARINADE

- *3 × 15 ml spoons (3 tablespoons) sunflower oil*
- *1 × 5 ml spoon (1 teaspoon) toasted sesame oil*
- *2 × 15 ml spoons (2 tablespoons) ginger juice, see page 10*
- *3 × 15 ml spoons (3 tablespoons) tamari*

FOR THE BROCHETTES

- *275 g (10 oz) regular plain tofu*
- *225 g (8 oz) baby courgettes, chopped*
- *1 orange pepper, de-seeded and diced*
- *1 green pepper, de-seeded and diced*
- *1 yellow pepper, de-seeded and diced*
- *50 button mushrooms*

● **MAKE THE MARINADE**

Mix all the ingredients together in a shallow mixing bowl.

● **PREPARE THE BROCHETTES**

Cut the block of tofu in two separate thinner layers. Cut each block into 25 pieces. Drain the tofu pieces on kitchen paper then add them to the marinade. Leave for 2–3 hours in a cool place, turning the tofu over from time to time to coat it thoroughly.

Preheat the oven to gas mark 6, 400°F (200°C).

Bake the tofu in the preheated oven for 20 minutes and cool. Thread the vegetables and tofu on to cocktail kebab skewers and bake again for 10 minutes in the oven, basting with the marinade, until the vegetables are tender. Serve hot.

GINGER SPICY FILO TRIANGLES

MAKES 50 TRIANGLES

These triangles freeze well.

FOR THE FILLING

- 50 g (2 oz) mung beans, soaked for a few hours
- 3 × 15 ml spoons (3 tablespoons) sunflower oil
- 3 onions, peeled and finely chopped
- 2 cloves garlic, crushed
- 1 × 5 ml spoon (1 teaspoon) salt
- 1 × 15 ml spoon (1 tablespoon) turmeric
- 1½ × 15 ml spoons (1½ tablespoons) cumin powder
- 2 × 5 ml spoons (2 teaspoons) whole cumin seeds
- 1 ×15 ml spoon (1 tablespoon) ground coriander
- ½ × 5 ml spoon (½ teaspoon) coarsely ground black pepper
- 1.5 kg (3½ lb) potatoes, cooked and diced
- 3 × 15 ml spoons (3 tablespoons) fresh root ginger, finely grated

FOR THE PASTRY

- 25 sheets filo pastry
- 225 g (8 oz) butter, melted

Bring the mung beans to the boil in 900 ml (1½ pints) of water. Boil fast for 10 minutes then simmer for 40 minutes or until the beans are completely soft. Drain well and reserve 150 ml (¼ pint) of the cooking liquid.

Heat the oil and fry the onions and garlic until the onions are soft and translucent and the mixture is slightly browned. Add the salt, turmeric, cumin powder, cumin seeds, ground coriander and black pepper and cook on a low heat for 3 minutes, stirring from time to time. Add the cooked mung beans and potatoes, grated ginger and the reserved cooking water, stir well and cook on a low heat for 3 minutes. Remove from the heat and cool a little.

Preheat the oven to gas mark 6, 400°F (200°C).

Place a sheet of filo pastry on your work surface; cut in half, so it is approximately 9 cm (3½ inches) wide. Brush one half with melted butter, using a large pastry brush. Place 1½ × 15 ml spoons (1½ tablespoons) of the filling at the base of the buttered sheet. Fold the pastry to shape into a triangle; fold the triangle over itself again and again until you reach the top of the sheet. Repeat with the rest of the pastry and filling until you have 50 triangles. Place on a baking sheet and bake in the preheated oven for 12–15 minutes or until crisp and golden. Cool on a cooling rack and serve warm on a garnished platter.

PINEAPPLE AND MALIBU GRANITA
SERVED IN EXOTIC ICE BOWL

SERVES 20

*T*o make the ice bowl, use a 20 cm (8 inch) wide freezerproof bowl 2 litres (3½ pints) in capacity, inside a larger freezerproof bowl 25 cm (10 inch) wide, 3.9 litres (7 pints) in capacity. The minimum width between the bowls should be 2.5 cm (1 inch), as otherwise the ice melts too quickly. For detailed instructions see the method. Any flowers or fruits may be placed in ice; try rose leaves, mint leaves, nasturtiums, strawberry slices, violets or lemon slices. Do not use leaves or flowers from buttercups, horse chestnuts, Christmas Roses, daffodils, foxgloves, lily of the valley, lupins, marshmallow marigolds or sweet peas as these are poisonous.

FOR THE ICE BOWL

- *6 slices star fruit 2 cm (¾ inch) thick*
- *5 slices orange*
- *10 leaves from pineapple tops*

FOR THE GRANITA

- *175 ml (6 fl oz) water*
- *175 g (6 oz) caster sugar*
- *2 large pineapples, peeled (removing the eyes) and cored*
- *2 × 15 ml spoons (2 tablespoons) Malibu*

● MAKE THE ICE BOWL

Place the star fruit slices to line the bottom of the large bowl and sit the smaller bowl over the fruit. Fill in between the bowls with 600 ml (1 pint) of water and freeze for 2 hours or until solid. Place the slices of orange around the bowl with the pineapple leaves between them; pour more water between the bowls, up to their rims. Add a weight inside the smaller bowl if necessary. Place in the freezer for 6 hours to allow for the whole ice bowl to freeze thoroughly.

● MAKE THE GRANITA

Place the water and sugar in a saucepan and bring to the boil. Boil for 3 minutes, uncovered, to make a sugar syrup. Chop the pineapples into pieces, place in a food processor and process until smooth. Add the sugar syrup and process again until fully incorporated. Cool thoroughly then add the Malibu. Place in an ice-cream maker or in the freezer and freeze until almost solid. If not using an ice-cream maker, stir the granita once or twice during freezing.

● TO SERVE

Remove the smaller bowl from the larger bowl by pouring some hot water into the small bowl first. Then sit the larger bowl over some hot water and remove the frozen ice bowl from its mould. Place the granita inside the ice bowl and serve from the ice bowl.

CHIFFON MACADAMIA
AND PISTACHIO FILO PASTRIES

SERVES 20

*T*he filling for these filo pastries is made from two different nuts in a sugar syrup which warms up and re-melts on being deep-fried. These filo pastries can be served hot or cold, sprinkled with plenty of icing sugar. The filling may be varied to include almonds, skinned hazelnuts or pine nuts.

- *12 sheets filo pastry*
- *65 g (2½ oz) butter, melted*

FOR THE FILLING

- *75 g (3 oz) caster sugar*
- *85 ml (3 fl oz) water*
- *65 g (2½ oz) unsalted pistachio nuts, peeled and chopped*
- *40 g (1½ oz) macadamia nuts*

Preheat the oven to gas mark 6, 400°F (200°C).

● **MAKE THE FILLING**

Place the sugar and water in a small saucepan and bring to the boil over a medium heat. Turn the heat right down and simmer, covered, for 2 minutes. Leave the sugar syrup aside for 5 minutes to cool a little.

Place the pistachio nuts in the preheated oven and toast for 5 minutes, stirring the nuts every 2 minutes so they toast evenly. Add all the nuts to the cooling syrup and mix well. Leave to cool thoroughly.

Place a sheet of filo pastry on your work surface; cut it into two equal long strips then cut each strip into three 9 cm (3½ inch) squares. Brush the squares with melted butter on both sides, using a large pastry brush.

Place a level teaspoon of the nut filling in the centre of each pastry square and wrap the pastry around the filling in the shape of a small purse. Twist the 'neck' a little and deep-fry in hot oil until golden and crisp. Drain on kitchen paper then dust with plenty of icing sugar rained through a sieve. Serve hot, warm or cold.

FAMILY CELEBRATION MENU

ASPARAGUS SAUCE MOUSSELINE

~

TWO-TONE CELEBRATION RING SERVED WITH
TOMATO SAUCE AND CREAMED CELERIAC

~

RASPBERRY, BLACKCURRANT AND
REDCURRANT CHARLOTTE

~

This is an excellent menu for family gatherings, as its
dishes are always successful and popular. The impressive main course centrepiece is made with filo pastry and has
two different coloured fillings.
The asparagus for the starter should be bought and prepared
on the day it is cooked. The celebration ring may be prepared
the day before and cooked on the day; it may also be frozen.
The charlotte should be made the night before.

ASPARAGUS SAUCE MOUSSELINE

SERVES 6

Choose small white or green asparagus for this recipe, as they taste sweeter. Make the sauce at the last minute or it will not taste as fresh and a skin may form on the top, which would mask the smoothness of the sauce.

- 1 kg (2 lb) fresh asparagus

FOR THE SAUCE

- 4 egg yolks
- 50 g (2 oz) butter, softened
- 2 × 15 ml spoons (2 tablespoons) water

- 2 × 5 ml spoons (2 teaspoons) fresh
lemon juice
- 300 ml (½ pint) crème fraîche
- salt and freshly ground black pepper

TO GARNISH

- 6 sprigs chervil

Chop about 1–2 cm (½–¾ inch) off the top of the asparagus and steam for 10–15 minutes (depending on their size) until the tips are soft and the stems tender.

● **MAKE THE SAUCE**

Place the egg yolks, butter, water and lemon juice in a heavy based frying-pan. Whisk all the ingredients together with a wire or wooden whisk and place the pan over a gentle heat. Keep whisking while the sauce is warming through until it has the same consistency as a light salad cream. Take the pan off the heat but keep whisking and add the *crème fraîche* and seasoning. Put it back on a low heat and whisk for another minute. The sauce will now have thinned down. Take it off the heat to rest for 5–10 seconds and whisk again; repeat this process of placing it on and off the heat, resting and whisking until the sauce thickens up to the same consistency as a light mayonnaise. Keep it warm by covering and placing the pan over a bowl of hot water.

● **TO SERVE**

Divide the cooked asparagus between six warmed starter plates and pour some of the sauce by the side. Garnish with some sprigs of chervil by the sauce and serve immediately.

TWO-TONE CELEBRATION RING SERVED WITH TOMATO SAUCE AND CREAMED CELERIAC

SERVES 8

*T*his filo pastry ring encases two fillings of different colours: one made of couscous and tomato, the other of mushroom and walnut. This is a particularly good combination of flavours since one is strong and the other milder; one has texture, the other is smooth.

When making this dish, make sure the walnuts are fresh otherwise it will make the filling bitter. This ring is suitable for serving at any time of the year and may be served hot, accompanied by the Tomato Sauce, or cold as part of a buffet, accompanied by small gherkins.

● *approximately 12 sheets of frozen
filo pastry*
● *100 g (4 oz) butter, melted*

FOR THE MUSHROOM AND WALNUT
FILLING

● *25 g (1 oz) butter*
● *750 g (1½ lb) mushrooms, chopped*
● *175 g (6 oz) walnuts, chopped*
● *2 × 15 ml spoons (2 tablespoons) tamari*
● *black pepper*

FOR THE COUSCOUS
AND TOMATO FILLING

- *2 × 15 ml spoons (2 tablespoons) olive oil*
- *1 onion, peeled and finely chopped*
- *2 cloves garlic, crushed*
- *1 × 400 g (1 × 14 oz) tin tomatoes*
- *125 g (5 oz) bulgur wheat*
- *50 g (2 oz) couscous*
- *1 × 5 ml spoon (1 teaspoon) fresh chopped oregano*
- *2 × 15 ml spoons (2 tablespoons) tomato purée*

- *150 ml (¼ pint) water*
- *2 × 5 ml spoons (2 teaspoons) bouillon powder*
- *salt and freshly ground black pepper*

TO FINISH

- *1 egg, beaten*
- *15 g (½ oz) sesame seeds*

TO GARNISH

- *few leaves round lettuce or lollo rosso, or 6 tomato roses (see page 16) and 12 sprigs parsley*

Let the filo pastry defrost for 3 hours before starting to prepare the dish.

● MAKE THE COUSCOUS AND TOMATO FILLING

Heat the oil in a frying-pan and fry the onion and garlic until soft. Add the tomatoes and bring to the boil. Cook the mixture, covered, for 3 minutes, breaking up the tomatoes from time to time with a wooden spoon. Add the bulgur wheat, couscous, oregano, tomato purée, water and bouillon powder; bring the mixture up to a simmer and cook, covered, on a low heat for 20 minutes. You will find that the water disappears quickly which is why the mixture should be cooked slowly. If you have the mixture on too high a heat, stir in a little extra water and then cook for a further 5 minutes. Season to taste and leave the mixture to cool, covered.

● MAKE THE MUSHROOM AND WALNUT FILLING

Melt the butter in a large frying-pan and add the mushrooms. Stir-fry on a high heat until the mushrooms start giving off their moisture content and the pan is moist. Take the pan off the heat and add the walnuts and tamari. Stir the mixture well then add black pepper to taste. Cool.

Preheat the oven to gas mark 7, 425°F (220°C).

Place one sheet of filo pastry on the work surface, short side nearest to you. Brush with melted butter using a large pastry brush. Lay another sheet of filo pastry over the buttered one, staggering it about 4–5 cm (1½–2 inches) to one side. Butter the second sheet of filo pastry and repeat the process with eight other sheets so you end up with a width of 40.5 cm (13 inches). Use the leftover filo pastry to strengthen the sides (where there are fewer layers of filo pastry) at either end. Place the mushroom and walnut filling in a straight horizontal line, almost along the base but leaving 2.5 cm (1 inch) of pastry clear at the bottom. Make sure there is the same amount of filling at one end of the roll as at the other. Roll the filo pastry over the walnut filling so that it is enclosed. Place the couscous and tomato filling along the fold and roll up the pastry, as though making a Swiss roll, enclosing both fillings.

Transfer the log on to a baking sheet and gently shape it into a circle, joining the ends neatly. Do not worry if the pastry splits; simply cover with buttered pastry trimmings. Brush the ring with melted butter then beaten egg and sprinkle with sesame seeds. Bake in the preheated oven for 30 minutes or until crisp and golden. Leave to stand for 5 minutes then serve either as a centrepiece or on individual plates.

● **TO SERVE**

Transfer on to a platter, and garnish with watercress, cress or lollo rosso. To serve on individual plates: transfer on to a chopping board and cut into neat slices with a serrated or sharp knife. Pour a little Tomato Sauce on to each plate then place one slice near the centre of the plate but slightly to one side and another slice next to it. Make sure different colours are opposite each other for the best effect. Place a tomato rose (page 16) above the slices. Serve with a selection of hot side vegetables such as new potatoes, Creamed Celeriac (see opposite) and french beans.

TOMATO SAUCE

SERVES 8

This is a simple but effective tomato sauce with a bright red colour and a good flavour. It should have a thin pouring consistency.

● 2 × 15 ml spoons (2 tablespoons) olive oil
● 1 large onion, peeled and finely chopped
● 1 × 800 g (1 × 28 oz) tin tomatoes
● 3 × 15 ml spoons (3 tablespoons) tomato purée

● 600 ml (1 pint) water
● 3 × 5 ml spoons (3 teaspoons) bouillon powder
● salt and freshly ground black pepper

Heat the oil and fry the onion until soft. Add the tomatoes, tomato purée, water and bouillon powder and bring to the boil. Simmer for 15 minutes then break up the tomatoes with a wooden spoon. Cook for a further 5 minutes and season to taste. Cool the sauce a little then blend in a blender until smooth. Pass the sauce through a sieve to remove the pips then reheat and serve as suggested above.

CREAMED CELERIAC

SERVES 6

*C*eleriac is one of my favourite vegetables and, although not the most attractive vegetable to look at, it makes the most delicious side dish when puréed with potatoes.

FOR THE PURÉE

- *500 g (1¼ lb) potatoes, peeled and chunkily chopped*
- *500 g (1¼ lb) celeriac, peeled and chunkily chopped*
- *garlic salt*
- *celery salt*
- *15 g (½ oz) butter*
- *freshly ground black pepper*

TO FINISH

- *15 g (½ oz) butter, melted*
- *sprig fresh parsley*

Preheat the oven to gas mark 5, 375°F (190°C).

Bring 600 ml (1 pint) water to the boil in a large saucepan. Add the potatoes and cook for 5 minutes. Add the celeriac, cover tightly and cook for a further 8–10 minutes or until both are tender. Drain, transfer into a mixing bowl and mash thoroughly. Add a good pinch of garlic salt and celery salt, the butter and some black pepper and mix well. Place the mixture in a shallow, greased, oven-to-table dish. Lightly brush the top with melted butter, using a pastry brush, and place in the preheated oven for 20 minutes or until heated through and golden on the top. Garnish with a sprig of parsley.

RASPBERRY, BLACKCURRANT AND REDCURRANT CHARLOTTE

SERVES 8–10

*A*lthough this charlotte sounds summery it may be served at any time of the year and, in fact, makes an excellent and refreshing alternative to Christmas Pudding!

Mixed frozen currants and raspberries are sold in most supermarkets and give this dessert a delicious flavour. I have given a recipe for boudoirs, or sponge fingers, in case you would like to make your own but it is not essential.

I used to dislike charlottes until I discovered how good they tasted when made with Greek yoghurt and a home-made coulis so do try it made this way too.

- *450 g (1 lb) Greek yoghurt*
- *2 × 15 ml spoons (2 tablespoons) soft brown sugar*
- *450 g (1 lb) fresh or frozen mixed blackcurrants, redcurrants and raspberries*
- *75 g (3 oz) soft light brown sugar*
- *450 ml (¾ pint) apple juice*
- *1 × 15 ml spoon (1 tablespoon) crème de cassis*
- *36 boudoirs, see opposite*

FOR THE RASPBERRY COULIS

- *225 g (8 oz) fresh or frozen raspberries, defrosted*
- *75 g (3 oz) sugar*
- *2 × 15 ml spoons (2 tablespoons) crème de cassis*

TO DECORATE

- *sprigs fresh mint*

Drain the Greek yoghurt through a cheesecloth or double layer of muslin for an hour. Mix with 2 × 15 ml spoons (2 tablespoons) of soft brown sugar and keep to one side.

Place the mixed fruits and remaining sugar in a medium saucepan and bring to the boil. Simmer for a few minutes on a low heat, uncovered. Take off the heat and leave to cool.

Mix the apple juice with the *crème de cassis*. Dip each of the boudoirs in the liquid for 6–7 seconds and line the base and sides of a 1.75 litre (3 pint) charlotte tin. Add another layer of the dipped boudoirs to the base so that the bottom layer is strong. Cover the base with one-third of the fruits; leave to stand for 2–3 minutes then cover with one-third of the Greek yoghurt mixture. Cover with a layer of the boudoirs, then another layer of fruits then another layer of the Greek yoghurt. Repeat once more and finish with a top layer of boudoirs. Cover loosely with food wrap, place the charlotte in the refrigerator and leave to stand overnight.

● MAKE THE COULIS

Place the fruits, sugar and 180 ml (6 fl oz) water in a saucepan, bring to the boil and boil for 7–8 minutes, covered. Take the pan off the heat, cool a little and sieve, making sure that no pips pass through the sieve. Stir the mixture and leave to cool. Add the *crème de cassis* and chill thoroughly.

● TO SERVE

Turn the charlotte out on to a platter, surrounded by fresh sprigs of mint and take to the table. Pour some raspberry coulis on to each plate and place a slice of charlotte on its side next to the raspberry sauce. Decorate with a fresh sprig of mint.

BOUDOIRS

TO MAKE 36 SPONGE FINGERS

*T*his recipe makes soft sponge fingers called *biscuits à la cuillère* in France. These are served with light fruit desserts such as fruit salads, and are delicious to eat.

● *150 g (5 oz) white flour*	● *1 × 5 ml spoon (1 teaspoon)*
● *salt*	*vanilla essence*
● *6 eggs, separated*	● *75 g (3 oz) icing sugar, for sprinkling*
● *150 g (5 oz) caster sugar*	

Heat the oven to gas mark 4, 350°F (175°C).

Grease and flour three baking trays each 23 × 33 cm (9 × 13 inches). Mark parallel lines with a little flour across the width of the tray about 3.5–5 cm (1½–2 inches) apart.

Sift the flour and salt together. Whisk the egg yolks with two-thirds of the sugar and beat for 10 minutes until pale in colour. Whisk in the vanilla essence. Beat the egg whites in a separate bowl until stiff. Whisk in the remaining third of the sugar until the mixture is glossy.

Using a spatula, alternately fold the flour and the egg whites into the egg yolk in three batches each.

Spoon the mixture into a piping bag with a plain nozzle 2 cm (¾ inch) wide. Handling it as little as possible, pipe fingers 10–12.5 cm (4–4½ inches) long, using the flour lines as a guide. Dust the tops with icing sugar.

Bake the sponge fingers in the preheated oven for 15–18 minutes or until just firm on the outside but still soft in the centre. Remove and allow to cool on the baking trays for 10 minutes then place on a wire rack to cool completely.

Summer Buffet

Fresh Coriander and Avocado Salsa
served with Nachos and Pitta Bread ♦★

~

Spinach, Feta and Filo Triangles ♦

~

Light Celery and Almond Croquettes ★

~

Curd Cheese and Tomato Quiche

~

Tabbouleh Salad ♦★

~

Mixed Leaf Salad with a
Walnut Oil Dressing ♦★

~

Cheeseboard

~

Petit Suisse Cakes

~

Individual Meringues Filled with Kiwi
and Fresh Raspberries

~

Chocolate and Strawberry Fondue

~

The dishes in this summer spread are colourful, light and tasty; there is a selection with flavours to suit everyone. The buffet finishes with a Chocolate and Strawberry Fondue which is simply wonderful! The quantities given below make enough to serve 20 people.
I have suggested a cheeseboard in between the salad and the puddings; serve it with star fruit, biscuits and grapes.

FRESH CORIANDER AND AVOCADO SALSA SERVED WITH NACHOS AND PITTA BREAD

Make twice the quantity of Avocado Salsa from the recipe on page 110. Serve with tortilla chips (see page 110) and warm pitta bread.

SPINACH, FETA AND FILO TRIANGLES

*T*he filling of these triangles is very tasty as it is based on feta cheese, spinach, spring onions and fresh herbs. The triangles may be served warm or cold.

- *10–15 sheets filo pastry, measuring 33 × 18 cm (13 × 7 inches), or the equivalent*
- *50–75 g (2–3 oz) butter, melted*
- *450 g (1 lb) fresh or frozen leaf spinach*
- *450 g (1 lb) boiled potatoes, diced*
- *225 g (8 oz) Feta cheese, crumbled*

- *1 × 5 ml spoon (1 tablespoon) fresh chopped parsley*
- *2 × 5 ml spoons (2 teaspoons) fresh chopped oregano*
- *6 spring onions, finely chopped*
- *salt and freshly ground black pepper*

Preheat the oven to gas mark 6, 400°F (200°C).

Make the filling. Cook the spinach until tender. Drain well and chop finely. Mix in the potatoes, Feta cheese, parsley, oregano, spring onions and season to taste.

Cut a sheet of filo pastry in half lengthwise to give two long strips. Brush half of this with melted butter. Place 1½ × 15 ml spoons (1½ tablespoons) of the filling at the base of each strip and fold the pastry over it, shaping it into a triangle. Fold the triangle over itself until you reach the top of the strip. Repeat with the other sheets of pastry. Bake on a greased baking sheet in the oven for 12–15 minutes or until crisp and golden. Makes 20–30 triangles.

LIGHT CELERY AND ALMOND CROQUETTES

- *1 × 15 ml spoon (1 tablespoon) sunflower oil*
- *225 g (8 oz) celery, finely diced*
- *350 g (12 oz) courgettes, finely diced*
- *2 cloves garlic, crushed*
- *150 ml (¼ pint) water*
- *1 × 15 ml spoon (1 tablespoon) bouillon powder*
- *225 g (8 oz) flaked almonds*
- *275 g (10 oz) granary bread*

- *2 eggs, beaten*
- *salt and freshly ground black pepper*

TO COAT

- *2 eggs, beaten*
- *175 g (6 oz) granary breadcrumbs*

TO SERVE

- *apple and tomato ketchup or a similar ketchup/sauce*

Heat the sunflower oil and fry the celery in a frying-pan until tender. Add the courgettes and garlic and fry for another 3 minutes. Add the water and bouillon powder, bring to the boil and simmer for 3 minutes. Take the pan off the heat.

Place the almonds and the bread in a food processor and process until fine. Transfer to a large mixing bowl and pour the vegetable mixture over. Mix well then add the eggs and season to taste. Leave to cool.

Shape into croquettes each the size of a large walnut. This recipe will make 40–50 croquettes. Dip first into the beaten egg and then into the breadcrumbs and deep-fry in hot oil until golden. Drain on kitchen paper and serve hot with an apple and tomato ketchup.

CURD CHEESE AND TOMATO QUICHE

This is a delicious and fresh-looking quiche which is made with curd cheese, fresh tomatoes, spring onions and herbs. The quantities below fill a quiche tin 28 cm (11 inches) in diameter and 3 cm (1¼ inches) deep.

FOR THE PASTRY

- *225 g (8 oz) wholewheat flour*
- *salt*
- *75 g (3 oz) butter, diced*
- *40 g (1½ oz) solid white vegetable fat, diced*

FOR THE FILLING

- *350 g (12 oz) curd cheese*
- *4 eggs, beaten*

- *5 large tomatoes, skinned and chopped*
- *8 spring onions, finely chopped*
- *2 × 5 ml spoons (2 teaspoons) dried basil*
- *1 × 15 ml spoon (1 tablespoon) fresh chopped basil*
- *salt and freshly ground black pepper*

TO GARNISH

- *sprig chervil*

● MAKE THE PASTRY

Preheat the oven to gas mark 6, 400°F (200°C).

Place the flour and a good pinch of salt in a mixing bowl. Add the butter and vegetable fat and rub into the flour with the tips of your fingers (note: this may also be done in a food processor). Add approximately 5 × 15 ml spoons (5 tablespoons) of water and mix to a soft dough. Some flours need more water than others, so add water accordingly. Roll the pastry out, place in the greased flan ring, prick with a fork and bake in the preheated oven for 10 minutes. Remove and cool. Turn the oven down to gas mark 5, 375°F (190°C).

● MAKE THE FILLING

Place the curd cheese in a mixing bowl and stir to soften with a whisk. Gradually add the beaten egg, stirring after each addition. Add the rest of the ingredients, mix well and season to taste. Pour into the part-cooked flan case. Bake in the preheated oven for 25 minutes or until set. Serve hot or cold with a sprig of chervil.

TABBOULEH SALAD

SERVES 20

*E*veryone's favourite, this salad is very pungent as it makes use of plenty of garlic and fresh mint in its dressing. Ideally, prepare it a day ahead so it has time to let the flavours mingle.

- *450 g (1 lb) coarse bulgur wheat*
- *1 × 5 ml spoon (1 teaspoon) salt*

FOR THE DRESSING

- *250 ml (8 fl oz) olive oil*
- *juice 4 lemons*
- *4 cloves garlic, crushed*
- *6 × 15 ml spoons (6 tablespoons) fresh chopped mint*

- *10 × 15 ml spoons (10 tablespoons) fresh chopped parsley*
- *salt and freshly ground black pepper*

TO SERVE

- *1 large cucumber, diced*
- *1.5 kg (3 lb) tomatoes, chunkily chopped*
- *8 spring onions, chopped, optional*

Place the bulgur wheat and salt in a mixing bowl. Pour 750 ml (1¼ pints) of boiling water over the bulgur, cover with a plate and leave to stand for 30 minutes. Do not remove the plate or stir the mixture.

● MAKE THE DRESSING

Mix all the ingredients together in a small mixing bowl. Pour over the bulgur wheat and mix well. Leave to stand until completely cold.

● TO SERVE

Add the vegetables to the salad and mix gently.

MIXED LEAF SALAD WITH A WALNUT OIL DRESSING

SERVES 20

*A*ny lettuce may be used to make a mixed leaf salad but the combination below makes an attractive salad bowl. The walnut oil dressing strengthens the flavour of some of the leaves and is made particularly tangy with the addition of wholegrain mustard.

FOR THE SALAD

- *1 small head radicchio lettuce, cored*
- *3 round lettuces, cored*
- *2 little gem lettuces, cored*
- *1 iceberg lettuce, cored*
- *heart of 1 frisée lettuce, chopped into pieces 4 cm (1½ inches) long*
- *a few heads of purslane lettuces, trimmed*
- *1 punnet mustard and cress, trimmed*
- *2 × 15 ml spoons (2 tablespoons) shredded fresh basil*
- *2 × 15 ml spoons (2 tablespoons) young leaves of continental parsley*

FOR THE DRESSING

- *6 × 15 ml spoons (6 tablespoons) sunflower oil*
- *2 × 15 ml spoons (2 tablespoons) walnut oil*
- *2 × 5 ml spoons (2 teaspoons) wholegrain mustard*
- *4 × 15 ml spoons (4 tablespoons) cider vinegar*
- *salt and freshly ground black pepper*

Cut the leaves of the first three leafy lettuces in half, down the centre stem. Chunkily chop the iceberg lettuce. Mix all the lettuce leaves, *frisée*, purslane, mustard and cress, basil and continental parsley together in a large mixing bowl. Make the dressing by mixing all the ingredients together. Pour it over the leaves at the last minute, stir it in and serve.

PETIT SUISSE CAKES

MAKES 24

*T*he filling for these sweet tartlets is Petit Suisses mixed with a little sugar to make a delicious, creamy and dry mixture on which the fruits sit. If Petit Suisses are not available use 450 g (1 lb) fromage frais that you have hung to drain in a double layer of muslin for 1 hour before using. All ingredients used for the filling should be chilled to make the tartlets very refreshing. If you prefer, other fruits such as ripe, thinly sliced peaches may be used.

2 quantities Pâte Sablée from the recipe on page 40

FOR THE FILLING

* *350 g (12 oz) Petit Suisses*
* *50–75 g (2–3 oz) caster sugar*

FOR THE TOPPING

* *450 g (1 lb) mixed redcurrants, whitecurrants and blackcurrants*

TO DECORATE

* *icing sugar*
* *small leaves fresh mint*

Make the pastry following the recipe on page 41 but omit the lemon. Roll out half the pastry at a time for easier handling. Use each quantity to line 12 deep bun tins by cutting the pastry into 12 rounds with a fluted 7.5 cm (3 inch) cutter. Bake the pastry as in the recipe. Cool.

● **MAKE THE FILLING**

Mix the Petit Suisses with caster sugar until smooth. Fill the tartlets with the mixture, top with the seasonal fruits and lightly rain some icing sugar over. Decorate with mint.

INDIVIDUAL MERINGUES FILLED WITH KIWI AND FRESH RASPBERRIES

MAKES 26–28 SMALL MERINGUES

The fruits should be chilled before filling and serving the meringues.

* *6 egg whites*
* *350 g (12 oz) caster sugar*

FOR THE FILLING

* *350 g (12 oz) Greek yoghurt*
* *350 g (12 oz) fresh raspberries*
* *3 kiwi fruits, peeled and thinly sliced*

Preheat the oven to gas mark 3, 325°F (160°C).

● **MAKE THE MERINGUE**

Whisk the egg whites until stiff. Add the sugar, a tablespoon at a time, and carry on whisking as you do so until all the sugar is incorporated. Transfer the mixture into a piping bag fitted with a 1 cm (½ inch) nozzle. Pipe 26–28 rounds of meringue each 6 cm (2½ inches) in diameter and bake in the preheated oven for 1 hour. Turn the oven down if the meringues start to brown. Cool on a cooling rack.

● **TO SERVE**

Top each meringue with a little Greek yoghurt and arrange the raspberries and kiwis on top.

CHOCOLATE AND STRAWBERRY FONDUE

*T*he chocolate sauce makes a 'butterscotch-like' accompaniment to the strawberries, and dipping the strawberries into it is a fun and delicious way to eat strawberries. The sauce may also be used as a topping or a filling for a chocolate cake. Note: boudoirs biscuits (see page 201) may be eaten with this dessert if you like.

FOR THE CHOCOLATE SAUCE

- *25 g (1 oz) unsalted butter*
- *6 egg yolks, beaten*
- *½ × 15 ml spoon (½ tablespoon) cocoa*
- *12 × 15 ml spoons (12 tablespoons) chocolate powder*
- *215 g (7½ oz) sugar*
- *12 × 15 ml spoons (12 tablespoons) milk*
- *6 × 15 ml spoons (6 tablespoons) double cream*

TO SERVE

- *1.5 kg (3 lb) whole ripe strawberries with hulls left on*

Melt the butter in a saucepan on a low heat. Take the pan off the heat and add the egg yolks, cocoa and chocolate powder and mix with a whisk until smooth. Place the pan back on the heat and warm through until the sauce thickens, whisking all the time – this should take no more than 3 minutes. Do not overheat. Add the sugar and milk and heat through, stirring all the time (especially around the edges of the pan), until the sauce thickens up again and is brought to its first boil. Take the pan off the heat, add the double cream and stir for another minute. Transfer into a serving bowl. Cool thoroughly.

Just before serving surround the chocolate sauce with strawberries, as though a dip.

*W*INTER *B*UFFET

BAKED CHERRY TOMATOES ◆

~

HARLEQUIN VEGETABLE RING

~

COURGETTE AND ALMOND RAISED PIE ★

~

RED ONION, CHIVE AND POTATO SALAD ★

~

EXOTIC RICE SALAD ◆★

~

EXOTIC FRUIT SALAD ◆★

~

CHOCOLATE CAKE

~

This is a good selection of dishes which starts with some baked cherry tomatoes with an unusual cheese filling; these should be served warm. The rest of the dishes, including the raised pie, should be served cold. The raised pie makes a good centrepiece; it is very satisfying as its filling is made with cashews and almonds so the slices should not be cut too thick. The quantities below make enough for 20 people as part of the buffet selection.

BAKED CHERRY TOMATOES

FILLS 40–50 CHERRY TOMATOES

*I*t is worth allowing 50 tomatoes to end up with 45 portions, as some cherry tomatoes split in the cooking process.

- 450 g (1 lb) minted halloumi cheese, cut into 50 dice, each 2 cm (¾ inch) square
- 50 cherry tomatoes, tops removed (and reserved) and de-seeded

TO SERVE

- shredded lettuce
- cress

Preheat the oven to gas mark 6, 400°F (200°C).

Fill the tomatoes with the pieces of halloumi cheese. Place on a baking sheet (keeping the tops on one side). Bake in the preheated oven for 10 minutes. Place the tops back on the tomatoes and serve on very finely shredded lettuce and cress.

HARLEQUIN VEGETABLE RING

SERVES 20

*T*o make this extremely colourful ring, make sure that the ingredients are not too moist or they will make the terrine taste watery. Once thoroughly cold, this terrine should be cut with a very sharp knife and served with a cumin and tomato coulis.

Notes: 1. If you prefer, you may vary the vegetables; fresh asparagus tips, for example, may be used.

2. To obtain a shiny effect, cover the terrine with a savoury agar-agar aspic, which is made using the same process as a sweet glaze (see page 28) but substitute a savoury light stock for the sweetened liquid. Pour it over the terrine and leave to set.

FOR THE TERRINE

- *1 red pepper*
- *2 yellow peppers*
- *25 g (1 oz) salted butter*
- *175 g (6 oz) large closed cup mushrooms, halved*
- *salt and freshly ground black pepper*
- *75 g (3 oz) green beans, topped and tailed and any strings removed*
- *2 egg yolks*

- *2 eggs*
- *4 × 15 ml spoons (4 tablespoons) milk*
- *300 ml (½ pint) double cream*
- *10 × 15 ml spoons (10 tablespoons) fresh chopped parsley*
- *100 g (4 oz) Edam cheese, grated*

FOR THE TOMATO COULIS

- *1 quantity of Cumin and Tomato Coulis, see page 122*

Make the Cumin and Tomato Coulis from the recipe on page 123. Chill it thoroughly.

Preheat the oven to gas mark 6, 400°F (200°C).

Place the peppers on a baking sheet and bake in the preheated oven for 20–25 minutes, turning the peppers round once during their cooking time so all sides of the peppers are blistered and charred. Take out of the oven and cover with a damp cloth; leave for 10 minutes then skin and de-seed the peppers, making sure that you don't break the flesh. Cut off the tops and bottoms and then cut them into two halves, then into quarters. Leave aside. Turn the oven down to gas mark 3, 325°F (160°C).

Heat the butter and fry the mushrooms on a medium heat, uncovered, for 7 minutes until the outside of the mushrooms are browned. Cover then cook for a further 8 minutes. The mushrooms will lose their moisture content at some point; when this happens, season the mushrooms and remove the lid to dry out the mushrooms a little as you cook.

Steam the green beans in a steamer for 12 minutes or until tender. Plunge them into iced water as soon as they are cooked then drain well.

Whisk the egg yolks, eggs and milk together and mix in the cream. Season to taste.

Grease a 1.2 litre (2 pint) savarin ring mould and place the quartered peppers lengthwise on the base of the ring, interchanging the colours. You will need three quarters of red peppers and three quarters of yellow peppers to line the base of the tin. Cover with 4 × 15 ml spoons (4 tablespoons) of the chopped parsley, then sprinkle half the grated Edam cheese over. Cover with the mushrooms, cut side down, then top with the green beans. Shred the remaining peppers and mix the two colours together. Sprinkle them over the green beans, add the rest of the cheese and finish with a sprinkling of the remaining parsley. Pour the cream and egg mixture over the vegetables and bake in a bain-marie in the oven for 1½ hours. Leave to cool completely for a few hours in a cool place.

● **T O   S E R V E**

Use a sharp knife to cut through the terrine neatly and place the slices on a bed of coulis.

C O U R G E T T E   A N D   A L M O N D   R A I S E D   P I E

MAKES A 25 CM (10 INCH) PIE

FOR THE FILLING

- 2 × 15 ml spoons (2 tablespoons) sunflower oil
- 750 g (1½ lb) carrots, peeled and diced
- 750 g (1½ lb) courgettes, chopped
- 2 red peppers, de-seeded and chopped
- 300–450 ml (½–¾ pint) water
- 1 × 15 ml spoon (1 tablespoon) bouillon powder
- 2–3 × 15 ml spoons (2–3 tablespoons) shoyu, or to taste
- 350 g (12 oz) mixed almonds, cashews and peanuts
- 350 g (12 oz) wholewheat bread, chopped
- salt and freshly ground black pepper

FOR THE PASTRY

- 750 g (1½ lb) wholewheat flour
- 1 × 5 ml spoon (1 teaspoon) baking powder
- 175 g (6 oz) solid white vegetable fat, diced
- 300–450 ml (½–¾ pint) boiling water
- extra boiling water at hand

TO GLAZE

- 1 egg, beaten

● **MAKE THE FILLING**

Heat the oil and fry the carrots in an open pan for 10 minutes. Add the courgettes and cook for a further 3 minutes. Add the red peppers, water and bouillon powder to the pan and bring to the boil. Add the shoyu. Place the nuts and bread in a food processor and process until smooth. Transfer into a large mixing bowl and pour the vegetable mixture over. Mix well and season to taste. The consistency should be that of a nut roast. Check the seasoning and cool.

● **MAKE THE PASTRY**

Preheat the oven to gas mark 7, 425°F (220°C).

Mix the flour and baking powder in a large mixing bowl. Bring the vegetable fat and the water to a fast boil; the fat should be entirely dissolved when the water comes up to the boil. Pour the liquid ingredients over the dry ingredients and stir with a wooden spoon. When a little cooler, use your hands to amalgamate the pastry into a soft dough, a little firmer than a scone dough. Add a little extra boiling water, if necessary, to gather together all the flour on the board, and mix well. Divide the dough into thirds. Cover one-third of the dough with a damp tea-towel and cool a little. Use the rest of the dough to mould the base and the sides of the pie tin by hand. Press against the sides, it should be between 5 mm and 1 cm (¼ and ½ inch) thick. Add the filling.

Roll out the remaining third of the dough to a circle 27 cm (10 inches) wide; in order to do this easily the pastry should have cooled down quite considerably. Dampen the edges of the filled pie; roll up the pastry on to the rolling pin and carefully unfold it over the top of the pie. Press the edges together into a decorative pattern and garnish the top of the pie with pastry leaves. Brush with the beaten egg to glaze, and bake in the preheated oven for 30 minutes. Reduce the heat to gas mark 5, 375°F (190°C) and cook for a further 45 minutes. Cool thoroughly and serve cold.

RED ONION, CHIVE AND POTATO SALAD

SERVES 20

*A*lthough Belles de Fontenay potatoes make a nice potato salad, it is possible to use any new or old potatoes to make this salad. The mayonnaise is flavoured with dill and is light and delicious.

● *1.75 kg (4 lb) Belles de Fontenay potatoes*

FOR THE MAYONNAISE

● *6 egg yolks*
● *1 × 5 ml spoon (1 teaspoon) English mustard*

- *2 × 15 ml spoons (2 tablespoons) cider vinegar*
- *600 ml (1 pint) sunflower oil*
- *1 × 5 ml spoon (1 teaspoon) dill vinegar*
- *1 × 5 ml spoon (1 teaspoon) garlic vinegar*
- *salt and freshly ground black pepper, to taste*

FOR THE SALAD INGREDIENTS

- *2 red onions, very finely shredded*
- *4 × 15 ml spoons (4 tablespoons) fresh chopped chives*
- *225 g (8 oz) radishes, sliced*

TO GARNISH

- *½ red onion, finely shredded*
- *1 × 15 ml spoon (1 tablespoon) chives*
- *few slices radishes*

Cook the potatoes in boiling, salted water for 15 minutes or until tender. Leave until completely cold then cut into slices 5 mm (¼ inch) thick.

MAKE THE MAYONNAISE

Place the egg yolks, mustard and cider vinegar in a large mixing bowl and stir until smooth. Add the oil, drop by drop, until 1 × 15 ml spoon (1 tablespoon) has been added. Then add it a few drops at a time until half the oil has been added. Then add the oil 1 × 10 ml spoon (1 dessertspoon) at a time. When all the oil has been added, add the dill vinegar and garlic vinegar and season to taste. Leave to cool thoroughly in a covered container.

Place the cooled potatoes in a large mixing bowl; add the mayonnaise and stir well but delicately. Add the red onions, chives and radishes and mix lightly again.

TO SERVE

Transfer into a serving dish; mix the garnishing ingredients together and sprinkle over the top.

EXOTIC RICE SALAD

SERVES 20

- *900 g (2 lb) basmati rice, soaked in 1.75 litres (3 pints) cold water for 20 minutes*

FOR THE DRESSING

- *8 × 15 ml spoons (8 tablespoons) sunflower oil*
- *4 × 15 ml spoons (4 tablespoons) rice vinegar*

- 3 × 15 ml spoons (3 tablespoons) fresh
  ginger juice, see page 10
- 2 × 5 ml spoons (2 teaspoons) toasted
  sesame oil
- 6 × 15 ml spoons (6 tablespoons) fresh
  orange juice
- 4 × 15 ml spoons (4 tablespoons) cider
  or white wine vinegar
- 4 × 15 ml spoons (4 tablespoons) shoyu
- salt and freshly ground black pepper

FOR THE SALAD INGREDIENTS

- 1.5 kg (3 lb) fresh beansprouts,
  well rinsed
- 225 g (8 oz) radishes, sliced
- 2 yellow peppers, de-seeded and chopped
  into fine strips 4 cm (1½ inches) long
- 2 orange peppers, de-seeded and chopped
  into fine strips 4 cm (1½ inches) long
- 10 spring onions, chopped

Bring the rice to the boil in its soaking water. When boiling, reduce the heat and simmer for 8 minutes. Do not remove the lid or stir during the cooking. At the end of the cooking time, keep the lid on and leave to cool for 5 minutes. Then place the rice in a large mixing bowl and cool.

Make the dressing by mixing all the ingredients together.

When the rice is cold, pour the dressing over it and leave to stand for at least 2 hours. Mix all the salad ingredients together in a mixing bowl. Reserve two handfuls of the mixture for the garnish. Gently mix the salad ingredients into the rice and place the reserved garnish over the top before serving.

EXOTIC FRUIT SALAD

SERVES 20

- 1 large pineapple, peeled, cored
  and chopped
- 3 oranges, cut into thin slices,
  see page 15
- 2 red pears, cored and thinly sliced
- 3 Cox apples, cored and sliced
- 3 passion fruits, halved and scooped out
- 1 mango, peeled, stoned and diced

- 1 paw-paw, peeled, de-seeded and diced
- 225 g (8 oz) dark seedless grapes
- 2 kiwi fruits, peeled and chopped
- 2 bananas, peeled and chopped
- 1 litre (2 pints) pineapple juice

TO SERVE

- Greek yoghurt or cream

Mix together all the fruits except the bananas in a mixing bowl. Add the pineapple juice and leave to stand for up to 2 hours. Add the bananas just before serving and accompany with Greek yoghurt or cream.

CHOCOLATE CAKE

MAKES 2 × 23 CM (9 INCH) CAKES

This cake is not a whisked sponge so it is not a super-light cake but it is flavoursome and keeps for a few days in an airtight tin.

- *1 × 15 ml spoon (1 tablespoon) cocoa*
- *65 g (2½ oz) chocolate powder*
- *450 g (1 lb) white flour*
- *6 × 5 ml spoons (6 teaspoons) baking powder*
- *350 g (12 oz) soft brown sugar*
- *450 g (1 lb) butter, softened*
- *10 eggs*

FOR THE FILLING

- *350 ml (¾ pint) double cream*

FOR THE ICING

- *750 g (1½ lb) butter*
- *450 g (1 lb) icing sugar*
- *15 × 15 ml spoons (15 tablespoons) chocolate powder*
- *12 × 5 ml spoons (12 teaspoons) cocoa powder*

TO DECORATE

- *fanned-out strawberries, see page 16*

Preheat the oven to gas mark 5, 375°F (190°C). Line 2 × 23 cm (9 inch) sandwich or spring mould tins with greased baking parchment.

Place the cocoa, chocolate powder, flour, baking powder and sugar in a large mixing bowl and mix well, using a whisk to distribute the baking powder evenly. Transfer half the mixture into a food processor, add half the butter and 5 eggs and process until smooth. Place this in a clean mixing bowl. Place the rest of the flour mixture and the remaining butter and eggs into the food processor and process again. Transfer into the mixing bowl and mix the two quantities well. Divide the mixture between the prepared tins and bake in the preheated oven for 40–50 minutes. Take out of the oven and leave to cool in the tins for 5 minutes. Turn out on a cooling rack.

● **MAKE THE FILLING**

Whip the cream until stiff then chill it thoroughly.

● **FINISH THE CHOCOLATE CAKE**

Trim the chocolate cakes so they are flat on both sides. Sandwich the cakes together with the whipped cream. Place all the ingredients for the icing in the food processor and process until completely smooth. Cover the whole cake with the chocolate icing, weave into a decorative pattern and decorate the top with fanned-out strawberries. Serve in slices.

CHRISTMAS MENU

PALM HEART AND CHERRY TOMATO
COCKTAIL IN LEAFY RADICCHIO BARQUETTES

~

LAYERED PINE KERNEL ROAST SERVED WITH
SPINACH AND CELERY SAUCE

~

SUGAR-FREE CHRISTMAS PUDDING ★

~

MANGO AND GINGER TRIFLE

~

I think a Christmas menu should be colourful and
satisfying without being too heavy. The starter is
light and tasty; the layered roast makes a great centrepiece;
followed by a traditional but sugar-free Christmas Pudding.
The exotic Mango and Ginger Trifle is an extra treat!

PALM HEART AND CHERRY TOMATO COCKTAIL IN LEAFY RADICCHIO BARQUETTES

SERVES 6

In order to make this cocktail look as good as possible, ask your greengrocer to reserve the freshest-looking radicchio; the head needs to be plump (don't buy a small head), healthy, with fresh outside leaves. The round lettuce also needs to be fresh; both are used to hold the cocktail of palm heart, avocado and cherry tomato.

FOR THE SALAD

- 1 round lettuce
- 1 head radicchio
- 1 × 400 g (14 oz) tin palm hearts
- 550 g (1¼ lb) cherry tomatoes
- 1 ripe avocado, peeled and stoned
- 2 small spring onions, sliced thinly

FOR THE PESTO AND BASIL DRESSING

- 1 × 5 ml spoon (1 teaspoon) pesto sauce
- 1 × 5 ml spoon (1 teaspoon) garlic vinegar
- 2 × 15 ml spoons (2 tablespoons) white wine vinegar
- 2 × 15 ml spoons (2 tablespoons) olive oil

- *1 × 15 ml spoon (1 tablespoon)
  sunflower oil*
- *a good pinch of celery salt*
- *1 × 15 ml spoon (1 tablespoon) fresh
  chopped basil, shredded thinly*
- *salt and freshly ground black pepper*

TO GARNISH

- *1 × 15 ml spoon (1 tablespoon) fresh
  basil, shredded thinly*

Choose six large, fresh, green leaves from the head of the round lettuce and place in a bowl of cold water for 30 minutes to refresh them. Choose six large, fresh leaves from the head of the radicchio and, if they look in need of reviving, add to the bowl of water.

Rinse the palm hearts in a sieve; leave to drain. Halve the cherry tomatoes. Cut the avocado into quarters and slice across.

Make the dressing by mixing all the ingredients together in a mixing bowl. Add the avocado, cherry tomatoes and spring onions. Slice the palm hearts into slices 5 mm (¼ inch) thick and add to the salad; mix well without breaking the slices. Chill.

● TO SERVE

Drain the large round lettuce leaves well. Place them on individual plates then top with the leaves of radicchio; these should actually sit inside the green leaves. Carefully divide the dressed salad mixture between the leaves of radicchio and garnish with a sprinkling of shredded basil.

LAYERED PINE KERNEL ROAST
SERVED WITH SPINACH AND CELERY SAUCE

SERVES 6

*L*ike turkey to the meat-eater, eating nut roast at Christmas has become a vegetarian tradition. Here is an interesting two-tone (white and green) roast for the festive season, which is tasty and satisfying. Serve with the traditional trimmings, such as roast potatoes and parsnips (cooked in vegetable oil), Brussels sprouts, carrots and peas.

This recipe serves no more than 6 people. If you wish to have some leftovers (this roast is nice served cold too, with a pickle) then it is best to make twice the quantity (and twice the sauce) and bake it in a 1 kg (2 lb) loaf tin. This way you will also have more of the sauce for the vegetables. The roast freezes well.

Fresh celery hearts are sold in supermarkets and at some greengrocers; if you cannot get any, use the hearty parts of 2 or 3 celery instead.

FOR THE ROAST

- 25 g (1 oz) butter
- 1 onion, peeled and finely chopped
- 120 ml (4 fl oz) dry white wine
- 2 × 5 ml spoons (2 teaspoons) bouillon powder
- 100 g (4 oz) whole pine kernels
- 100 g (4 oz) cashew nuts
- 175 g (6 oz) white bread
- 1 egg, beaten
- salt and freshly ground black pepper

FOR THE FILLING

- 25 g (1 oz) butter
- 450 g (1 lb) celery hearts, finely chopped
- 100 g (4 oz) fresh spinach
- 1 × 5 ml spoon (1 teaspoon) fresh chopped marjoram
- 40 g (1½ oz) white bread
- 1 egg, beaten
- salt and freshly ground black pepper

FOR THE SPINACH AND CELERY SAUCE

- 300 ml (½ pint) water
- 2 × 5 ml spoons (2 teaspoons) bouillon powder
- salt and freshly ground black pepper

Preheat the oven to gas mark 5, 375°F (190°C). Line a deep 450 g (1 lb) loaf tin with greased baking parchment. This is important to ensure the roast will turn out successfully.

- **PREPARE THE ROAST**

Melt the butter and fry the onion until soft; do not brown. Add the white wine and bouillon powder and simmer for 2 minutes, covered. Meanwhile place 50 g (2 oz) of the pine kernels on a baking sheet, place in the preheated oven and toast until golden. Place the rest of the pine kernels, all the cashew nuts and bread in a food processor and process until the bread is reduced to breadcrumbs and the nuts are finely ground. Transfer into a mixing bowl and add the toasted pine kernels, onion mixture, beaten egg and seasoning and mix well. Leave aside.

- **PREPARE THE FILLING**

Melt the butter and fry the celery until tender, this will take approximately 10 minutes. Remove the stalks from the spinach and rinse thoroughly; drain, chop and add to the pan, together with the marjoram. Cook for 3 minutes and remove from the heat. Cool a little then process in a food processor until fairly smooth (but not completely liquid). Remove from the food processor and keep to one side. Grind the bread into breadcrumbs in the food processor and transfer into a mixing bowl. Add one-third of the reserved spinach mixture, the egg and seasoning and mix well. (The other two-thirds of the spinach mixture will be used to make the sauce, so keep to one side.)

Spoon a little less than half of the pine kernel mixture into the base of the prepared loaf tin and level the top. Spoon the prepared spinach and bread filling over the pine kernel mixture and level the top. Finally, spoon the remaining pine kernel mixture over the top and level it. Bake in the preheated oven for 35 minutes.

● **MAKE THE SAUCE**

Place the reserved two-thirds of the spinach and celery mixture into a blender and process until completely smooth. Add the water and blend again. Transfer into a saucepan, add the bouillon powder and seasoning and simmer, covered, for 5 minutes.

● **TO SERVE**

Loosen the roast with a knife and turn out on to a warmed platter. Surround with roast potatoes and other vegetables. Cut into slices and serve with the spinach and celery sauce as accompaniment.

SUGAR-FREE CHRISTMAS PUDDING

MAKES 1 × 1.5 LITRE (2½ PINT) PUDDING

*T*his is a delicious Christmas pudding which relies on the sweetness of dates and figs to sweeten it; it also has molasses and dark beer to help flavour it. If you prefer, you can microwave it (cook for 17 minutes on full power, and leave to stand for 5 minutes).

- *225 g (8 oz) stoned dates, chopped*
- *100 g (4 oz) figs, chopped*
- *200 ml (7 fl oz) dark beer*
- *2 × 5 ml spoons (2 teaspoons) molasses*
- *1 apple, grated*
- *175 g (6 oz) currants*
- *175 g (6 oz) sultanas*
- *175 g (6 oz) raisins*
- *100 g (4 oz) wholewheat breadcrumbs*
- *50 g (2 oz) solid white vegetable fat, chilled and grated*
- *50 g (2 oz) self-raising wholewheat flour, or use plain wholewheat flour mixed*
- *with ½ × 5 ml spoon (½ teaspoon) baking powder*
- *3 × 15 ml spoons (3 tablespoons) brandy*
- *½ × 5 ml spoon (½ teaspoon) cinnamon*
- *½ × 5 ml spoon (½ teaspoon) mixed spice*
- *25 g (1 oz) stem ginger, finely chopped*
- *rind and juice 1 orange*
- *rind and juice 1 lemon*
- *2 eggs, beaten*

TO DECORATE

- *few holly leaves*

Place the dates and figs in a small saucepan, cover with the beer and bring to the boil. Simmer, covered, on a low heat for 5 minutes. Keep the pan covered, and leave to stand for 1 hour. Add the molasses and give the mixture a good stir, then cream with a wooden spoon until the fruits are almost puréed (this can also be done in a food processor). Mix the rest of the ingredients in a large mixing bowl. Add the date and fig mixture and mix again.

Pour the mixture into a greased 1.5 litre (2½ pint) pudding basin and cover with a layer of greaseproof paper, greased on the inside. Cover with a double layer of foil and secure with string so water cannot reach the pudding mixture during steaming. Steam for 4 hours. Once cooked, let the pudding stand for 5 minutes then turn out.

Decorate with holly leaves and serve with single or double pouring cream.

MANGO AND GINGER TRIFLE

SERVES 6–8

*T*rifles came about as a variation on syllabubs, then cake was added to trifles to make them more substantial. Since this trifle is served as part of a Christmas meal, which is already very filling, I find that a lighter cake-free trifle is best. It is flavoured with stem ginger and has plenty of 'zest'.

FOR THE COINTREAU AND ORANGE JELLY

- 2½ × 5 ml spoons (2½ teaspoons) agar-agar powder or 7½ × 5 ml spoons (7½ teaspoons) agar-agar flakes
- 600 ml (1 pint) orange juice
- 2 × 15 ml spoons (2 tablespoons) Cointreau
- 25 g (1 oz) soft light brown sugar
- rind ½ orange
- 1 × 15 ml spoon (1 tablespoon) stem ginger, finely chopped

FOR THE FRUITS

- 2 oranges, cut into segments, see page 15
- 2 bananas, thickly sliced
- 1 mango, stoned and chopped

FOR THE CONFECTIONER'S CUSTARD

- 600 ml (1 pint) milk
- 3 eggs, beaten
- 50 g (2 oz) white or soft brown sugar
- 25 g (1 oz) unbleached white flour
- few drops vanilla essence

FOR THE TOPPING

- 300–450 ml (½–¾ pint) double cream
- 25 g (1 oz) stem ginger and/or crystallised fruits, chopped

● MAKE THE JELLY

Mix the agar-agar with the orange juice in a small saucepan. Bring to the boil, stir once and simmer, covered, for 2 minutes if using the powder, 10 minutes if using the flakes. Add the Cointreau, sugar, orange rind and stem ginger. Cool a little.

Place the prepared fruits in a 1.75 litre (3 pint) trifle dish and pour the jelly over. Leave to cool and set.

● MAKE THE CUSTARD

Heat the milk to boiling point. Whisk the eggs, sugar and flour together in a mixing bowl. Gradually pour the hot milk over the egg mixture and whisk all the ingredients together. Place in a clean pan and bring the mixture to the boil on a very low heat, stirring all the time, until the custard thickens. Simmer for 2–3 minutes, stirring from time to time. Take the pan off the heat and add the vanilla essence. Cool a little and pour over the set jelly. Leave to cool thoroughly; the custard will also set. Whip the cream to a soft peak in a mixing bowl and refrigerate it while the custard is cooling.

● TO SERVE

Once the trifle is cool, spoon or pipe the cream over the custard and decorate with the stem ginger and/or the crystallised fruits just before serving.

$\mathscr{I}$ N D E X

Italic numbers refer to photographs